Patrick Lo, Allan Cho and Dickson K.W. Chiu
World's Leading National, Public, Monastery and Royal Library Directors

Patrick Lo, Allan Cho
and Dickson K.W. Chiu

World's Leading National, Public, Monastery and Royal Library Directors

Leadership, Management, Future of Libraries

DE GRUYTER SAUR

ISBN 978-3-11-065241-3
e-ISBN (PDF) 978-3-11-053334-7
e-ISBN (EPUB) 978-3-11-053091-9

Library of Congress Cataloging-in-Publication Data
A CIP catalog record for this book has been applied for at the Library of Congress.

Bibliografische Information der Deutschen Nationalbibliothek
The Deutsche Nationalbibliothek lists this publication in the Deutsche Nationalbibliografie; detailed bibliographic data is available on the internet at http://dnb.dnb.de.

© 2019 Walter de Gruyter GmbH, Berlin/Boston
This volume is text- and page-identical with the hardback published in 2017.
Cover Image: © Hejduk, Austrian National Library
Typesetting: Compuscript Ltd., Shannon, Ireland
Printing and binding: CPI books GmbH, Leck

♾ Printed on acid-free paper
Printed in Germany

www.degruyter.com

Foreword

This book has come along just as the world of information is called to reflect on itself following the explosion of social networking and digital content. Technology has overtaken the profession by storm; after the storm always creates a new balance. Yet unknown opportunities await for those who enter an expanding profession in librarianship, knowledge management, and cultural preservation, all to the future of a profession that is still evolving.

Contributors are interviewed from their individual perspectives where successes are celebrated, challenges and overcome, and all share a dedication both to the profession and to cultural gatekeeping. A few found models to emulate, some relied on networking in broadening their positions, while others found their own way into leadership positions. All share a passion that uphold the unique and important mandates of their libraries and organizations.

Libraries can be seen as cultural and educational centers in their communities since the beginning of their existence. We may have overlooked how much we have advanced in bringing the leadership into our communities, by being too engaged in keeping our libraries current with technology. Libraries have long been designated as community spaces for exhibits and programs, but what we have seen in recent years is a profound expansion in how these spaces are being reinvented and re-envisioned.

This is an important work that enables readers to walk out of their own positions wherever they may be and the types of programs and services that the needs and priorities of patrons with other cultural identities. The reader will great a much richer insight into the libraries of the world, by reading the stories of successful programs and partnerships; they will become wiser in their own realms professionals and will benefit the world that they had entered to serve their users.

Mauro Guerrini
Professor of Library Science, Cataloging and Classification, University of Florence;
Former President of Italian Library Association;
President of the Italian Committee for 2009 IFLA, Milan;
Founder and Editor of Jlis.it <Jlis.it>, an academic open access journal on LIS.

Acknowledgements

This is our fourth book on practicing library professionals, but very first joint interview book project that is dedicated to documenting on such a worldwide scale, the senior leadership and managerial skills, strategic planning as well as professional developments, etc. – all the skills and attributes that an 'effective total leader' absolutely needs in the world of librarianship today. The world of librarianship today is struggling to evolve alongside with new and fast-changing technological trends, as well as the changes in political and socio-cultural environments. Libraries regardless of size, specialities and user groups are stretching their manpower and resources to the fullest – to perform both traditional as well as non-traditional roles – with the aim of revitalising neighborhoods and underprivileged communities, in order to stay relevant with society and in the digital age.

Each individual library director appearing in this book is highly reputable and greatly respected for their integrity, endeavors and contributions in their own right. Their participation in this interview book project, sharing with our readers, their valuable professional practices, unparalleled experiences and unique perspectives, etc., has created such valuable and boundless professional learning opportunities for these practicing library professionals to communicate with each other on a cross-national, as well as on a cross-cultural level.

As renowned management scholar Henry Mintzberg of McGill University theorises, "managing is about influencing action. Managing is about helping organizations and units to get things done, which means action. Sometimes, managers manage actions directly. They fight fires. They manage projects. They negotiate contracts."[1] So as the individuals profiled in this book will tell us, their roles are manifold and multi-fold, involving a range of tasks and abilities that require experience, dedication, and creativity that not only keep the library's operations afloat but thrive under their guidance. We are fortunate that these busy leaders of knowledge are able to generously share with us their time and knowledge in the making of this book. It was simply a pleasure to learn through their experiences and expertise by "picking" their brains about how these library managers not only shape the missions of their respective libraries, but also how they are shaped by their own experiences into become current leadership positions.

---

[1] Mintzberg, Henry. (1973). *The Nature of Managerial Work*. New York, N.Y.: Harper & Row. (pp. 92–93).

Finally, we would like to thank our publisher, De Gruyter Publishers, and in particular, Claudia Heyer (Editor) for having such faith in our book project, as well as her continuous support on the journey of getting this book published by one of the finest academic publishers in the world.

I am most indebted to Professor Susan L. Robertson (Graduate School of Education, University of Bristol), a specialist in globalisation of education who served as the supervisor of my Doctor of Education dissertation from 2007–2009, for giving me much support – even from a distance – during my doctoral research. I am immensely grateful, and I would like to dedicate this book to her

–Patrick Lo.

I am most indebted to Keith Bunnell of the University of British Columbia Library, a humanities and social sciences librarian for more than thirty-five years, for his mentorship and guidance throughout my years as a librarian. His knowledge and professionalism as a librarian are sui generis.

–Allan Cho

I am most indebted to Professor Steve Andrews, Dr. Daniel Churchill, and Dr. Maggie Wang, of Faculty of Education, The University of Hong Kong, who provided the opportunities for me to start my research in LIS, together with the supportive colleagues in the faculty. I also thank Dr. Patrick Lo and Allan Cho who have helped me convert my previous research experiences into the LIS profession.

–Dickson Chiu

Contents

Foreword —— v

Acknowledgements —— vii

Introduction —— 1

National and state libraries

1   David S. Mao, Acting Librarian, Library of Congress —— 7

2   Dr. Johanna Rachinger, Director General, Austrian National Library —— 19

3   Caroline Brazier, Chief Librarian, British Library —— 25

4   Ana Santos Aramburo, Director, National Library of Spain —— 37

5   Marie-Christine Doffey, Director, Swiss National Library —— 47

6   Andris Vilks, Director of the National Library of Latvia —— 63

7   Prof. Dr. Renaldas Gudauskas, Director General, Martynas Mažvydas National Library of Lithuania —— 79

8   Alberto Manguel, Director, National Library of Argentina —— 87

9   Jelena Djurovic, Director, National Library of Montenegro —— 95

10 Dr. Claudia Lux, Librarian, Project Director of the Qatar National Library in Doha IFLA President 2007–2009 —— 111

11 Oren Weinberg, Director, National Library of Israel —— 129

12 Dr. Ismail Serageldin, Director, The Library of Alexandria (Egypt) —— 147

Public and city libraries

13 Pam Sandlian Smith, Director, Anythink Libraries,
    Adams County (Colorado) —— 163

14 Christopher Platt, Chief Branch Library Officer,
    New York Public Library —— 177

15 John F. Szabo, City Librarian, Los Angeles Public Library —— 193

16 David Leonard, President, Boston Public Library —— 207

17 Felton Thomas, Jr., Director of Cleveland Public Library —— 219

18 Mary Anne Hodel, Director/CEO, Orange County Library System —— 235

19 Misty Jones, Director, San Diego Public Library —— 249

20 Marcellus Turner, City Librarian, The Seattle Public
    Library System —— 257

21 Kate P. Horan, MLS, Library Director, McAllen Public
    Library (Texas) —— 267

22 Dr. Hannelore Vogt, Director, Cologne Public Library —— 279

23 Christine Brunner, Director, Stuttgart City Library —— 287

24 Sandra Singh, Chief Librarian, Vancouver Public Library —— 295

25 Shih-chang Horng, Director, Taipei Public Library —— 307

Other libraries

26 Father Maximilian Schiefermüller O.S.B., General Director,
    Admont Abbey Library —— 317

27 Dr. Cornel Dora, Director, Abbey Library of Saint Gall —— 327

28 Oliver Urquhart Irvine, The Librarian & Assistant Keeper, The Queen's Archives —— 337

Conclusion —— 353

About the authors —— 365

Introduction

Have you ever noticed the public library around your neighborhood, the central library nestled in the center of the downtown area, and the national library that is located in the very heart of your country's capital? What about those breathtakingly beautiful baroque monastery libraries located in some far-off and tranquil mountains in Europe? While academic libraries have traditionally been the nexus of the campus experience, and focused on building collections, providing research support to students and faculty, and offering information literacy instruction, they are increasingly integrated into the broader aspirations of the institution, especially in terms of connecting and even influencing its surrounding community.

National libraries are usually notable for both their physical size and collections, when compared to that of other city or academic libraries in the same country. As part of their mission to preserve nationwide information and documentary heritage, national libraries are also expected to function as legal deposits – serving as preeminent repository of literature, as well as many other types of published information of the whole nation, both within and outside the country. On the other hand, public or central libraries are public places that help shape an important part of our public culture. They are also of great importance as social and public spaces, and are responsible for connecting people of the local community and beyond with learning, recreation as well as culture, etc. In fact, city or central libraries also believed to be some of the powerful public spaces offering boundless opportunities for enhancing the lives of the individuals in society, fostering social inclusion, and more importantly, feeding the souls of those in need of either knowledge or inspiration. Furthermore, public libraries are established with the mission and capacity to support self-sufficiency and independent learning of each person, who enters either the physical or virtual doors. For such reasons, public libraries often appear to be less exclusive (both socially and culturally) than other cultural institutions, such as museums, art galleries, theatres, opera houses and concert halls.

Leadership, management and library directors
It is never easy to determine or sometimes even justify in quantitative terms the status and social values of most public spaces, particularly libraries. Traditionally, great importance is attached to libraries' political and cultural influences, as well as social values. This importance has not diminished over the past decades, despite of the tremendous convenience brought by Internet connectivity. Even with a common political and public consensus on the libraries' social, cultural,

educational and national importance, it is not often that libraries would make the front pages of the newspapers, or featured as cover stories of a lifestyle magazine or in the media spotlights. Meanwhile, in comparison to museums, art galleries, opera houses, and theatres, libraries as public social places simply do not hold a certain status or even attention in the social and political arena.

"Leadership" and "Management" may be the words that most people would associate with large profit-making corporations, rather than with arts, cultural and educational institutions. Until we hear some of the internationally foremost directors in the world of librarianship to speak on the subjects. Sometimes, the simplest but most innovative ideas in culture and education are those we most often overlook, or do not understand. For any service-providing institutions, or professionals practicing in the field of library and information science (LIS), understanding the fundamentals is unarguably the key to creating an enduring relationship with a sustainable user group.

Without doubts, the minds of our communities could be enriched, and a nation's identity could be firmed when we have access to libraries that provide opportunities and resources for creating knowledge, connecting people to the world of information, fostering creative ideas and preserving national heritage, as well as creating flexible spaces for community engagement and recreation.

Aims of this book

What new services and cutting-edge projects are the world's foremost library directors and their teams of library staff working on? What are the most promising recent developments in the field of library science? In *World's Leading National, Public, Monastery and Royal Library Directors*, chief librarians and general directors behind some of the most cutting-edge public and national libraries reveal the thoughts, philosophies, strategic planning, management, and execution process, as well as collaborations (at both national and international levels) that have guided their efforts – from conception to developing, producing some of the most innovative and creating library and information services in different socio-cultural and political contexts.

This book amounts to a great deal more than just a series of informal conversations with general directors who have all made their marks in the field of librarianship. Speaking from a variety of perspectives, including economic, social, educational, cultural developmental, and political, the discussions here could no doubt increase our understanding of the managerial decisions, and other factors that affect the decisions and determine the library's overall policy and operations – listening to the minds, dedications and passions of top leaders in the world of librarianship. With this book, we aim to provide our readers with thoughtful essays outlining the diverse political, social, cultural and economic developments of our current society that is driven by communications technology and networked information.

Choice of methods

Over the past year, we had the opportunity to talk, via Skype or written emails, with some of the most insightful, passionate, as well as inspiring directors in the world of librarianship, from national, city central, monastery libraries, Library of Congress (U.S.) to the Royal Library belonging to Elizabeth II, Queen of the United Kingdom, etc. In this book, we feature the conversations that help shape our understanding, and inspire us with their dedication to become more informed, better educated, better prepared and more confident citizens for the future.

Qualitative interviews were used to illustrate the underlying reasons for individual interviewees' professional practices and actions as well as decisions. Interview techniques enabled participants' attitudes and opinions to be fully expressed in their own words and allowed space for a variety of sometimes contradictory points of view to be aired. In addition to allowing individual library directors to fully articulate their answers, such natural and free conversational interviews also enabled maximum flexibility for more open, spontaneous, and instant exchanges of ideas without any preconceived expectations on our side. Not only does the interview approach provide opportunities for open discussions where both participants and researcher can "construct meaning" together, but it is also "essential for the understanding of how participants view their world."

In this book, the authors and the interviewees together explore topics like the influence of libraries in public culture, impacts and relations to our current information-driven society, the growth of democracy in former communist countries, the acceleration of immigration in Western Europe, or innovative methods for developing library services through harnessing social media, etc. These inspiring exchanges from some of our most leaders in the field of librarianship, presenting thought-provoking ideas and practical insights into the profession that plays a central role to the emergent information society. In summary, interviewing the general directors of the world's leading libraries provides an effective way to comprehend the matrix in which their contributions arise.

Intended readership

This book is valuable on many levels. The more or less casual readers with a general sense for the issues might read these interviews for enjoyment. The library and information science (LIS) students and practitioners who are struggling to construct a coherent picture in time for their future and current profession will find them of tremendous value. As authors, we suspect that many practicing LIS professionals and students will learn a great deal about every area.

For current students and graduates who are planning to enter a career in libraries, this book could provide them with insights into the careers of leadership positions in libraries. All the directors appearing in this book come with many years of training and professional experiences, yet each had interesting and diverse paths before landing his or her current position. By asking these top-level managers of large institutions to describe in their own words the necessary professional skills, knowledge, and personalities that are required for working at different world's leading institutions with varying size, nature, and composition, we intend to enlighten those who with lofty ambitions the inspiration and perhaps tools for career mobility.

For instance, for an MLIS graduate who wishes to seek employment outside homeland, what are the career opportunities and options available? What unique skills should these MLIS graduates acquire and possess in order to contribute to a career in leading a library? The aspiring readers of this book might be able to find answers and inspiration through the interviews of seasoned senior library managers appearing in the pages of this book. Undeniably, this book is for educators of all levels and, particularly, to government officials responsible for public policy formulation concerning social inclusion and the development of educational and cultural institutions in historical and contemporary sociocultural and political contexts.

National and state libraries

1 David S. Mao

Acting Librarian, Library of Congress

Introduction

Founded in 1800 and situated in the capital city of the United States, the Library of Congress (LC) is the official library serving the US Congress. It also serves as the de facto national library of the United States and is said to be the largest library in the world. As of 2016, LC's collection contains more than 164 million items on approximately 838 miles of bookshelves. Items in the LC collection include more than 38 million books and other printed materials, 3.6 million recordings, 14 million photographs, 5.5 million maps, 8.1 million pieces of sheet music, 70 million manuscripts, and multiple petabytes of digital information. LC's collection is truly universal, as it is not limited by subject, format, or national boundary.

David S. Mao served as the Acting Librarian of Congress from the retirement of the 13th Librarian James H. Billington in September 2015 until the confirmation of the 14th Librarian Carla Hayden in September 2016. Trained in both law and librarianship, Mao worked at a number of law firms and research libraries before joining the LC in 2005. In the following interview, Mao discusses the challenges of filling the shoes of his predecessor as well as the ultimate job satisfaction derived from managing the overall operations, resources, and finances of the most influential library in the world.

DOI 10.1515/9783110533347-002

Fig. 1.1: Deputy Librarian of Congress David S. Mao (Photo: Shawn Miller).

Fig. 1.2: Exterior of the Thomas Jefferson Buildings of the Library of Congress, Washington D C. (Photo: Shawn Miller).

Fig. 1.3: More than 1.7 million visitors tour the Thomas Jefferson Buildings's Great Hall each year (Photo: Shawn Miller).

Fig. 1.4: The Library of Congress Main Reading Room (Photo: Shawn Miller).

Could we begin this interview by first introducing yourself, for example, your professional training and education background? Could you also describe in detail your current roles, and areas responsibilities as the Acting Librarian of the Library of Congress (LC)?

I am a graduate of George Washington University[1], where I majored in international affairs with a minor in Chinese language and literature. I studied law at Georgetown University Law Center[2], and then worked in private practice for several years before embarking on a master's program in library science at The Catholic University of America.[3] I worked at the Georgetown University Law Library[4] and in the research library of the international law firm Covington and Burling LLP[5] before joining the Library of Congress Congressional Research

---

1 The George Washington University – Homepage. Available at: https://www.gwu.edu.
2 Georgetown University Law Center – Homepage. Available at: http://www.law.georgetown.edu.
3 The Catholic University of America – Homepage. Available at: http://www.cua.edu.
4 Georgetown Law Library – Georgetown University – Homepage. Available at: http://www.law.georgetown.edu/library/.
5 Covington and Burling LLP – Homepage. Available at: https://www.cov.com/.

Service[6] in 2005. I also taught as an adjunct professor at the University of Maryland[7]-College Park. As Acting Librarian, I am the chief executive of the institution, with final decision-making authority over all aspects of the institution. I work with other senior Library executives to set policy, oversee spending, and work with the Congress. I speak and write on behalf of the Library and help arbitrate issues that arise within, and among, divisions of the Library.

Based on my understanding, you practiced law for a few years before choosing a career in librarianship. Librarianship is never known to be a well-paid profession. In the librarian profession, promotion and career advancement are often based on seniority, and not on competency or performance – so what made you undertake such as major career change?

I realized that I enjoyed the type of work librarianship offered, and that there were numerous opportunities to combine librarianship with my legal education and experience. In my observations of the American library profession – uniformly across various settings including academic, government, and the private sectors – I see competence and performance strongly supporting promotion and career advancement.

Could you tell us more about your career path to becoming the Acting Librarian of Congress?

My fascination with libraries probably began in high school. I spent a lot of time in the school's library – I volunteered during the school year and even worked one summer shelf-reading the collection. While in law school, I had a work-study assignment in the law library and really enjoyed it. Before graduation, I consulted with several librarians about a career in law librarianship; however, they advised me that I needed a library degree.

At the time it wasn't fiscally prudent for me to think of going back to school for another graduate degree. It wasn't until a few years later that I had an opportunity to work in a law library and attend graduate school to study library science. My first library position was at Georgetown University, followed by several library positions at the international law firm Covington and Burling LLP. From there I moved to the Congressional Research Service at the Library of Congress. In 2010, I transferred to the Law Library of Congress as Deputy Law Librarian. I was

---

6 Congressional Research Service (Library of Congress) – Homepage. Available at: http://www.loc.gov/crsinfo/.
7 University of Maryland-College – Homepage. Available at: http://www.umd.edu/.

appointed Law Librarian of Congress in January 2012, and in January 2015 I was named Deputy Librarian of Congress. When the former Librarian of Congress, Dr. James H. Billington retired after almost 28 years of service in September 2015, I became the Acting Librarian of Congress.

Could you describe your management and leadership style? Mentorship is such an important theme in leadership – both mentoring and being mentored. Could you please tell us about your experiences about both? Do you still have mentors that you go to?

I believe in leadership that reaches out to employees at all levels. My colleague Robert Newlen – the Library's Chief of Staff – and I hold regular roundtable-style meetings with employees and invite people to bring us their questions and concerns. We recognize that good leadership begins with good listening. While Library of Congress management has a formal structure, I generally like to keep action low-key. I also believe in an organization that emphasizes collaboration and efficiency. A first initiative while I was Law Librarian of Congress was to reorganize the Law Library's organizational structure.

Similarly, the Chief of Staff and I launched a major reorganization of the Library shortly after starting in our roles to improve and streamline Library operations and functions. Mentorship plays a very significant role in professional development and I strongly encourage it. I have many colleagues that I consider to be mentors and that have helpfully guided me throughout my career. I believe sharing my experiences with newer colleagues may be helpful to them, but perhaps more importantly, I learn from their perspectives as well.

The General Director of the LC is to be appointed by the President of the United States, with the advice and consent issued by the United States Senate. Could you explain why the General Director of LC needs to be appointed by the US President? What are the US Senate's criteria for selecting the Head of LC?

Presidential nomination of the Librarian of Congress dates back to Thomas Jefferson's time in 1802. Congress added the requirement of Senate confirmation of the nomination in 1897. The Library's appointment-and-confirmation practice is consistent with many agencies across the United States federal government.

What is the current size of the LC collections, including its special collections? Could you also describe what you deem are the highlights of the collection?

The Library currently holds more than 162 million items including books, manuscripts, prints and photographs, films and sound recordings, and other material types. Many items are categorized as "top treasures," and although the following examples are too limiting, highlights include the Waldseemuller Map of 1507 (the first document to use the word "America"); Stradivari, Amati, and Guarneri stringed instruments; a draft of the Declaration of Independence in Thomas Jefferson's handwriting, with edits by Benjamin Franklin and John Adams; the contents of Abraham Lincoln's pockets on the night he was assassinated (such as eyeglasses, a handkerchief, and a Confederate five-dollar note); and, one of our more recent acquisitions, the manuscript papers of Civil Rights pioneer Rosa Parks. Library exhibitions feature items from the collection and many materials, including many of those mentioned, are digitized for permanent online display and access.

Does the LC work closely with other libraries outside the United States? If so, could you tell us about such cross-national or global collaborative projects? What are some highlights?

Indeed the Library works closely with many libraries around the world, including national libraries, academic libraries, and subject-specific libraries, to describe a few. An example of international library collaboration is the World Digital Library (WDL).[8] A United Nations Educational, Cultural and Scientific Organization (UNESCO)[9] – supported project led by the Library of Congress since 2009, WDL makes available free of charge on the Internet – digitized versions of top treasures of the world's major libraries and research collections (including explanations in seven languages). In several nations or regions where major libraries are not established the Library has its own offices to help collect books and other documents for the Library of Congress collection, as well as many United States libraries' collections.

Do you speak Chinese? How does your Chinese heritage influenced the way you manage or work as a librarian?

Yes, I do speak Chinese as I studied it in college, and also have lived in China for an extended period. From time to time, it comes in handy with Library visitors or guests who either speak Chinese as their native language or wish to share information about the Library in that language. For example, a California-based journalist

---

8 World Digital Library (WDL) – Homepage. Available at: https://www.wdl.org/en/.
9 United Nations Educational, Cultural and Scientific Organization (UNESCO) – Homepage. Available at: http://en.unesco.org/.

recently visited the Library. She produces a Chinese-language radio program out of San Francisco and appears on Bay-area television. At her request, I spoke to her and her family at length in Chinese about the Library and she thereafter created a radio program to acquaint her listeners with the Library and what it holds that may be of interest to them as visitors themselves.

Compared with other national libraries worldwide, would you say that the LC has staff coming from the most number of ethnic groups, cultural backgrounds, and language skills? If yes, what are the major challenges in working for such a multi-cultural and multi-ethnic organization?

I'm really not sure how we compare to national libraries worldwide, but the Library has staff from many backgrounds, cultures and nations, and many of them speak multiple languages. The multiculturalism and multi-ethnicity is not a problem – indeed, the Library often has public programs that bring forward these culturally fascinating offerings. Moreover, with a collection, more than half of which is not in English and that encompasses more than 460 languages, having a diverse staff is really an asset. As a U.S. federal agency, the Library strives for an overall workforce that represents generally the makeup of the nation.

After 28 years of leadership of the LC by James H. Billington, what change have you made in your time as Librarian of Congress? Have you faced considerable challenges in filling James Billington's shoes?

Dr. Billington was a gentleman and a scholar, and in his long tenure here made many key changes in the digital sphere, and with outreach and fundraising. It would be a challenge for anyone to try to fill his shoes! I am proud of the work accomplished during my time as Acting Librarian, and I believe the Library is positioned well to meet the needs of the 21st century. Through reorganization information technology governance, management, and staffing has improved; administrative operations are more efficient; and national and international outreach is better coordinated.

For many decades, the Library of Congress has set the standards for the sharing of library resources, as well as the standards for professional practices on an international scale in many respects. For example, many English-speaking and non-English-speaking countries have abandoned their own national standards and adopted MARC21, LC Classification Scheme, LC Subject Headings and LC Name Authority File, etc. (for the convenience of resources sharing on a global scale, as well as saving manpower from developing/maintaining their own national files/standards). In your view, what roles do you expect the LC to play in the international library community in the next 20 to 30 years?

I believe the Library of Congress will continue to help lead the international community in making digital and traditional analogue assets available. Working together in collaboration, the world library community will help create efficiencies that will allow for greater resource sharing and access.

Please describe the overall staffing structure at the LC? The Library of Congress has more than 3,000 employees.

Most staff work in one of three buildings on Capitol Hill in Washington, D.C., at special alternative storage facilities in Maryland, and a special Virginia facility focused on storage, conservation and preservation of audio-visual materials. The Library also has overseas offices to help with acquisitions in certain parts of the world. Organizationally, the Library includes five major divisions: the Congressional Research Service that provides unbiased research, analysis, and consultation to Congress; the U.S. Copyright Office that provides information support, conducts law and policy functions, and manages recordation and registration systems related to copyright; the Law Library of Congress that is the world's largest repository of legal information; Library Services that performs the work of a national library; and National and International Outreach, that is responsible for the Library's outward-facing programs, exhibitions and special public events. These many divisions work together well to provide service and information to the nation.

Could you describe your typical day at work? Is there ever a typical day at work? Who are the majority users of the LC? That is, who comes to see you about your collections, programs, and services?

It is very hard to describe a "typical day" for me. As Acting Librarian, I may be meeting with Library staff; speaking with a Member of Congress; greeting a foreign official; reviewing Library operations; advocating through congressional testimony; and addressing visitors and luminaries – all in the same day. People come to the Library, whether online or in person, to delve into unparalleled collections for research, scholarship, and learning. Increasingly, though, visitors include members of the public who want to see the beautiful and historic Thomas Jefferson Building – now more than a million visitors a year – and people attending the Library's museum-like exhibitions and many special events. For example, many do not know that the Library presents a free series of classical-music concerts throughout the fall and winter months, and into the spring, in the Coolidge Auditorium.

And the Library offers numerous free public events including lectures, author talks, folk-music concerts, and story hours for the young.

What are the major challenges that the LC is currently facing? As you said, "has been a constant challenge for us over the last few years, primarily because of the fiscal challenges." In fact, many arts and cultural organizations in the United States have been closed down. The health care system in the United States is also not comparable to its Canadian counterpart. When you get to meet the next new US President, what would be the first thing you want to say to him or her?

Despite an increasingly digital world, I don't anticipate any time in the near future where the Library will significantly decrease the physical material it adds to the collection. Finding adequate storage space continues to be an issue. Adequate staffing for the Library to fulfill its mission also is a major challenge. The Library has a first-rate staff and they do terrific work, but I know they would greatly enjoy the company of additional colleagues. If I had the opportunity to speak with the next president about the Library, I would urge him or her to make room for cultural spending even in tough times. Knowledge, creativity, and invention are the hallmarks of American progress and innovation, and are all the more important in time of fiscal restraint.

Which part(s) of your job as the Librarian do you find most rewarding? What is the most frustrating?

Working with the Library of Congress collection certainly is an amazing privilege; however, even more rewarding is working with the Library of Congress staff – employees who are high-calibre, innovative, and committed to public service. It is frustrating, though, that fiscal challenges hold back what could be greater progress and accomplishment.

I understand the staff at the LC carry the US Official Passport (which is different from the ones that held by a regular citizen). When you go through custom in a foreign country, would they sometimes assume that you work for the Whitehouse or the CIA?

Generally speaking, all United States government employees traveling abroad on official business use a special issuance passport.

I know that there has been a controversy going on with the LC about eliminating the use of the term "illegal alien" as a bibliographical term. Some legislators are fighting to keep that term for whatever reason. We are interested in learning more about it from your perspective (See: http://www.latimes.com/nation/la-na-library-congress-alien-20160403-story.html).

Indexing is a core business in library work. Because the Library creates cataloging materials and shares them with many other libraries around the country and the world, Library staff keep an eye on terminology and its changes. After all, the reason for creating catalogs is to help researchers efficiently find what need. Out-dated terms stay in the mix, but might not be the main access point. At times users approach the Library with recommendations. In early 2016, the American Library Association[10], representing the U.S. library community, asked the Library of Congress to amend a subject heading. The Library received the request, analyzed it, and proposed somewhat different subject headings. At present the Library is following its long-established procedure and receiving comments on the proposed change.

Further readings

David S. Mao [YouTube]. Available at: https://www.youtube.com/watch?v=7L2UA0Ulz_g.
DC Law.Gov 3.3 – David Mao [YouTube]. Available at: https://www.youtube.com/watch?v=jZ2QO1xrkEg.
Interview with David S. Mao [YouTube]. Available at: https://www.youtube.com/watch?v=4jJ-C9WbZY0.
The Law Library of Congress: Acquisitions, Access, and Authenticity [YouTube]. Available at: https://www.youtube.com/watch?v=pfesgiJpgAg.
*The Law Librarian of Congress: David Mao visits Diamond Ba*r [YouTube]. Available at: https://www.youtube.com/watch?v=WD3NPtYywgY.
Thomson Reuters – Tom Leighton and David Mao on the Magna Carta [YouTube]. Available at: https://www.youtube.com/watch?v=bgdUKhdP09o.

---

10 American Library Association – Homepage. Available at: http://www.ala.org/.

2 Dr. Johanna Rachinger

Director General, Austrian National Library

Introduction

Dripping with opulence and bursting with grace, this breathtakingly beautiful Baroque-style State Hall inside the Hofburg Palace in Vienna is a part of the Austrian National Library, and it is considered to be one of the most beautiful library halls in the world. The origin of the Imperial Court Library of the House of Habsburg dates back to the 14th century; the famous Baroque library building as part of the Hofburg was built in order of emperor Charles VI in the first half of the 18th century. Not until 1945 was it renamed "Austrian National Library". In addition to its large collections of incunabula of immeasurable value, the collection of the Austrian National Library contains handwritten notes and numerous scores and original printings of the works of legendary composers such as Wolfgang Amadeus Mozart, Anton Bruckner and Richard Strauss. In the following interview, Dr. Johanna Rachinger shares with us her unique management style and the rewards derived from managing this magnificent library that comes with centuries of information and tradition.

Fig. 2.1: Director General Dr. Johanna Rachinger (Photo: Sabine Hauswirth, Austrian National Library).

Fig. 2.2: Austrian National Library, Heldenplatz (Photo: Austrian National Library).

Fig. 2.3: State Hall (Photo: Hejduk, Austrian National Library).

Fig. 2.4: Augustinian Reading Room (Photo: Austrian National Library).

Could we begin this interview by first introducing yourself, for example, your training and background (what did you study at university), and your major roles and duties as the Director of Austrian National Library?[1] Have you always worked in libraries? Could you tell us more about your path to becoming the director of a National Library?

Having attended a higher secondary school with a focus on economics, I eventually graduated as doctor of philosophy in a humanities subject (theatre studies). In my professional career, I have concentrated on books from the very beginning. Following various job assignments, I worked for Austria's leading publishing house for many years, first as a project manager and finally as chief executive officer. When the position of the Austrian National Library's Director-General was advertised, I felt extremely tempted to apply. The post not only involved a new legal basis on which the library would operate in the future, but also and above all the challenge of the institution's fundamental reorientation in the digital age. We have succeeded in transforming a venerable library whose history stretches

---

[1] Austrian National Library – Homepage. Available at: http://www.onb.ac.at/ev/

back as far as the fourteenth century into a modern and service-oriented institution of the twenty-first century that innovatively makes use of state-of-the-art technologies.

Could you please provide a brief introduction about the roles and responsibilities as the Director of the Austrian National Library?

The tasks the general management is responsible for comprise all of the divisions of our institution, ranging from human resources and budget management and the strategic and administrative planning and implementation of defined priorities to public relations, sponsoring, etc.

What best prepared you for your work as Director of Austrian National Library?

Besides my chief interest in the book as a medium, my experience as CEO of a major publishing house has been extremely important. This involves strategic planning, innovativeness, decision-making, leadership in personnel matters, and, last but not least, economic thinking.

Could you describe your typical day at work? Is there ever a typical day at work?

My daily schedule resembles that of the manager of a big company. My day is filled with numerous appointments. In between, I always try to allow for time during which I can work in peace and go through important documents, reply to e-mails, etc. A major part of my work includes negotiations with political decision-makers and contacts with sponsors and international partners.

Could you describe your management or leadership style? Mentorship is such an important theme in leadership – both mentoring and being mentored. Could you please tell us about your experiences about both? Do you still have mentors that you go to?

In my professional career, I have always been fortunate enough to meet people who challenged and simultaneously fostered my talents. I still feel very grateful to them for their encouragement. At the same time, I have committed myself to impart my knowledge. This is why I have become a mentor who supports first and foremost young women on their way to management positions.

What is the current size of the Austrian National Library collections, including its special collections? Could you also describe the highlights of the Collections at the Austrian National Library?

Currently, the Austrian National Library's collections comprise as many as 11.6 million objects, a large part of which are digital objects. On the one hand, these are born-digital media, such as web content (about 1.7 million units); on the other hand, they include permanently archived digital copies of analogue media (about 1.3 million units). In addition, there are roughly 3.8 million printed documents, more than 3 million pictorial documents, as well as other media, such as manuscripts and correspondences, papyri, sound recordings, etc.

Its roots, which reach back as far as the fourteenth century, have left their imprint on what is now the Austrian National Library. As heir to the Imperial Court Library, it preserves a substantial part of written documents that are considered part of the World Cultural Heritage, and whose origins lie far beyond today's national borders. These documents particularly include medieval manuscripts, incunabula and early prints, historical maps and globes, musical autographs, portraits, and even antique papyri. The global significance of our historical collections also finds expression in seven successful nominations to UNESCO's Memory of the World Register. (http://www.onb.ac.at/)

The Austrian National Library holds eight special collections and has four museums that are affiliated to it (Esperanto Museum, Globe Museum, Literature Museum, Papyrus Museum). In addition, special exhibitions are held at the Baroque State Hall on a regular basis. These are examples of the close and synergetic connection between conservation (archiving), exploration (research), and public presentation.

Which part(s) of your job as the Director do you find most rewarding? What is the most frustrating?

One of the most positive and at the same time, most challenging aspects of my job is that, in extremely dynamic times marked by the change from analogue to digital media, I must make far-reaching decisions impacting the library's future. New ideas are indispensable in order to secure the library's position in tomorrow's society. It goes without saying that at the same time it is also important to secure the funds for these complementary tasks and projects.

3 Caroline Brazier

Chief Librarian, British Library

Introduction

The British Library is the national library of the United Kingdom, and it is the second-largest library in the world in terms of its collection size. In 1973, the British Library Act 1972 detached the library department from the British Museum, but it continued to host the library in its building until 1997. As the legal depository of the UK, the British Library collects copies of all materials published in the UK and Ireland as well as a significant proportion of overseas titles distributed there.

A graduate of the University of Edinburgh, Caroline Brazier received her MA from University College London in Library and Information Studies. She has been serving as Chief Librarian of the British Library since 2013. Prior to that, Brazier was the Director of Scholarship and Collections (2011–2013), Associate Director of Operations and Services (2009–2011), Head of Resource Discovery (2008–2009) and Head of Collection Acquisition and Description (2002–2007) of the British Library. Before joining the British Library in 2002, Brazier spent almost 20 years working as an academic librarian mainly at Dublin City University and Trinity College Dublin.

Being a member of the Library's Executive Team, Brazier reports directly to the Chief Executive of the British Library. In the following interview, Brazier discusses the rewards and challenges derived from being the Chief Librarian of the second-largest library in the world, as well as the professional roles that the British Library plays with libraries in the UK and internationally and, in particular, the world of global librarianship.

Fig. 3.1: Caroline Brazier, Chief Librarian, British Library (Photo: British Library).

DOI 10.1515/9783110533347-004

Fig. 3.2: The British Library (Photo: Jack 1956).

Could we begin this interview by first introducing yourself, for example, your professional training and education background? For example, what did you study at university? Could you also describe your role as Chief Librarian of the British Library?

I graduated with an MA in history from Edinburgh University[1], followed by a professional diploma and MA from University College London[2] in Library and Information Studies (LIS). After qualifying I worked in a variety of professional library roles within the university sector, mainly in Ireland, from 1982 to 2002.

I joined the British Library[3] in 2002. I have held several roles in the Library since then, including Head of Collection Acquisition and Description (responsible for the large-scale collection management services and the systems which underpin them), and Associate Director for Operations at the Library's Boston Spa site (in addition to Collection Acquisition and Description also responsible

---

1 The University of Edinburgh – Homepage. Available at: http://www.ed.ac.uk/
2 University College London (UCL) – Homepage. Available at: http://www.ucl.ac.uk/
3 The British Library – Homepage. Available at: http://www.bl.uk/

for the development of the Library's international document supply service). In 2010, I was promoted to Director of Scholarship and Collections and my current role as Chief Librarian follows on from this.

As Chief Librarian, I am responsible for all aspects of the curation and management of our collections, in both physical and digital formats. Staff in my area work across a wide range of professional library, archival, curatorial and research roles, including curation, acquisitions, cataloging and metadata, conservation, preservation, digitization and research support. The division has c. 600 staff, who work at our sites at St. Pancras in London and Boston Spa in Yorkshire. The main departments and functions include:
- Collections and Curation, including Contemporary British Collections, Western Heritage Collections, European and American Collections, Asian and African Collections;
- Collection Management, including Conservation and Preservation, Cataloging and Processing, Metadata Services, Resource Discovery and Collection Development;
- Research Services, including service and content development for researchers in Arts and Humanities, Social Science and Science, Technology and Medicine;
- Digital Scholarship, including digital research and digitization management;
- Cultural Engagement, broadening the cultural reach of the collections across the UK and internationally, through exhibitions and events;
- Learning, serving the needs of learners of all ages, from schools to lifelong learners;
- Business services, including the development of a UK wide network of Business and Intellectual Property Centres;
- Higher Education, developing strategic links with the UK research sector;
- International Office, which coordinates and manages the international collaboration and diplomatic engagement of the Library.

I am also responsible for the Eccles Centre for American Studies [at the British Library][4], and the British Library Qatar Foundation program.[5]

---

[4] Eccles Centre for American Studies at the British Library – Homepage. Available at: http://www.bl.uk/eccles/
[5] British Library Qatar Foundation program – Homepage. Available at: http://www.bl.uk/qatar/

Have you always worked in libraries? Could you tell us more about your path to becoming the Chief Librarian of the British Library?

Yes, I have always worked in libraries! I have always loved being a user of libraries in my personal life, and I was lucky to be helped by some wonderful librarians as a child and throughout my education. This is what inspired me to think about a career as a librarian. Since qualifying as a librarian, my whole professional career has been in library services, in higher education and national libraries. With each role, I have tried to gain more experience both in professional expertise but also in leadership and strategic management.

The roles I have worked in, including major projects, span areas such as developing new generations of library services for teaching and research, introducing major new IT systems, managing new library building projects, and managing changes in legal and regulatory frameworks such as copyright and legal deposit. Staff management and team building have also been a major focus in every role, in both large and small libraries. I have also tried to be active in the wider profession throughout my career, through membership with professional library associations, serving on the management boards of library sector organizations, writing and giving presentations at professional conferences and symposia.

Could you please provide a brief introduction about the Chief Librarian of the British Library?

As the Chief Librarian, I lead a team of senior staff who are responsible for all aspects of strategic development and management of the Library's collections to ensure they remain world class, relevant to all the Library's audiences and accessible for research and scholarship. I am responsible for delivering on the Library's core mandate to develop, preserve, curate and make available the British Library's collection of over 150 million items. As well as meeting the needs of researchers in the UK and around the world, the Library also tries to make its collections available to cultural visitors and learners of all ages, through a growing program of exhibitions and cultural and educational events. I am strongly committed to ensuring the Library shares its collections as widely as possible nationally and internationally.

One of our key areas of work is the development of digital library services, particularly implementing digital legal deposit in the UK. With my colleagues we are working hard to understand and deliver the new skills, standards and infrastructure we need, both as an individual institution and also as part of the wider information profession to make this transformation.

In my current role, I am deeply involved in collaboration and partnership across the library world. I am currently a Board member of Research Libraries UK (RLUK), of SCONUL (Standing Conference of National and University Libraries), and of the UK Research Reserve[6] which are all working towards better collaborative and shared services to support library users in the UK. I am also actively involved at European level collaboration through the Conference of European National Libraries (CENL)[7], where I currently serve as Treasurer.

What is the current size of the British Library collections, including its special collections? Could you also describe what you deem are the highlights of the collection?

This is a very difficult question to answer. Our collections span over 3,000 years, include many formats including written texts in manuscripts, printed books, journals, newspapers and digital documents, as well as maps, stamps, music, prints, photographs, sound recordings, film, broadcasts and web sites, etc. We estimate we have between 150 and 200 million unique items representing every age of written civilization. There is almost no subject, no part of the world, no faith, and no language on which we cannot help researchers shed more light.

It is extremely difficult to pick individual "highlights" out of the collection because of its scale and complexity. The most famous and iconic include items such as copies of Magna Carta, the Lindisfarne Gospels, original manuscripts of major literary figures such as Charlotte Bronte and Jane Austen as well as major cultural figures such as The Beatles. Many of our highlights are collections, such as our collections of newspapers, or the UK Sound Archive, rather than individual items. We do identify some of our most iconic 'Treasures' on our website and I would recommend anyone to start exploring here (See details at: http://www.bl.uk/highlights/)

Does your Library work closely with other libraries across the United Kingdom? What about the rest of the world? If so, could you tell us about such cross-national or global collaborative projects? What are some highlights?

---

6 UK Research Reserve – Homepage. Available at: http://www.ukrr.ac.uk/
7 Conference of European National Libraries (CENL) – Homepage. Available at: http://www.cenl.org/

Yes, we work closely with the higher education sector, and with the public library network on various initiatives. Collaboration and partnership are core to our philosophy and the way we work. In our Living Knowledge vision (http://www.bl.uk/projects/living-knowledge-the-british-library-2015-2023) we set out our fundamental purposes which are:
- Custodianship: We build, curate and preserve the UK's national collection of published, written and digital content;
- Research: We support and stimulate research of all kinds;
- Business: We help businesses to innovate and grow;
- Culture: We engage everyone with memorable cultural experiences;
- Learning: We inspire young people and learners of all ages;
- International: We work with partners around the world to advance knowledge and mutual understanding.

Under each of these purposes we seek to work collaboratively with the library and wider cultural and educational sectors across the UK and internationally. Some of our major collaborations include:

UK Research Reserve. This is a major custodianship collaboration with the university library sector across the UK. To enable university libraries to make better use of their spaces and to de-duplicate the number of copies of low-use runs of scholarly journals held across the UK, we have worked in partnership with the HE community to take in and de-duplicate any research journals which we did not already hold. This has resulted in over 90 km of journal storage being released for other purposes in the universities.

British Library Business and Intellectual Property National Network. This is a major collaboration in support of our business purpose. Having successfully set up and developed a business and intellectual property information service at our St. Pancras site, we have also worked with major city public libraries around the UK to support them to develop similar services. These services are directed at supporting entrepreneurs and smaller businesses to grow their business and create new jobs. They provide free access to databases, market research, journals, directories and reports, as well as a program of free and low-cost workshops on a range of topics including business planning, marketing and intellectual property. The original network consisted of 6 partners in Birmingham, Leeds, Liverpool, Manchester, Newcastle and Sheffield and we are currently working on plans to expand it to 20 partner city libraries (See details at: http://www.bl.uk/business-and-ip-centre/national-network)

International digitization partnerships. To support our custodianship, research and international purposes we collaborate with national libraries and other organizations around the world to digitize and share our collections digitally. These projects are often also done in partnership and with the support of philanthropic organizations who are working to advance education and culture in many countries around the world. The largest international partnership has been the **British Library Qatar Foundation Partnership.** We have worked in partnership with the Qatar Foundation and the Qatar Digital Library to digitize many of the archival records in our collections relating to the history of the Gulf region, as well as many Arabic scientific manuscripts which highlight the contribution of Arab science to scientific development. This content is freely available through the Qatar Digital Library, a bilingual, online service from the Qatar National Library (See details at: http://www.qdl.qa/en)

Cultural and learning partnerships. We also work in partnership to develop our cultural and learning purposes. Following the success of the national network for business services, we are developing a similar network with UK public libraries to share our collections, events and exhibitions more widely around the UK. The first of these partnerships has been between the British Library and the Library of Birmingham, the public library of the city of Birmingham. The partnership has already delivered a major Shakespeare exhibition, focussing on the relationship between Shakespeare and his native county. The partnership brings together the world class collections on Shakespeare in the Library together with curatorial, exhibition design and conservation expertise from the British Library. http://www.libraryofbirmingham.com/event/Events/ourshakespeare. A second exhibition and events series is planned on the theme of the South Asian experience in Birmingham, using local and national sources and expertise.

Please describe the staffing structure at the British Library?

The British Library is governed by a Board appointed by UK government to oversee its strategy and development. Responsibility and delegated authority for the management of the British Library rests with the Executive Leadership Team, under the leadership of the Chief Executive, who as Accounting Officer, is responsible to UK Parliament. In December 2014, the Chief Executive announced a new structure to be effective from 1st April 2015, with an executive team consisting of the Chief Executive, the Chief Operating Officer and the Chief Librarian (See details at: http://www.bl.uk/aboutus/annrep/2014to2015/annual-report2014-15.pdf).

The executive team of the British Library consists of:

Could you describe your typical day at work? Is there ever a typical day at work?

It is really difficult to answer that question as there is no typical day. Most of my work is done through meetings, both internal and external. I am heavily involved in the day-to-day management of the library and this work is done through a series of governance meetings, executive meetings with the Chief Executive and Chief Operating Officer, strategy and business meetings of the Library's Senior Leadership Team, meetings to oversee our major programs of work which I chair, as well as many discussions with my direct reports, each of whom is responsible for a major area of library activity.

Because the Library works in a very collaborative way, there are also many meetings in the UK and internationally with partners. I represent the Library at many external meetings on national projects such as UK Research Reserve or the National Monograph Strategy.

I also regularly give professional talks and presentations, as well as writing occasional professional articles and book chapters. These all require time to research and prepare so that also takes up a lot of time!

What scholarly and professional associations are you a part of, and how do they inform you in your work?

I am a member and also currently a Trustee on the Board of CILIP, the Chartered Institute of Library and Information Professionals[8] in the UK. I believe that access to information, improving knowledge through literacy and supporting learning for everyone are vital public services and that libraries are an essential part of that service. Library and information services in the UK, as well as internationally, are going through a period of unprecedented challenge and change and so in my role in the British Library I try to be a strategic voice to advocate for libraries and for information professionals. I also look for ways in which the British Library can work alongside other organizations to promote our shared goals and common values.

I am also a Board member of both Research Libraries UK (RLUK http://www.rluk.ac.uk/), and the Society of College, National and University Libraries (SCONUL http://www.sconul.ac.uk/). Both organizations represent the interests and promote the major research libraries and university libraries across the UK. Our shared vision of the future of the modern research and educational library is important to the British Library's strategy. I see my role as ensuring that we are aware of how the research world is changing and that the British Library adapts its services and collections to make sure we are still relevant as a major partner in the UK and internationally.

I am also currently the Treasurer of CENL, the Conference of European National Librarians. CENL is a network of 49 libraries from 46 European countries, who share a common vision of making the rich cultural and heritage collections of Europe's national libraries known and available to all. (http://www.cenl.org/). Through CENL, I also engage with other international organizations such as LIBER and CDNL (Conference of Directors of National Libraries), which meets annually at IFLA. These international links are core to the British Library's strategy and help shape our priorities. Whether it is working together on shared international standards to support libraries in a digital age, or work on transnational legal issues such as copyright reform or digital legal deposit, or building new collaborations to develop digital collections or share new technologies, my work with the international library community is a very important part of my remit.

You gave a talk called "Living Knowledge: the value of national libraries" to the Library and Archives Canada (LAC) explore the different ways in which we can look

---

[8] Chartered Institute of Library and Information Professionals (CILIP) – Homepage. Available at: http://www.cilip.org.uk/

at the benefits which come from national libraries. Could you elaborate on how the British Library exemplifies these core points?

There are many different "types" of national library around the world, different in size, in function and in structure. But while we all work in different ways, we all have a common purpose to deliver public value for the nations and communities we serve. This can be through the way we collect, preserve and make available our national memory (through legal deposit and other archival services). It can also be through the services we offer to our users and the support we give them to meet their educational and informational needs, such as through our reference, business and research services. Increasingly, it is through our role as cultural organizations and the ways in which we can inspire people and help them achieve their goals. Through bringing our collections to life and by being innovative in the ways we serve people, we aim to reach the widest possible audience, to be open, welcoming and make them feel they belong. This does not detract from our role in serving the highest achieving researchers and scholars, rather it complements it and makes us more aware of everyone's needs. I hope I conveyed this in my talk at Library and Archives Canada (https://www.bac-lac.gc.ca/eng/about-us/events/Documents/Living-Knowledge-value-national-libraries_en.pdf).

National Information Policy – what are the aims and the core essence of the national information policy in your country?

There is no single formal statutory national information policy in the UK. We work within a framework of national regulations, including Public Sector Information, Open Data and information governance, as well as regulations specific to the role of the British Library such as legal deposit regulations. The British Library is charged with systematically collecting and archiving the UK's national published output and since 2013 this covers material published digitally and online, including e-books, e-journals and websites.

The range of UK policies aim to maintain a balance between the rights of access to information for research and commercial reuse and the rights of creators and subjects of information, through copyright and data protection and privacy.

Who are the majority users of the British Library? That is, who comes to see you about your collections, programs, and services?

We serve a wide range of visitors who come for many reasons. We can broadly categorize these as:
- Academic researchers – people involved in formal academic work whether as senior academics, postgraduates or undergraduates who come to use the collections and consult our curatorial and reference experts.

- Work and personal researchers – people outside formal academic life who come to consult the collections for professional reasons, such as journalists, for creative reasons, such as writers and artists or for personal reasons such as entrepreneurs to our Business Centre or family history.
- Cultural and leisure visitors – people who come to visit an exhibition, attend an event, meet friends for coffee or just enjoy our building and facilities.

At any one time in the building the people you see around you are roughly split equally between these three types of visitor. However, it is the academic researchers who visit most frequently so they make up the majority of our total number of visits. There were c. 380,000 visits to our Reading Rooms in 2014/2015. However, this compares with over 19 million "visits" to our website and online services including catalogs, collections pages and online services such as booking tickets. Our online annual reports give more details (http://www.bl.uk/aboutus/annrep/).

For many decades, the Library of Congress has been taking up leadership roles in setting policies and standards for both resources sharing and professional/operational practices worldwide. Given the sheer number of Commonwealth of Nations around the world, what roles does the British Library play in this context?

The British Library has a long history of working collaboratively at international levels to provide leadership in standards and infrastructure development. We have worked alongside Library of Congress and other national libraries in the development of the RDA standard for description of information assets; we make a major contribution at European and global level to policy on reform of copyright and related legal issues on use of library collections. We are major partners in leading international library consortia where we try to solve problems and to advance the skills and knowledge of the library sector together. One good example is the IIPC (International Internet Preservation Consortium)[9] through which major national libraries work in partnership to develop new infrastructures and workflows for the efficient collecting and preservation of websites. The web is global, but the laws under which we collect the web are national, so it is only by working collaboratively to ensure we can do this together that we will be able to recreate today's web environment for future generations of researchers.

---

9 International Internet Preservation Consortium (IIPC) – Homepage. Available at: http://www.netpreserve.org/

Could you describe your management and leadership style? Mentorship is such an important theme in leadership – both mentoring and being mentored. Could you please tell us about your experiences about both?

I have learned through my own experience that people work best when they have a sense of ownership and control over their work and feel that their ideas and views are valued. I try to make time for people, to listen a lot and to ensure that people have opportunities to develop themselves. I was fortunate enough in the early parts of my career to work for librarians who gave me challenges, which stretched me professionally and broadened my experiences. I try to do that for others.

Which part(s) of your job as the Librarian do you find most rewarding? What is the most frustrating?

I get huge pleasure from the sense of progress and change in our ability to serve library users. The most rewarding thing is seeing something that you have worked on from the earliest stages come to fruition and be successful, whether it is a new service, a new building or delivering a major IT project.

The most frustrating thing is probably too many meetings, especially those which do not really contribute to the progress and change I am hoping for. So one of my main aims is to make sure that meetings have a purpose!

Further readings

British Library Labs Presentation at Open Repositories 2016 [YouTube]. Available at: https://www.youtube.com/watch?v=e9T5zP2iZIM

The British Library – the World's Knowledge. Available at: http://www.bl.uk/

Caroline Brazier Appointed British Library Director of Scholarship & Collections. Available at: https://www.bl.uk/press-releases/2010/november/caroline-brazier-appointed-british-library-director-of-scholarship--collections

Chief Librarian – British Library. Available at: http://www.bl.uk/aboutus/foi/pubsch/pubscheme1/DirectorofCollections.html

GLAM-Wiki 2013 - Caroline Brazier opens the conference [YouTube]. Available at: https://www.youtube.com/watch?v=s3XZQwhNEgQ

Presentation to the 2015 British Library Labs Competition winners [YouTube]. Available at: https://www.youtube.com/watch?v=SaDNUHlug6A

Welcome to the Launch of British Library Labs [YouTube]. Available at: https://www.youtube.com/watch?v=K4zVg2lQRro

What the Library has learned from the British Library Labs project [YouTube]. Available at: https://www.youtube.com/watch?v=WHPnhzGuq3M

4 Ana Santos Aramburo

Director, National Library of Spain

Introduction

The national libraries of Europe were founded mostly as private archives or personal libraries of different royal households. They would then be open to the general public and became national libraries by the end of the 19th century. Taking the National Library of Spain as an example, it was originally founded by Philip V at the end of 1711, and opened its doors in March of the following year as Royal Public Library. In 1836, the Library stopped being property of the crown, and the ownership of the Library was transferred to the Ministry of Home Affairs. In that same year, it received for the first time the name of National Library. With reference to the scope of its collections, at the end of the nineteenth century, a decree ordered the seizure of archives, libraries and art collections held by different cathedrals, monasteries and military orders, among others – so that valuable works from the cathedrals of Avila and Toledo were transferred to the Royal Library of Spain. Between 1936 and 1939, during the Civil War, the Seizure Board collected nearly 500,000 volumes with the intention of safeguarding books and works of art originally preserved in religious centers, palaces or private homes.

Ana Santos Aramburo became the Director of this National Library of immeasurable historical and cultural values in 2013. Santos, who graduated with a degree in History, began her career as a librarian at the University of Zaragoza more than thirty years ago. In the following interview, Santos addresses the challenges she faces in guiding this century-old institution, as well as the strategies she develops for drawing a new future marked by an environment increasingly channeled through digital technology.

Fig. 4.1: Ana Santos Aramburo, Director of the National Library of Spain (Photo: National Library of Spain).

DOI 10.1515/9783110533347-005

Fig. 4.2: Main facade of the BNE (Photo: National Library of Spain).

Fig. 4.3: Hall of entrance to the BNE (Photo: National Library of Spain).

Fig. 4.4: General Reading Room (Photo: National Library of Spain).

Could we begin this interview by first introducing yourself, for example, your training and background? Could you also describe your described role as the Director of the National Library of Spain?

I have been a librarian for more than 30 years. I started as a library assistant at the University of Zaragoza, although most of my career has been spent at the Library of the Complutense University of Madrid (UCM).[1] In this institution, I held various positions of responsibility such as being responsible for the computerization in the 1990s, the Historical Library Director or Director of the Library of the UCM.

At the National Library of Spain / Biblioteca Nacional de España (BNE)[2], I was the Director of Culture for more than four years, and since 2013, I have been the Director of the Library. My responsibility is to guide this institution so that its enormous value can benefit the culture and adapt to the digital environment, so that it can continue to fulfil the missions of National Library of Spain that began more than 300 years ago.

---

1 Complutense University of Madrid – Homepage. Available at: https://www.ucm.es/english
2 National Library of Spain / Biblioteca Nacional de España (BNE) – Homepage. Available at: http://www.bne.es/en/LaBNE/

Your responsibility is to liberate this institution – to "liberate" – does it mean to try as much as possible – making the collections and other valuable materials of the National Library of Spain available for the general public to access?

More than "to liberate" would be "to make available" the collections and open the institution for cultural enjoyment.

Which university did you attend, and what subjects did you study at university?

I attended the University of Zaragoza[3] (Spain), and I studied History. After that, I took different courses focusing on library sciences.

How many different languages have you mastered?

Spanish is my native tongue, and I also have intermediate-level English and French.

Have you always worked in libraries? Could you tell us more about your path to becoming the Director of the National Library of Spain?

Yes, as I have already mentioned, I belong to the Project Scale Library of the Complutense University for more than 25 years. I have had the privilege of doing a job that I love, and I have had various responsibilities throughout my career from lending and placing books in the stacks to leading the university library, which has provided me a very valuable experience. I have already been familiar with the National Library of Spain before becoming its director, because I was responsible for its cultural schedule for almost five years. This gave me a vision of the institution, which finally was very useful at the time when I took up the managerial responsibilities.

Could you please provide a brief introduction about the National Library of Spain? When the National Library of Spain was first established by King Philip V of Spain in 1712, what kind of vision did he have in mind? What roles did King Philip V want the National Library of Spain to play?

The National Library of Spain is the oldest cultural institution in Spain founded by the first monarch of the Bourbon Dynasty in Spain, Felipe V, in 1712. When he began his reign, he thought that a good way to get the Spanish people to be more educated was to create a [public] library, which would be available for all. The King [Felipe V] did so by adding his own [personal royal] library as a part of the library of the Habsburg Empire. In the following years, major [royal] libraries

---

3 University of Zaragoza – Homepage. Available at: http://wzar.unizar.es/servicios/ingles/prese.htm

were enriched by seizing from the other noble families in Europe who had lost the War of the Spanish Succession – and this became the core foundational works of immense heritage value for Spain. A few years later, the nationwide legal deposit regulations was approved so that everything that was published in Spain would be deposited. In short, one of the core missions of the National Library of Spain is to preserve the cultural memories of the country of Spain, as well as to transmit knowledge – thereby cultivating for the future generations in order to not lose our own unique cultural identity.

"The King [Felipe V] did so by adding his own [personal royal] library as a part of the library of the Habsburgs" – how has the library collection of the Royal House of Austria end up being a part of the library of the Habsburgs?

One of the heartlands of the house of Habsburg was what is Austria today. In the 16th century, Spain, like many other countries, was under the Habsburg rule, too.

What is the current size of the National Library of Spain's collections, including its special collections? Could you also describe what you deem are the highlights of the collection?

The collection is over 32 million copies of all types of materials: manuscripts, books, magazines, newspapers, CDs, videos, sheet music, prints, drawings, maps, etc.; and recently, we have begun to preserve digital contents, e.g., digital books and Spanish websites, etc. It is very difficult to choose the most emblematic copies since the origin of the National Library of Spain was the [former] Library of the Spanish Royal Court – containing works of great historical and cultural values, and there are also very valuable copies, which were bought later with the addition of other libraries of the noblemen. Over the following centuries, the National Library incorporated libraries of important bibliophiles with copies of great value and all kinds of materials. It is therefore very difficult to select individual works from the collection of the National Library of Spain that could simply be called highlights of our Library's collection. But, many of us would agree that the original manuscript copy of *Song of the Cid*, the *Beatus of Liebana*, the *Madrid codices of Leonardo de Vinci*, etc. – are undoubtedly some of the most valuable Spanish documentary heritage belonging to the National Library of Spain.

Do you also work closely with other libraries across Spain and Europe? Such as on cross-national or globally collaborative projects? What are some highlights?

We work in close cooperation with associations representing librarians' collectives. In Spain, we coordinate the Cooperation Committee with Regional Libraries within the Library Cooperation Council. In Europe, we are members of the Consortium of European National Librarians (CENL) and Latin America of the Association of Ibero-American National Libraries. We highlight some important projects we have developed cooperatively as the Digital Library Heritage Ibero-American grouping collections of national libraries from 12 countries. In Spain, we coordinate the legal deposit of electronic publications for other regional libraries and of course in Europe participate in Europeana.

Please describe the staffing structure at the National Library of Spain. For example, what are the working relationships between the various Heads of subject/cataloging departments and the branch heads in such a vast and large system?

Below is the organizational structure of the National Library of Spain:

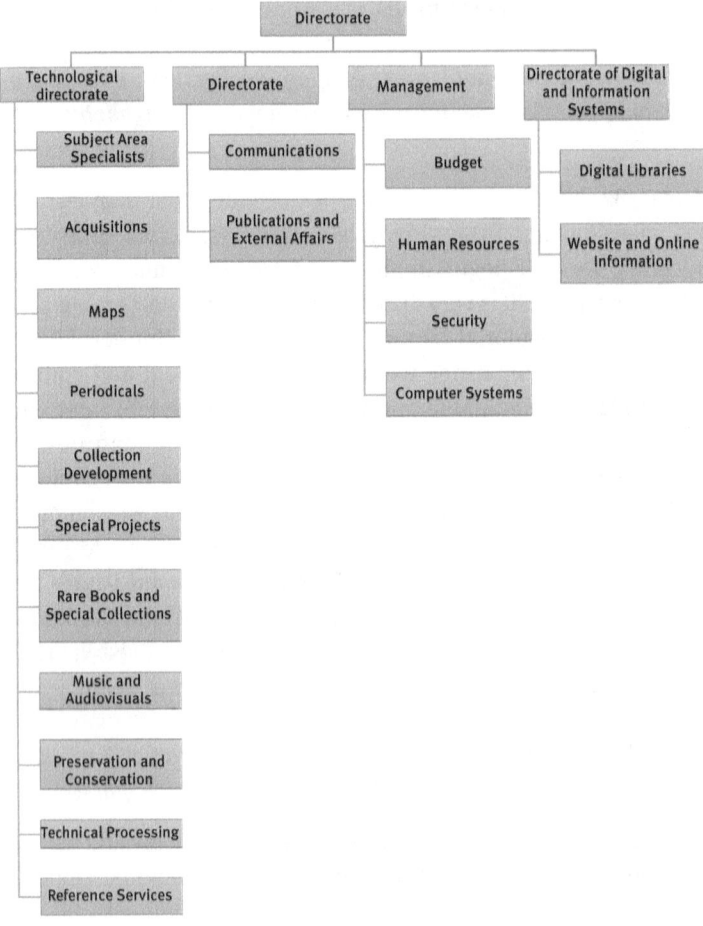

The relationship also hierarchical, functional – defined according to the 2015–2020 Strategic Plan: http://www.bne.es/webdocs/LaBNE/PlanEstrategico/Plan_estrategico_2015-2020.pdf

A series of actions involve different departments, and this is very changeable according to different projects that are underway.

Could you describe your typical day at work? Is there ever a typical day at work?

I do not have any days that are similar to each other. Each day changes according to different circumstances. Usually several meetings, receiving professional visits, and I also try to have some time for personal work in order to struggle with paperwork or think about certain issues.

What scholarly and professional associations are you a part of, and how do they inform you in your work?

I am part of the Iberianamerican States' Association for the Development of the Nationals Libraries of Iberianamerica (ABINIA), and the Cooperation Council Library (CENL).

Who are the majority users of the National Library of Spain? That is, who comes to see you about your collections, programs, and services?

They are mainly researchers and scholars majoring in the Spanish culture seeking for consultations on works that can only be found in our collection. But, every time we have more people coming to the National Library of Spain to enjoy their cultural activities, students doing the practices of their studies or research groups working closely together on projects related to our collections. In other words, our users are becoming increasingly diverse.

Could you give examples of types of new programs and services at National Library of Spain, which you've found successful or innovative?

All have to do with the two main areas of development: digital Library and digital services and cultural programming.

Some examples include the Hispanic Digital Library, the Digital Newspaper Library, the legal deposit of online publications. These are all new projects that provide a service of great value and unstoppable growth. On the other hand, everything can be something related to a cultural activity that allows us to show the National Library of Spain as an open institution, where anyone is welcome to come to learn.

In 2015, it was finally drafted into law that gave the National Library of Spain greater autonomy and a similar status to the Prado Museum[4] and the National Museum Centro de Arte Reina Sofía.[5] How has this all changed the Library and how has the new law enabled your role in managing the resources of the Library more autonomously?

The law is fundamental to give the National Library of Spain the value it deserves as an essential institution for the preservation of Hispanic culture (worldwide). In addition, in order to improve its status and consideration it has account creation management bodies that will work more autonomously once the statute is approved by this law.

Upon your appointment, you have emphasized on the launch of the digital legal depository as one of your priorities in your mandate as Director, and you helped prepare a royal decree to regulate the legal deposit of digital content. How has this change affected the acquisitions of digital materials?

The Spanish Royal Decree has already been approved in July 2015, and since then, we are working to implement this project; however, the technological challenge is of great importance. This will also allow us to preserve digital materials and contents of the Spanish web, which is essential at this time. This new project changes how to enter the materials and their consultation and use. For the former, we have worked with publishers, and we facilitate the deposit and issues regarding the use and dealing with the copyright issues.

What is the role of technology and innovation at National Library of Spain?

Technological development and constant adaptation to changes occurring in the world of information is essential to the National Library of Spain, which is brought by technology, tends to be strategic.

Since April 2009, the National Library of Spain had been keeping copies of web documents in the Internet Domain, which is under an agreement with Internet Archive. This information becomes stored in the servers of National Library of Spain, and it will expand its capacity to preserve digital videos. How much has your library needed to prepare for this project in both technological needs and staffing needs?

---

4 Prado Museum – Homepage. Available at: https://www.museodelprado.es/en
5 Museo Nacional Centro de Arte Reina Sofía – Homepage. Available at: *http://www.museoreinasofia.es/en*

This project is a major challenge for the National Library of Spain. In April of this year, the digital collections that were conserved in California reached the National Library of Spain's servers, and from that moment collections continue to enrich us, including specific issues such as a general dominion, which we just launched a few days ago. We had to acquire IT infrastructure and people engaged in this project, both computer and librarians have had to make an effort on training. Fortunately, we have had significant supports from both the IIPC and the National Library of France, which have especially helped us in training issues; as the public entity that has given us financial support, without which there would not have been possible to put this project on track. We have also enjoyed the cooperation of other [public and private] sectors such as the Union of Publishers or other associations that have contributed to that today, fortunately, what was once a project is a reality nowadays.

Could you describe your management and leadership style? Mentorship is such an important theme in leadership – both mentoring and being mentored. Could you please tell us about your experiences about both? Do you still have mentors that you go to?

With reference to my management style, I try to be as participatory and as open as possible – encouraging communication, and involving people in achieving the different objectives, etc. I consider the staff at the National Library of Spain to be a fundamental value (core assets), and that they are the true "architects" or "engineers" behind many of our achievements. There have been people whom I would consider teachers or mentors throughout my career, and now, if you consult with experts in the case of difficult decisions, I think it is essential that they can provide a different point of view and contribute, so therefore, to take decisions for future and continuous improvements.

Some of the previous Directors of the National Library of Spain have been intellectuals who don't have a background in libraries – individuals such as writers and artists. How important is it for the position of Director to have a background or training in librarianship?

I think it is very important to professionalize the position of the director, especially since it requires significant knowledge such as in public administration management as much as skills in the librarian sphere/community. It is also important that a post of this nature ceases to be politicized, and is chosen in an open procedure, where prevail the values of professionalism, competence and experience for their performance, and be selected by an independent expert committee. This is what provides the Law (the philosophy behind the service) of the

National Library of Spain – and this is why I was chosen to become to General Director of the National Library of Spain, and this will also the criteria for selecting my successors for leading this Library.

Which part(s) of your job as the Director do you find most rewarding? What is the most frustrating?

The greatest satisfaction is to see how people come to discover and to enjoy the services and the variety of cultural programs carried out by the National Library of Spain. People of different social classes and any political views, and those who desire to learn can do it right here in our living rooms at the National Library of Spain as a reader, or as a participant of the cultural programs carried out by our Library. The contributions of the National Library of Spain could more compensate for many shortcomings and downfalls in society. Also, the positive attitudes and feedbacks from the staff working for the National Library of Spain – telling me that the newly implemented projects that they have engaged in have generated good results and high user satisfaction. I suppose that collective consciousness is essential for the ongoing operations and success of any cultural organization. What gives me the greatest frustration is the lack of support, especially since the enormous effort that needs to be done to get some things that are logical but prevents administrative operations with more complicity. Meanwhile, the failure to make decisions on major issues could also make me feel helpless at times.

5 Marie-Christine Doffey

Director, Swiss National Library

Introduction

Situated in Bern, the capital city of Switzerland, the Swiss National Library is part of the Federal Office of Culture, and it is both a cultural memory institution and a research library that is open to all members of the general public.

A graduate of Antiquity Studies from the University of Fribourg and Arts Management from the University of Basel, Marie-Christine Doffey became the Director of the Swiss National Library in 2005. In the following interview, Doffey discusses her pragmatic management style as well as the advantages of having a team of library staff coming from many different linguistic regions, cultures, and ways of thinking – working side-by-side together in a country that has four different official languages.

Fig. 5.1: Marie-Christine Doffey, Director of the Swiss National Library (Photo: Swiss National Library).

DOI 10.1515/9783110533347-006

Fig. 5.2: The Swiss National Library in Bern. This listed building was inaugurated in 1931 and is the only Swiss library built in the style of "Neues Bauen" (close to Bauhaus). The NL was founded in 1895 and housed in various locations in Bern before moving to this building in 1931 (Photo: Swiss National Library).

Fig. 5.3: Staircase leading to reading rooms, study areas and reference section, and Swiss Literary Archives. (Photo: Swiss National Library).

Fig. 5.4: The main reading room, with furniture in the style of the 1930s (Photo: Swiss National Library).

Could we begin this interview by first introducing yourself, for example, your training and background, and your major roles and duties as the Director of Swiss National Library? Have you always worked in libraries? Could you tell us more about your path to becoming the director of a National Library?

I have been Director of the Swiss National Library[1] since 2005. I hold a degree in Antiquity studies from the University of Fribourg[2] (1983), and a Master of Advanced Studies in Arts Management from the University of Basel[3] (2002). I started my career as a subject indexer at the Fribourg Cantonal and University Library before moving to the Swiss National Library in 1991, where I have worked in a number of departments (head of the national union catalog of serials, head of the Collections Section). I became Vice Director of the Swiss National Library in 2003, and Director in 2005.

---

1 Swiss National Library – Homepage. Available at: https://www.nb.admin.ch/?lang=en
2 University of Fribourg – Homepage. Available at: http://www3.unifr.ch/home/en/
3 University of Basel – Homepage. Available at: https://www.unibas.ch/en.html

What best prepared you for your work as Director of Swiss National Library?

My experience in and knowledge of different departments of the library, combined with a good understanding of the federal and local environment of Switzerland, especially in the library and wider cultural sphere, plus the MAS (Master of Advanced Studies in Arts Management) were excellent preparation for the challenge of leading the Swiss National Library. Excellent knowledge of three of the four national languages (French, German, Italian) enabled me to develop contacts across the different linguistic regions – and with the staff – and of course English was an important factor for international activity.

Could you please provide a brief introduction about the roles and responsibilities as the Director of Swiss National Library?

The Swiss National Library is part of the Federal Office of Culture[4], which is attached to the Federal Department of the Interior. It is managed by the Director, who is responsible for our three sites, the main building in Bern, our small museum the Dürrenmatt Centre[5] in Neuchâtel, and since January 1st 2016, the Swiss National Sound Archives in Lugano[6]. The Library is therefore present in the three main linguistic regions of Switzerland.

Working with the members of the Management Committee, and the Deputy Director, who is in charge of day-to-day operations across the sections, I ensure that the National Library's strategy and activities are innovative, up-to-date, and in line with our mandate from the government as well as respect our traditions. Our general mandate is to collect, catalog and preserve Helvetica as well as make them available to the public, now and in the future.

The term Helvetica covers:
1. the literary and informational production published in Switzerland;
2. all publications published abroad, ancient and modern, dealing with Switzerland and its inhabitants;
3. works and translations of works by Swiss authors in all languages.

This mandate includes "digitally born" publications such as, for example, e-books, e-journals, sound and websites.

---

4 Federal Office of Culture, Switzerland – Homepage. Available at: http://www.bak.admin.ch/
5 Museum the Dürrenmatt Centre – Homepage. Available at: http://www.bundesmuseen.ch/cdn/index.html?lang=en
6 Swiss National Sound Archives in Lugano – Homepage. Available at: http://www.fonoteca.ch/index_en.htm

Switzerland is unusual as there are no Swiss national regulations relative to the legal deposit of documents. However, the NL has established mechanisms to ensure the on-going development of its collections through its complimentary deposit convention with the two main publishing associations: the ASDEL (**A**ssociation **S**uisse des **D**iffuseurs, **E**diteurs et **L**ibraires, formerly SLESR) and the SBVV (**S**chweizerischer **B**uchhändler- und **V**erleger-**V**erband), and SUISA, the Cooperative Society of Music Authors and Publishers in Switzerland. These agreements are non-binding and the publishers deposit their publications on a voluntary basis. The Swiss ISSN agency also encourages authors and publishers to deposit a copy of their work at the national library when they request ISSN numbers.

Another unusual aspect of the Swiss National Library is that it is also mandated to lend its material both to the general public and the research community, not only in reading rooms, but also outside the library, in homes or offices.

The law on the National Library SR 432.21 determines our mandate; the Application Ordinance defines our collection policy. The goals within a particular legislative period are set in discussion with the [Federal] Office of Culture[7] and the Department of Home Affairs[8], and with advice from the Swiss National Library Commission, an extra-parliamentary commission that is elected for a four-year period by the Federal Council. Its function and its responsibilities are regulated by the Federal Act of 18 December 1992 on the Swiss National Library (432.21) and by the Ordinance of 14 January 1998 on the Swiss National Library (432.211).

In addition, as Director, I also support and encourage cooperation and networking at both the national and international level. The following list gives some idea of the breadth of those responsibilities:
- Vice Chair, Conference of European National Librarians (CENL) (2011–)
- Vice Chair, Conference of Directors of National Libraries (CDNL) (2012–2016)
- Member of the Management Committee, The European Library (2008–2011; 2013–2015)
- President of Memoriav (Association for the preservation of the audio-visual heritage of Switzerland) (2013–2016)
- Vice President of the Board of Trustees, Swiss National Sound Archives (2005–)
- Member of the Board of Trustees, Graphica Helvetica (2005–)

---

7 Federal Office of Culture, Switzerland – Homepage. Available at: http://www.bak.admin.ch/
8 Department of Home Affairs – Switzerland – Homepage. Available at: https://www.admin.ch/gov/en/start/departments/department-home-affairs-fdha.html

- Member of the Steering Committee, Swiss RISM (part of the International Inventory of Musical Sources) (2005–)
- Member of the Conference of Swiss University Libraries (CBU-KUB) (2005–)
- Member of the Steering Committee, Swiss Conference of Cantonal Libraries (SKKB-CSBC) (2011–)

Could you describe your typical day at work? Is there ever a typical day at work?

As you might guess from the list of responsibilities above, there is no typical day at work! My day starts early, and depending on travel commitments, for example, to meetings of the CENL (Conference of European National Librarians)[9] Executive Committee, discussions in Lugano or meetings of different commissions around Switzerland, plus of course cultural events at the library or elsewhere, it may finish very late. The only constant is the flow of emails, but I am not alone in that.

Could you describe your management or leadership style?

My management style is open and pragmatic. In Switzerland, we are accustomed to working towards consensus through discussion, though it is necessary to know at what point discussion has to stop and decisions, however difficult, have to be taken – by the Director. I try to be available for my staff from all hierarchical levels; when possible, I practice an open door approach but of course the number of meetings and commitments makes that a challenge. When I can, I eat in the library's cafeteria, or take a coffee there: this provides a good opportunity for contact with staff who do not report directly to me. I meet each member of staff who reports directly to me at least once every three weeks for a bilateral discussion about their activities, goals and objectives. Of course, we have discussions on strategy, projects, etc., at other times too. I am aware of the need for flexibility to enable staff to manage work and home life balance so that if necessary, staff may work from home on some days.

Please describe the staffing structure at the Swiss National Library.

The Library's organization chart is available here: http://www.nb.admin.ch/org/organisation/00782/index.html?lang=en

There are 145 FTE in total. Activities are described in the Annual report: http://www.nb.admin.ch/org/01549/05099/index.html?lang=en

---

9 CENL (Conference of European National Librarians) – Homepage. Available at: http://www.cenl.org/

The staff represent a wide variety of professions: librarians, archivists, researchers, conservators, book-binders, IT specialists, sound specialists, assistants, managers and accountants, etc. We have a strong training program for library school students.

Based on my understanding, the Swiss National Library has a team of staff, with people of diversely different backgrounds and cultures. Could you tell us what are the advantages of having staff members of different nationalities, cultures and ways of thinking?

Switzerland is located at the crossroads of the German, French and Italian speaking areas in Europe and is a multilingual and multicultural country. Around 63% of its population are German speakers, 23% French speakers, and 8% Italian speakers. There are also small Romansh speaking populations in the Alpine region to the south-east of the country (0.5%). In the most recent statistics for 2014:

(http://www.bfs.admin.ch/bfs/portal/en/index/themen/01/05/blank/key/sprachen.html) a total of "other languages" reached 20%. Combined, this reaches over 100% because respondents could indicate that they had more than one main language. This also reflects the high non-Swiss population (24.3%) – many from the surrounding countries. So, the country itself is very diverse. The Swiss National Library's staff in 2016 almost mirrors these figures for the four national languages: German 66%, French 21% Italian 12% and Romansh 1%.

Given this wide linguistic and cultural mix (since the different linguistic regions also represent different working styles and approaches), pragmatism, tolerance and patience are a must. Staff at senior level are expected to master (speaking, reading and writing) at least two national languages, while at other levels they should at least understand and read one other national language even if they cannot write it. Language courses are provided through the federal administration, and conversation tandems are encouraged (informal chats over a coffee break in alternating languages). In meetings, those present may speak their own language and others attending are expected to understand. When presentations are given, slides should be in one language (e.g., German), and the speaker may use another (e.g., French).

Staff evaluation discussions take place in the language of the member of staff being evaluated. When I speak to the staff at our information afternoons (at least once a year) or in other contexts, I make sure to switch between languages to include all members of staff, even though my first language is French.

In such a diverse context, it is necessary to be patient, to check that one has been understood, and be ready to reformulate questions or replies to make comprehension easier. This mix brings a wealth of viewpoints and enables us to ensure that the Swiss National Library is there for all the country, not just one linguistic group. And it also mirrors the federal administration's strategy to seek to ensure a balance of languages in the different departments.

What is the current size of the Swiss National Library collections, including its special collections? Could you also describe the highlights of the Collections at the Swiss National Library?

The Swiss National Library is both a memory institution and a research library open to all, including the general public. Founded in 1895, it collects texts, images and sounds that have a link with Switzerland. In addition to the library itself and the Swiss Literary Archives in Bern the NL also comprises the Centre Dürrenmatt Neuchâtel and since 1 January 2016, the Swiss National Sound Archives in Lugano. The Swiss National Library's holdings are listed in catalogs and databases and are available onsite and, increasingly, online.

The general Helvetica collection held 4,504,046 units at the end of 2015. The 2,972,661 monographs make up the largest part of the collection, followed by the 878,006 volumes of newspapers and magazines. The Prints and Drawings Department contains 80 individual collections – including works by Swiss Petits Maîtres, photographic views, posters, prints, special editions and artists' archives, etc. The Federal Archive for Monuments is also part of the Prints and Drawings Department and holds an estimated 1.2 million individual documents. The Swiss Literary Archives had at year-end 353 archives and literary estates of authors, scholars and publishers from all parts of the country.

At the end of 2015, about 12.1 million pages, or about 5.7 per thousand of the printed books, and volumes of newspapers and magazines volumes made up the digitized collection and are accessible online. The collection of born digital electronic publications contained 45,291 units.

The paper collection occupies some 65,000 linear meters in the stacks, while the digital collection amounts to 10.0 TB.

The library catalog Helveticat was accessed 571,216 times during the year, the archive database Helvetic Archives 146,583 times, and 6,247 people borrowed or consulted a total of 69,605 individual documents, folders and archive boxes. The Swiss National Library employees responded to 20,075 requests for information. They provided 2,681 photographs, 26,293 copies and 152 e-books.

The collection of born digital publications is being built up on a selective basis. It currently covers online theses from Swiss universities, online publications from selected Swiss publishers, online official publications from selected federal agencies and cultural heritage websites selected by cantonal and other special libraries. And, since March 2106, we collect self-published e-books and those produced by small publishing houses. These are deposited in our e-collection by the authors or publishers following registration – and checks as to whether the items are Helvetica. Our digitization strategy focuses on making important and intensively used collections available. We work with institutions around the country to digitize newspapers and journals that would otherwise be difficult to access. As part of our strategy, we digitize rights' free monographs on demand for our users.

Do you also work closely with other public libraries across Switzerland and Europe? Such as on cross-national or global collaborative projects?

Part of our legal mandate is to work in close cooperation with institutions in Switzerland and abroad, mostly in Europe. At the national level, we are active in digitization partnerships with a variety of libraries. Our goal is to share expertise, resources and avoid duplication. A good example of this is the cooperative catalog for Swiss posters, whose members include museums as well as libraries. As indicated above, we work closely with cantonal libraries who select websites for us to collect for long term preservation in our e-helvetica webarchive. We also work with university libraries within the Conference of Swiss University Libraries on national projects such as the metacatalog swissbib (www.swissbib.ch), or the implementation of RDA. Internationally, we work mainly with other national libraries taking part in CENL activities at a European level (e.g., Copyright group), or in the RDA discussions as active participants representing European interests (especially language questions) as well as with the Conference of Directors of National Libraries (CDNL)[10] and IFLA at an international level (where several of my staff are active).

It says that the Swiss Union Catalog was created by the Swiss National Library in 1928. Could you describe what kinds of procedures and technical operations were involved in creating this Swiss Union Catalog during the 1920s? What format was this Union Catalog in? 1928 – why did the Swiss National Library choose such a time to create this catalog?

The inauguration of the Swiss Union Catalog (CCS/GK) on 15 July 1928 brought to a close over a century of discussion. Philippe Albert Stapfer was the first to conceive of such a catalog in 1799, when he served as Minister of Arts and Sciences during the period of the short-lived Helvetian Republic.

---

10 Conference of Directors of National Libraries (CDNL) – Homepage. Available at: http://www.cdnl.info/

It was not until 1919, however, that Marcel Godet, Director of the Swiss National Library, presented a proposal to the Federal Council for the creation of a union catalog of all foreign publications held by Swiss libraries with an indication of their whereabouts, and in 1927 the Swiss executive agreed to release the requisite funds. At the close of its first year of operation, the "General Catalog of Swiss Libraries and Information Offices" comprised 11,743 titles at 89 libraries.

It was dubbed the "Swiss Union Catalog" in 1945, when it also began to come into its own: it contained 2 million titles in 1961, 3 million in 1970, and 5.2 million in 1990, with 350 libraries reporting their holdings to the CCS/GK.

Participating Swiss libraries sent copies of descriptions of their holdings to the National Library where they were cut up, glued to catalog cards and inserted in the union catalog. The rules used for cataloging and sorting were those managed by the Swiss Library Association.

In 1979 the Swiss Union Catalog, which had been under the management of the Swiss Librarians' Association (the forerunner of the BIS), became an integral component of the Swiss National Library.

Swiss libraries were changing rapidly, and, as they automated their management systems, most of them also created their own union catalogs, grouped into regional networks. In 2002, therefore, since the libraries were no longer reporting new acquisitions to the CCS/GK, it was decided that new entries would be accepted from just 15 more libraries, and, in early 2003, after those institutions had submitted their file cards, the CCS/GK was closed.

The file cards comprised by the CCS/GK have been microfilmed and are still available to the employees of the «Information Retrieval Service».

Today, the holdings of Swiss libraries are available in www.swissbib.ch, the catalog of all Swiss university libraries, the Swiss National Library, several cantonal libraries and of other institutions.

During World War II (WWII), Switzerland became a haven for refugees from many different European countries – since many of these refugees were educated and wealthy individuals (including: literary writers, scholars, professors, artists, merchants, etc.) – I wonder such a major political and social movement also brought any impacts on the collections and operations of the Swiss National Library during that time? Could you also describe the operations and conditions of the Swiss National Library during World War II? Did the Swiss National Library continue to operate at any level during WWII?

The guiding principle for the Swiss National Library at the outbreak of war in 1939 was to maintain the normal course of work as far as possible, but inevitably the war had an impact from the start and throughout the following years. In the first phase (1939–1940), the number of users decreased, as men were conscripted into the military service. The mobilization of the army also had an impact on staff numbers, and thus necessitated a reduction in opening hours. In addition, during the winter the library was closed on Saturdays to save fuel. Book production decreased in Switzerland and the number of publications by Swiss authors published abroad also diminished. International interlibrary loan dropped sharply. As a precaution, precious books and manuscripts were moved to a vault, while the card catalog (situated in a vulnerable area with a glass roof) was moved to a better-protected area of the library. Some offices were commandeered for the war effort as well.

In 1941–42, there was curiously enough a marked increase both in numbers of users and loans, despite the continuing conscription and the reduced opening hours. In addition, book production increased, reaching higher figures than even before the war. This can be explained in part by the fact that the Swiss authors previously published abroad sought publication in Switzerland. In addition, more foreign authors were published – this was thought to be the result of the better paper available, better conditions, neutrality and greater freedom. There was an increase of translations of English and US works that would normally have been published in Germany, and also French authors who would normally have been published in Paris, turned to Swiss-French publishing houses, making Switzerland a refuge for books. In addition, the restrictions on publishing abroad and thus reduction of imports (or their increased price) opened the home market for Swiss publishers. There was also an increased demand for Swiss books in many European countries and the US.

This situation continued in 1943–44, when statistics rose on all levels. More people used the reading rooms even though the opening hours were still reduced as an economy measure. There was a significant increase in the number of volumes mailed to users outside Bern (a specificity of the Swiss National Library) as well as interlibrary loans. This reflected not only the conscription of civilians into the army but was also the results of loans to internment and refugee camps. As the war moved closer to the borders and the risk of bombing increased, the special collections were once again moved to a more secure area (they had been previously been put back to their usual place).

It was during this time that the use of the union catalog increased sharply since it was so difficult to obtain material from abroad. There was again an extraordinary increase in publishing and in translations, especially from English.

As the war drew to a close, and continuing through 1946, fuel shortages meant that opening hours were further reduced. There was a dramatic decline in use of the reading rooms of the national library but also of all research libraries in Switzerland: internees and refugees were leaving, while the need to invest in the economy meant that there was less free time. However, there was an increase in lending, mostly of literature probably as a result of increased costs, which hindered private sales. The report from 1945–46 notes that this gave rise to some damage to heavily requested material and necessitated costly duplication of acquisitions. With the return of staff from military service, the library started to catch up on some of the tasks that had of necessity been left during the war years. And as international contacts started once again, the demand for photographic reproductions from abroad, especially from the United States and allied countries, increased, as libraries sought to complete or replace their damaged collections. Once again, publishing output increased as did translations, despite a paper shortage.

As 1945 came to a close, the Swiss National Library celebrated its fiftieth anniversary, and took its leave of the Director, Marcel Godet who retired over three years later than planned after accompanying the library throughout the war, keeping to his goal "business as usual" as far as possible and providing a strong library service.

You are currently Vice Chair of the Conference of European National Librarians (CENL). What has it been like and how does it complement position as Director? How do you find time doing both?

As Vice Chair of the CENL, I have a great opportunity to network with colleagues from libraries from across Europe, and in doing so share experience, and gain innovative ideas for application in my own context. As the Swiss National Library hosted the annual meeting of the CENL in 2015, it has been a very heavy workload, especially as we have also prepared a new strategy for the CENL. In these preparations I have naturally been able to count on strong support from my teams and colleagues at all levels, and from the CENL Chair, Secretariat and other members of the Executive Committee. 2016 has also been busy as there are decisions to be taken in a number of areas and so face-to-face and telephone meetings have been frequent. How do I find time? Sometimes, I don't know! However, technology is a boon: access to files and mails while on the road is facilitated today by the infrastructure we have available.

Who are the majority users of the Swiss National Library? That is, who comes to see you about your collections, programs, and services?

Our users represent a wide spectrum from students and researchers and include the general public. A free user card is issued to persons 15 years of age or older residing permanently in Switzerland. Documents may be ordered online and many items (except newspaper, journals and special collections), published in the past

50 years may be borrowed for home use. Other documents are used in the reading room. Like many other libraries, we are seeing a decline in on site visits as users prefer to access material online. Some of the material in our e-Helvetica deposit may be viewed online, while for copyright reasons some is only available on site – or in the reading rooms of our partner cantonal libraries. Literary evenings and readings are very popular – mostly with the older generations, as are exhibit openings. We take part in Bern's annual museum night which draws all ages, as we have special programs to appeal also to children. Each year, we organize an event for World Book Day and another for the World Day for Audiovisual Heritage, reaching a new public who may be unaware of the range of our collections. Any event which allows people to see behind the scenes (especially the stacks) is very popular. In 2015 we held a daylong Sunday event: invited guests explained how they created new works in, or thanks to, the Swiss National Library.

Simon Jäggi, the singer of the band Kummerbuben, revealed how he researched old Swiss songs in the Swiss National Library, re-used them and is now interpreting them for a contemporary audience. Wilfried Meichtry offered an insight into the genesis of his biography of Mani Matter, which drew on the resources of the Swiss Literary Archives. An interactive presentation offered animated, three-dimensional images of artists' books. Also on display was Gugelmann Galaxy, which was created at the cultural data hackathon in February. Leading the packed program for children was Yakari. A section of the underground stacks was also opened up exclusively for the day. In 2015, a total of 9,387 people visited an exhibition or attended an event, guided tour or course at the Centre Dürrenmatt Neuchâtel, while the figure for the NL was 8,722.

Could you give examples of types of new programs and services at Swiss National Library, which you've found successful or innovative? What are the challenges and difficulties currently faced by the Swiss National Library?

As indicated above, the open day was very popular. Also, for some time, the NL has been experimenting with the production of three-dimensional data. The first visible result was a three-dimensional projection of artists' books during the Sunday opening day, which visitors could view from all sides using hand movements. It is accessible online at http://nationalbibliothek.ch/3d/

A web app for mobile devices was also developed for that day, offering an insight into the various collections. I am also very pleased that we are making our content and metadata available free of charge, wherever possible, to encourage their re-use. For example, we are involved in the Swiss open government data portal, publish attractive images on Wikimedia Commons, the media collection of Wikipedia, and supplied data for the cultural data "hackathon", an experimental event for software developers. This was the first time, Switzerland played host to a cultural data hackathon. Around a hundred software developers, data providers and researchers met at the NL to use the open data of cultural institutions for their own purposes, discuss their experiences and program together. "Hacking" the data revealed new interconnections, allowing them to be used for creative projects such as Mathias Bernhard's Gugelmann Galaxy. We are also part of the Metagrid project, which aims to achieve the interlinking of a wide spectrum of resources for the humanities. The Bibliography on Swiss History has recently been linked to the portal Rechtsquellen Online, the collection of Swiss law source materials. We have been working with a newspaper publisher and a digital humanities lab to offer innovative access to one of our digitized newspaper titles, and are also working with on a test for automatic indexing.

Our challenges and difficulties are shared by many of our sister institutions in Europe and across the world: shrinking budgets (but still large numbers of printed items being produced) mean we have to find ways to maintain essential services but also innovate to respond to user expectations. As indicated above, the number of on site visitors is decreasing while the demand for online material is expanding. However, copyright restrictions mean we need to be careful what we digitize and make available. We are lucky that for a number of newspapers and journals partnerships with publishers enable us to make even recent material available for free online. However, in the field of books, it is more difficult: our collection is relatively young as we were founded in 1895 and our mandate is to collect Helvetica from 1848 onwards. Older titles (manuscripts and incunabula above all) are held in the cantonal collections. This means that much of our collection falls under copyright, or may be orphan works but rights' clearance is very time-consuming. We are awaiting the results of a consultation on copyright law in this regard. So we need to manage the past and create the future.

Other challenges coming up: we are integrating the Swiss National Sound Archives, bringing in a new site, welcoming colleagues who will discover the federal culture and meaning increased travel across the country for several staff or Skype meetings. We will send out a call for tender for a new IT system: this is a very structured and lengthy process, which will require staff to be open to new approaches. So in both cases, change management is going to be a central point in the next years.

Which part(s) of your job as the Director do you find most rewarding? What is the most frustrating?

I find it immensely rewarding to be part of a dynamic cultural institution, which is open to such a wide public and which is seeking to promote and improve access to Swiss culture here and abroad. I am very happy and proud to have such dedicated staff who are open to trying out new approaches and who respect one another's linguistic cultures.

I think the most frustrating part is the lack of time and the increase in bureaucracy! We are all juggling different tasks and doing our best to meet deadlines. At least we can say that we are continuing to live in interesting and exciting times with many new opportunities.

6 Andris Vilks

Director of the National Library of Latvia

Introduction

As a national cultural institution under the supervision of the Latvian Ministry of Culture, the National Library of Latvia (NLL) was formed in 1919 after the independent Republic of Latvia was proclaimed in 1918. Today, the Library plays an important role in the development of Latvia's information society, providing Internet access to residents and supporting research and lifelong education. One of the characteristic cornerstones of the NLL, which characterizes every national library, is the formation of the collection of national literature, its eternal storage and long-term access. Andris Vilks is one of the most prominent specialists of the library and information sciences. He has contributed significantly to the development of the library sector and advancement of information and knowledge society in Latvia and the Baltic States. In the following interview, Vilks shares with the readers his experiences and his first-hand witness account of Latvia gaining independence together with the fall of the USSR – from the perspective of a public librarian.

Fig. 6.1: Andris Vilks, Inauguration ceremony. 29 August 2014 (Photo: National Library of Latvia).

Fig. 6.2: Exterior of the Castle of Light. Front square (National Library of Latvia, photo by Indriķis Stūrmanis).

Fig. 6.3: Interior of the Castle of Light. Central staircase (National Library of Latvia, photo by Indriķis Stūrmanis).

Fig. 6.4: Interior of the Castle of Light. People's Bookshelf (National Library of Latvia, photo by Indriķis Stūrmanis).

Could we begin this interview by first having you introduce yourself?

My name is Andris Vilks. I was born in 1957 in Riga, Latvia. I earned my bachelor's degree in 1979, and master's degree in 1993, and I graduated the doctoral program of the Library and Information Sciences (LIS) at the University of Latvia in 2006.[1] I am an Honorary Doctor and Honorary Member of Latvian Academy of Science.[2] In fact, I have been working for the National Library of Latvia[3] since 1978. I spent 11 years working in the Library Department of Rare Books and Manuscripts (at the National Library of Latvia), and eventually, I became the Director of this National Library in 1989.

Since 1989, we [librarians] have witnessed many major social and political transitions with the fall of the Soviet Union, and the beginning of an independent Latvia. There was also a more democratic shift in leadership, policies, practices, managerial culture within the organizational structure of the National Library of Latvia. In 1989, I was elected by all of my [library] staff to become the Director of the National Library of Latvia – which would never be possible nowadays, because of all the governmental protocols and red tape that we must observe. For

---

[1] University of Latvia – Homepage. Available at: http://www.lu.lv/eng/
[2] Latvian Academy of Science – Homepage. Available at: http://www.lza.lv/index.php?mylang=english
[3] National Library of Latvia – Homepage. Available at: http://www.lnb.lv/en

example, there should be fair and equal opportunities for every eligible person [within the same governmental agency] to compete for the same position, and so on. There will be a special committee that are responsible for selecting the eligible person to become the next Director of the National Library or the Minister for Culture, and so on. But, at that moment, it was somewhat "vox populi," and I am still very proud about it.

Do you come from a family of librarians?

No, my father died when I was very young (in 1965), and I was born in 1957. But, he worked in a construction field. My mother worked as a book accountant. After high school, I had many ideas of where to go after studying, and I was interested in many different fields, for example, geography, history, art, and literature, and so on. Somehow, I managed to bring all of these diversely different subject fields and interests together, and finally considered librarianship as my lifetime career.

Were you ever a keen user of the public or school library when you were a young child and a student?

Yes, I did read many books when I was young. We had a large collection of books at home, and it was a typical Latvian tradition, that is, many of us have really large "libraries" at home.

How many languages have you mastered?

Besides my mother tongue Latvian, I also speak Russian, English (though not very well), a little bit of German, and I also speak Lithuanian.

Do you speak Czech or Hungarian?

No, but I can speak a little bit of Polish.

Back in 1989, what kinds of technical skills, knowledge and professional qualifications were needed to become the Director of the National Library of Latvia?

At that moment, the most pressing issue for the National Library of Latvia was to deal with these major political changes brought by the fall of the Soviet Union. And my very first and foremost objective [as the Director] was to liberate the National Library from the Communistic ideology, and "liquidate" the special (closed) collections.

I had gained some useful leadership experience as the Head of the Rare Books and Manuscripts Department, before I became the Library Director at the

[National Library of Latvia]. From the beginning, I very much preferred teamwork. As the Director of the National Library of Latvia, I would like to make everyone, including myself, feel as though we are members of one big family. What I really disliked was being treated as someone special, who would expect special favors, treatments or privileges. I have always been a true believer of teamwork and collaboration that is based on trust, mutual respect and fair play.

When you first became the Director of the National Library of Latvia in 1989, how many staff were there in total working for the Library at that time?

Back in 1993, we merged together with the National Bibliographic Agency, which was separate from the National Library of Latvia. At its peak, it was quite possible that we had as many as 650 people working for the National Library during the Soviet Union era. But, in the recent years, we have begun to downsize in the number of employees. Today, despite being in this huge, new [library] building, we have only about 380 people in total working for the National Library of Latvia.

The Soviet Union era versus now – what are the major differences in terms of the missions, objectives, functions and services of the National Library of Latvia?

During the Soviet era, the main missions of the National Library of Latvia were to serve as a vehicle for "Communist version" of public education. In other words, instead of fulfilling the information needs of the general public, as well as preserving the documentary heritage of the country of Latvia, the public and national libraries were expected to serve as an instrument for supporting the Soviet system of governance for educating and wide-spreading the Communist ideology. During the Soviet Union era, every year, we had to organize these exhibitions on a regular basis – with themes and subject matters focusing on the anniversaries of important or new political leaders, events, and movements of the Communist party – for instance, the Hundredth Anniversary of Lenin's Birth, and so on.

The National Library of Latvia, at that time, was also responsible for the professional developments of the public library sector of the whole country, which was called at that time, the "Mass Libraries." For these Mass Libraries, we produced many "recommended" materials and also bibliographical tools for achieving the same set of "political" agendas, that is to continue wide-spread and reinforce the same message: "The Communist Party is the key to building and sustaining a harmonious and unified society." We would prepare lists of books or other forms of publications – with themes or topics focusing on building socialism, communism's impacts on World War II, and Communist Party's immeasurable contributions to the world, and so on.

During the Soviet Union era, was there very strict censorship imposed by the central government, in terms of buying or ordering books from the USA, England or from other countries in Western Europe?

Absolutely! *Censorship* in the Soviet Union was pervasive and strictly enforced. For example, Latvian-language materials published outside the Soviet Union Empire were completely prohibited or censored. It was simply impossible to get our hands on any materials from the Latvian exile communities. Meanwhile, the Latvian communities worldwide produced about 10,000 titles during the 1940s, 50s, and 60s. The Latvian communities had publishers located in many different countries, namely: Australia, United States, Sweden, and Canada, and so on.

You can imagine that it was quite an impressive amount of [Latvian-language] literature available, but it was completely prohibited in Latvia. Almost all Latvian publications from 1918–1940 and 1941–1944 were prohibited, as well. Furthermore, materials coming from other Western countries were completely censored – only a small amount of such materials were allowed to be kept in the special (closed) collections at the National Library of Latvia. Exile Latvian materials from 1972 were kept only in the Library of the Academy of Sciences. Each library user had to ask for special permission in order to gain access to those "special collection" books that were published outside the Soviet Union.

How would the central government prevent these censored books from coming into Latvian soil during the Soviet Union era? How would the Latvian Government officials inspect the shipments of books that were to be delivered to the National Library of Latvia?

They inspected absolutely everything! There was a special committee "Glavlit" under the KGB (**K**omitet **g**osudarstvennoy **b**ezopasnosti/Committee for State Security of the Soviet Union) that would prepare a list of prohibited authors and prohibited books. This list was not only delivered to individual libraries, but were spread to all Soviet Republics – to every single border custom for access control. Overseas tourists were controlled, mail shipments were also controlled – in short, everything was controlled!

During the Soviet Union era, were you happy with your work as a librarian? Did you understand what was going on outside of the Communist Latvia?

Of course we understood! We tried to listen to the radio programs in Latvian and Russian languages from the voices of freedom from Europe, and from Washington (USA). I was also able to obtain some illegal (censored) materials to read, for example, newspapers and magazines from outside of the Soviet Union. You know, our grandparents remembered the former times in Latvia as an independent country before 1940. My grandmother, for instance, had memories of freedom before 1940. And for me, since early childhood, I was aware that this [Communist] system was wrong, and I was always surrounded with people who spoke about freedom and independence before 1940, and not about the Communist ideology.

How did you gain access to those censored materials in Latvia during the Soviet Union era?

As I mentioned earlier, the Soviets controlled all the tourists, but with Latvian exiles in the 1970s and the people who managed to travel back to Latvia during the 1980s, they did try to bring in books and other forms of publications from the outside world. Of course, they controlled all the borders, but from time to time, some journals or newspapers from the West got sneaked into Latvian soil, and they managed to circulate amongst people like me.

Would one get arrested for being in possession of those censored reading materials coming from outside of Soviet Union?

Yes, it was possible to be arrested. For instance, father of my best friend was arrested in 1983, and spent time in prison for years, because he was found in possession of those censored publications.

After the fall of the Soviet Union, and followed by Latvia becoming independent, what kind of major changes actually took place at the National Library of Latvia?

First of all, we reconstructed and restarted the National Library – that is, to resume all the normal functions and services that any regular national library is expected to perform – while also being free from any political oppression, unpleasant surveillance, influence and interference imposed by the central government.

After resuming all the normal library functions, our library's first and foremost objective was to rebuild a full and comprehensive collection of materials that could represent the depth and diversity of the national documentary heritage of our homeland. In order to achieve this, we tried to acquire any and all materials published in the Latvian language (whenever and/or wherever these Latvian books were published) – that is including all the books and other publications that were previously censored by the Communist Party of Latvia. The second objective was to create full bibliographic records of all the materials published in Latvian, in Latvia, and about Latvia. In other words, we focused mainly on reconstructing a full scope of functions and services to be performed by the National Library of Latvia.

Can you tell me what is the current size of the collection at the National Library of Latvia, and the highlights of the collection?

As of April 2016, the National Library of Latvia has over four million items – we focus on national resources, at the same time, you should also know that we are a small nation. We are one-fourth the size of Hong Kong (in terms of population)! It means that our collections of materials that are published in the Latvian language are still very small, in comparison to many other European countries. Therefore, we need to compensate this by enriching our collection with other foreign-language materials. Despite our efforts invested into rebuilding a comprehensive collection of "Latvian" materials, only less than half of our library's entire collection is in Latvian. In other words, the remaining materials in our collection are in other foreign languages, that is including: Russian, English, and German, French, etc.

The National Library of Latvia also has a special collection of considerable size. In fact, we have the largest and most important collection of [geographic] maps, and also sound recordings and other graphic materials. Because of our long history and rich culture, we also have quite an impressive collection of manuscripts. We have a good collection of old prints that were produced in Latvia, and some of them date all the way back to the 16th century – it is indeed a very comprehensive collection of such rarities. We are interested in discovering national history from past centuries, we therefore sometimes do not worry about having duplicate titles, especially printed before 1830. For example, if it is a biblical title, we can afford to collect up to fifteen copies, since each Bible has its own history and you can create your own story about each of them.

In 1989, you were working hard on developing a project on the National Library of Latvia, the Castle of Light, which involved the construction of new buildings of the library. Could you tell us more about your participation in this project and your vision in shaping the new building?

About the new building for the National Library, in our community, debates already began in the 1920s, the 1930s, and also during the Soviet-controlled period after 1944. There were several attempts to construct a new National Library because until 1989, the National Library had no specifically designed building for the library. We were distributed in many different locations -- they were not built for libraries, but for different purposes. Finally, in 1989, we started to develop this particular project, and I was involved since the very beginning with designing, planning and programming. After finding the right architect, [after unsuccessful competition, an architect with Latvian origins, Gunnar Birkerts (USA), has agreed to design the new building, by the way, schematic design phase – free of charge], I was involved all of these years in the definition of this library functionality, size and services, and so on. It was my main role and core duty of what I did in the library.

In 2014, there was a major event called "The Book Chain," and the books were moved from the old building to the new one. So, as the Director of the National Library of Latvia, you were overseeing this massive project. Can you tell me about the logistics of this project and what kinds of challenges you faced during the course of this project? Can you describe your experiences as the manager who was responsible for overseeing this relocation?

We have moved books from one building to another building for many decades now, so it is not new. The basic technology behind all these was to form a chain of librarians. We always used "human labor" in a smart way for transferring books from one building to another during the 1950s, 60s, and 70s. But, a very important point was that in 2010, when the old building was in an emergency situation – about 70,000 books simply dropped into the basement. It was very important that we rescued these books by taking them out of the basement. We called people [from the general public] to help us, and not only librarians, but many people came and made this "human" chain (conveying belt). This time more for symbolic reason. Immediately, we collected these books out of this basement. It was the idea we had discussed with the transfer of the library from the old building to the new building. We felt we could use this same "human" method because during the emergency, people came and helped – even as they have departed, they reminded us, "If you need us, just call again!" That is why we were confident that we could call on the people [from the general public] again to come to form this human chain (conveying belt). Frankly speaking, I never expected that even the temperature was below –14 degrees even, over 14,000 people from the general public came to form this human chain – to help us relocate the books. What I originally anticipated was four or five thousand at the most. Therefore, it was really a manifestation of people's positive attitude towards the library and to this project. We expected much fewer people, and the result of it was just overwhelmingly fantastic. There were not any managerial or logistical tools behind the whole thing.

You were instrumental in the development of a countrywide library network, and the establishment of a national digital library. Could you describe your role in leading this collaborative structure?

When we heavily discussed with politicians, journalists, mass media, and also our colleagues about the urgent need for a new library, we felt that it was impossible just to construct a single building in the capital city. After discussing with my closest friends and colleagues, we developed ideas that this project should be much broader than just having a single library building. Also in that period, there was a similar program in Singapore. There was this idea that we should combine the physical library with a whole library network in the country. There were three pillars behind this program, namely: *The Castle of Light*, *Light Net*, and *Lighthouse* – meaning, the digital library. In other words, there were three ideas about light. This project was also sympathetic for politicians and also for the community. We got many benefits from this triangle because it was also very important for the library that it has a physical building to enable it to carry out all its missions, objectives, functions and services, and so on.

In your speech, you talked about the digital library bringing the archives, museums, and libraries all closer together. Can you comment a bit on that?

In 2001, I participated in a workshop and a seminar in London (U.K.) mainly because the British were the first to start this development of libraries archives, and museum (LAM) collaborations. I was very inspired by this seminar, and when I returned to my home country, we started to organize several activities towards this idea of closer collaboration amongst LAMs. Now, during these years, we have been trying hard to translate this idea into action (closer collaboration). I believed that this kind of collaboration should be more on the digital level – but not necessarily having to match or merge together with other institutions and organizations. It is more important to put together these digital resources on a common platform that would allow convenient access and resources sharing amongst the general public, who simply don't actually care where the materials [physically] lie – because they just need to have access to such materials, in order to fulfil their instant gratification of information needs. Frankly saying, initially, this collaboration between LAMs was not so easy. Speaking about the future, right now, we are starting a new project on digital cooperation between different memory institutions. I am looking forward to 2020, when we achieve this digitalization project of cultural memories, and cultural heritage with LAMs, and other memory institutions. Still, I am aware that the main goal of what we are doing should focus on collaboration between LAMs, but not merging them together.

Who are the majority of users of the National Library of Latvia?

Now, we are at a very interesting time – our audience is changing. The main audience is students and also scholars and professors, but it is a quite typical target group. But now, especially on weekends, we have a new public, and they are mostly families. It is very different from working days, so we started developing some programs for children. We have an auditorium for concerts, exhibition areas, and a restaurant offering brunch on Sunday mornings. The library's restaurant is outsourced, but people are staying in the library, exploring the library exhibitions, and almost every day, we are having events inside our library building. This is something new that we had never faced before in the previous library building. People in the community who are normally spending the weekends window-shopping at malls – some of them are now coming to the library. But, it is only weekends. Quite certainly, you could now divide our audience into several categories: students, scholars, everyday life, and weekends and excursions on weekends.

How are the public activities carried out by the National Library of Latvia different from those at the nearby cities or public or central libraries with the same city?

The content, nature, and scope our public service activities differ from the rest. We have set a very clear division between the other local public library's services in terms of our scope, nature and contents. We do not focus on the promotion of fictions or popular literature. We have a large quantity of unique and rare materials, and we try to use them to attract these unique materials to create different theme-oriented exhibitions and seminars that are based on our special collections of maps, manuscripts and rarities, and so on. If you compare the two collections, there is a great difference. Moreover, in Riga, we do not have a central metropolitan public library. We do have the Riga Central Library, but it is comprised mostly of library branches. Our library network in the city is mostly organized in various branches. However, we don't have any branches – we are a single unit.

Can you tell me about the staffing situation at the National Library of Latvia? How many different operational divisions and departments are there in total at your Library?

We have seven main divisions: we have (1) Data Division responsible for creating data and bibliographical records, and also subject cataloging. Its second main function is acquisition of analogue and digital materials; (2) Services Division, which has many subdivisions, mostly reading rooms; (3) Special Collections Division, that is where our rarities, art, music and audio-visual materials, small prints and maps are being managed by. In addition, Letonica and Baltic Center with corresponding reading room and group of researchers is part of this structural unit; (4) Development Division, which deals mostly with the overall development of the whole library network. With this Division, we provide training and consultations via this whole library network, and there is also a center for children's literature and a center of excellence for the digital library, that is to handle the management of the digital library; (5) Technical Division for ICT; (6) Communication Division that is in charge of PR, visual identity, space rental, exhibitions and other library events and (7) Housekeeping Division – the name of this Division speaks of its functions itself.

As the Director of the National Library of Latvia, could you describe your typical day at work?

My week usually starts on Sunday, because on this day, I prepare myself for the following whole week. I first list out all the tasks that need doing, and then prioritize them according to the library's goals and objectives. I then divide and group all the waiting-to-be-done activities and tasks, according to the deadlines and the amount of time I have in the following week.

On a typical Monday, we have regular weekly meetings with heads of all departments or divisions within the National Library. Then on Tuesdays, we have operational meetings with the whole library management team. But, mainly, the morning part is for writing, the mid-day is mostly meetings with people outside and inside, and often I try to be in the library four days a week, and in average one day is devoted for activities outside the library (at the ministry or universities, other institutions, and so on). Then, the evenings, after 5:00 p.m., when I am alone, I devote all my time to answering emails and phone calls.

Can you describe your management style and leadership style?

The staffing situation at the National Library of Latvia is now very much different from what it was 20 years ago. We have a totally different organizational structure. For instance, about 60% are only librarians, and the remaining 40% are in other professions, possessing other non-library-related skills, knowledge and qualifications. In terms of generational age differences, we try to pair elderly employees with younger one. We are getting the best specialists from our LIS master's program. For Eastern Europe, we have a very good balance of gender. We have one-third men – which is rather unusual in our part of the LIS world, since it's not typical that we have so many men.

Would you say that during the Soviet Union era, people working at the National Library of Latvia were not encouraged to exercise their individual thinking and judgement?

We librarians used to lead a dual life in Latvia during the Soviet Union era. People only needed to follow orders, instructions and protocols at work. But when they were at home in the kitchen, they were always thinking and talking. It is called "kitchen politics," that is, many families would meet at home in the kitchens, and then felt free to speak of anything that were in their minds – things that former

Communist central government would not necessarily approve of. Therefore, in the library, there are many who are very dedicated professionals, but they are shy or afraid to express opinions publicly and to visitors.

When you were studying Library Science at the university, do you think that the Communist Party had much influence in the contents of your studies?

Yes, of course! There was a History of the Communist Party course, and the philosophy behind this course was Marxist Philosophy. In every semester, there were special courses. It was really stupid with this integration of Soviet ideology. On the other hand, there were plenty of other courses on the history of literature, also some interesting programs that were eliminated from LIS like having some basis in physics, biology, chemistry, and so on. We really had the best professors in these subjects. Frankly speaking, the attitude is that we can't say that Communist ideology and politicization made up all of our studies at university.

During the Soviet Union era, for the courses and lectures that you had to take as a university student, what kinds of assignments or coursework did you have to write?

The whole university program was very much exam-oriented. Nature and formats of exam questions would depend a lot on the individual courses that one was taking. An examination paper would usually involve about 15 questions. You would have to select a few out of all 15 questions, and answered them accordingly. Then, in the exam auditorium, you would be given about one hour to answer these questions, without using any supporting tools – in other words, they were not open book exams. You basically had to memorise all the facts and details. If it was an exam the History of the Communist Party, questions would be like, "When was the second congress of the Bolshevik Party, and what were some of the important decisions?" and what is said in Lenin's literary works, and so on. You should quote directly from the texts by Lenin or Marx or Engels. It was mandatory to give citations of Lenin when answering these exam questions.

In order to get a high grade at the university exams, did you have to follow some kind of model answer set out by the university or by the Communist party? Or if you said something that went against the Communist ideology, how would the professors handle your answers?

There was simply no room for expressing one's personal opinions or viewpoints. To do so was considered to be very dangerous, as you could risk being expelled from university. Only during lectures, when you felt – this particular professor has different historical or philosophical points of view, very heedful debates were possible.

The university exam questions, would they also ask you to criticize other Western European countries and capitalism?

Of course! It was an important part of the Communist ideology. The examination questions would be like, "What kinds of resistances are there in America towards communism?" and there were questions about Communist parties in France, Italy, and in Western countries, and so on. We would always be asked about unemployment situations in other Western countries. And of course, militarism, NATO (North Atlantic Treaty Organization), and these impossible military aggressions. Also for us, there was one day of military training for everyone. I had to spend one day at the military campus when I was still studying at university. At university lectures, we were introduced to possible enemies and aggressors to our country – of course, these possible enemies were West Germany and/or the United States.

Could you tell us what styles of management and leadership were favored by the senior management in the library setting during the USSR era?

In previous times, dictatorship was not only privilege of the main leaders of the system, but also very much favored by many arts and cultural organizations during the USSR era, that is including public and national libraries, but I simply hated that kind of dictatorship style.

Can you describe how such dictatorship-style management would work in the library context?

It was a very simple management system with only vertical decision-making. All the guidelines come from above, and there were very few times that you would be able to express your opinions and exercise your expertise and judgments. I like very much the horizontal management environment in my office – I personally like different working groups and different committees discussing and working together for decision-making. For instance, we have a data committee. For the top management, there is no need to interfere because there are competent people throughout the whole library from almost all divisions to form this data committee. They are making decisions on how to organize data in our library. In my opinion, I think that "competence" is the most important thing in terms of choosing the most suitable person to lead the library.

In the old days during the Soviet Union era, how would they select a person to lead the library?

The director was part of a *nomenklatura*. There were people within the Communist Party who were from time to time rotated into other positions, simply because they were leaders of the Communist Party. One day, he was head of the collective farm and the second day he would be the director of the library. His only specialization was being a member of the Communist Party!

In the old days, what were the main concerns, priorities, and challenges of the library?

I did not work as the director during the Communist era. When I arrived in 1989, the Communist system had already collapsed, and we started everything from scratch. I can't compare because I was the very first Director of the National Library who was not a Communist. At that time, we were dependent on and responded to the Minister of Culture. It was already a governmental system in which we organized our work that not related with the Communist Party anymore.

Can you give a list of cultural programs or services carried by the National Library of Latvia, under your leadership, that you found to be very successful?

The digital library is one success story. Another one is the Center for Children's Literature because it's not just a reading room for children, but a center where we librarians could provide reading materials, along with a range of activities aiming at cultivating a habit of voluntary reading amongst the children in the local community. The audience of this Center are made up of 19,000 children in the whole country of Latvia. With the activities and programs launched via this Center, we intend to cover children throughout the whole country, and also other Latvians living in overseas.

Our library has also been conducted a lot of research studies on the history of books. In fact, we have more than 10 people, who are Ph.D. holders, working in our library, who devote most of their time on studying our library's collections from a history scholar's perspective.

Then we have another new program, which is quite successful, which is focusing on the generation, which was standing before a decision where to go to university to study. This was a very crucial period, and we have a standard reading room devoted to these young people. I think our exhibition programming is also very successful. Now, in the new building, we have several very interesting exhibitions and also some publications that we did in recent years that won awards.

As the Director of the National Library of Latvia, which part of your job do you find the most frustrating?

I think the most rewarding part of my job is when you see that you have satisfied your audience whom you are serving. In addition, your colleagues are happy with what they are doing. If the audience and my colleagues are satisfied, then I am satisfied too. I think that we – users and colleagues – should be one big family. We are a very small community, and it is much easier to know each other personally, when compared with other large national libraries in major cities.

What aspects of your work as the Director of the National Library of Latvia do you find more frustrating?

Bureaucracy and formalism always frustrate me! The state has many forms of bureaucratic systems – not only for money, but different regulations, rules, and also legislation.

What is the average age of the population? In some developed countries, the whole population is getting older and older. What is the trend in your country?

The situation here is similar, and we are also becoming older and older. We have fewer and fewer young people than it was 20 years ago. That is the reality.

What are your plans for the next five to ten years as the Director of the National Library of Latvia?

It is quite complex, but I think that we would like be more proactive in the development of education for the whole country – that is, to try to do more cooperation with other educational institutions. We would like to become some kind of alternatives in local education system. The second thing, we would like to have more involvement in research, and we are very much looking forward to doing digital humanities in the library context. Behind me, there is a new building for the University of Latvia just five minutes from here, therefore, I think that we should develop this synergy between the University and the National Library. I think the most challenging issue is to be more proactive in the environment of research and education.

7 Prof. Dr. Renaldas Gudauskas

Director General, Martynas Mažvydas National Library of Lithuania

Introduction

Founded in 1919, the National Library of Lithuania (NLL) was established with the mission to accumulate and preserve Lithuanian documentary cultural heritage. In 1988, the Library was named after Martynas Mažvydas, the author of the first Lithuanian book (published in 1547). In addition to serving as a research library that is open to the general public, this Library also functions as a parliamentary library. One of the newer features of the National Library of Lithuania will be a Jewish research center – established in the renovated premises of the library.

In 2010, Dr. Renaldas Gudauskas was appointed the Director General of the Martynas Mažvydas National Library of Lithuania. In the following interview, Dr. Gudauskas discusses the various sociopolitical roles the Library played during the Soviet era, as well as how it strives to become the modern-day multifunctional center of culture, science, and politics in the Lithuanian capital under his direction.

Fig. 7.1: Prof. Dr. Renaldas Gudauskas (Photo: National Library of Lithuania).

DOI 10.1515/9783110533347-008

Fig. 7.2: Main building of the National Library of Lithuania (Photo: National Library of Lithuania).

Fig. 7.3: National Library of Lithuania interior (Photo: National Library of Lithuania).

Fig. 7.4: National Library of Lithuania reading room (Photo: National Library of Lithuania).

Could we begin this interview by first introducing yourself, for example, your training and background, and your major roles and duties as the Lithuanian National Library?

My brief biography is as follows:
- Vilnius University, Faculty of History[1], a diploma in library and information sciences.
- The Saint-Petersburg Institute of Culture, Social Sciences, Ph.D. "Higher education of information professionals at universities";
- Certified knowledge manager of the Knowledge Management Professional Society (KMPro), USA;
- My primary duty at the Martynas Mažvydas National Library of Lithuania[2] (hereafter NLL) is to enable this national institution to become the strategic center for shaping the nation's progress and competitive advantage.

The key areas of your research interest include: knowledge management, information management, contemporary management, strategic management and change

---
[1] Vilnius University, Faculty of History – Homepage. Available at: http://www.vu.lt/en/scientific-report-2012/faculties-and-institutes/faculty-of-history.
[2] Martynas Mažvydas National Library of Lithuania – Homepage. Available at: http://www.lnb.lt/en/.

management – all these are unarguably key concepts in modern-day management for any profit and non-profit organizations. How have your active and diverse areas of research in the field of management helped inform you in your daily work at a library?

My strategic competencies in diverse areas of classical and contemporary management help me deal with solutions in developing ICT, and change management of libraries, as well as addressing critical situations in these areas. Integrated managerial and leadership competencies make it easier for our Library as an organization to achieve institutional goals.

Could you describe your leadership and management style? Mentorship is such an important theme in leadership – both mentoring and being mentored. Could you please tell us about your experiences about both? Do you still have mentors that you go to?

Mentorship is always important. At present, I act as a mentor myself. I would describe my leadership and management style as transformational leadership. In my opinion, it is the only solution for NLL to establish a proactive, perspective-oriented, creative, effective and unique strategic management system.

In your C.V., it lists "The Art of War" as an area of research interest. Could you elaborate on this, and how can this help libraries?

"The Art of War" may help in any business area including libraries as organizations. It is about how to create critical masses of core competence, and to build a sustainable library ready for competitiveness in the new information business environment.

Have you always worked in libraries? Could you tell us more about your path to becoming the director of a National Library?

I started working in the library field in 2010 when I was appointed the Director-General of NLL. My professional career: Master of Library and Information Sciences (MLIS), Doctor of Social Sciences, Professor of Information and Communication; Dean of the Faculty of Communication at Vilnius University (12 years); Director of UNESCO's Centre for Knowledge Economy Management at Vilnius University (4 years).

What best prepared you for your work as Director of the Lithuanian National Library?

It was my academic activities at various universities as well as the experience gained during the position as an advisor to the President of the Republic of

Lithuania for information and communication and an advisor to the Prime Minister of the Republic of Lithuania for information society and knowledge economy (6 years), the Vice-Minister for information and information science at the Ministry of Management Reform and Municipal Affairs of the Republic of Lithuania (2 years), and my activities as an international business consultant (12 years). This blend of economical, political and business experiences has prepared me for my current work in this position.

Could you please provide a brief introduction about the Lithuanian National Library? What roles (politically, culturally, socially and educationally) did the National Library of Lithuania play during the Cold War, and also during the Communist Era when the country of Lithuania was so heavily influenced by the Soviet Union?

During the Soviet era, all functions of NLL were heavily influenced by state policies of the Soviet Union. Since the restoration of Lithuania's independence in 1991, we have been seeking to expand cooperation between libraries and business structures, institutions of local authorities and non-governmental organizations, and to consolidate the potential of Lithuanian research libraries. The encounters of the competitive supremacy of the State are big data, interoperability between strategic information systems, open government and position of libraries within the new reality of universal open access.

Communist era versus now – has the Lithuanian National Library undergone any major changes in terms of its missions, goals and operational/foreign policies after the Communist rule in Lithuania came to an end in 1989?

The current mission of NLL is ensuring satisfaction of the needs of the Lithuanian knowledge society for the documentary and digital information. NLL fundamentally contributes to realizing the principles and goals of the national information policy, by ensuring access to information for the public and providing opportunities to use information as a strategic resource for the development of all activities and/or areas of the society.

What is the current size of the Lithuanian National Library's collections, including its special collections? Could you also describe the highlights of the Collections at the Lithuanian National Library?

NLL provides access to collections of books, periodicals, serial and information publications, manuscripts, microforms, video and audio documents, old and rare printings, compact discs, and documents of Lithuanian, foreign and international organizations. The collection consists of 6.58 million physical units and 1.21 million titles.

Do you also work closely with other libraries across Lithuania and Europe? Such as on cross-national or global collaborative projects? What are some highlights?

We work closely with public and research libraries not only at the national level but also in Europe and other countries. We collaborate with the Royal Library of Denmark, the British Library, the National Libraries of the Netherlands, France, Estonia, Latvia and Germany and other countries.

Below there is information about NLL's most significant international project "Libraries for Innovation" implemented together with the Bill & Melinda Gates Foundation (http://3erdve.lt/media/public/Ataskaitos/bibl-paz-2015-web2a-en.pdf).

Reference is slowly fading away. Some library schools don't even teach it anymore, or teaches a different variation – such as Human Computer Interaction (HCI). What are your thoughts on reference services? Does the National Library of Lithuania offer it anymore?

We are still involved in the reference service, thus enabling us to change our information service strategies. Web–science and human–computer interactions, big data, open access solutions and cyber security issues have become a serious challenge for NLL in its pursuit to manage digital complexity.

Please describe the staffing structure at the National Library of Lithuania. For example, what are the working relationships between the various heads of subject/cataloging departments and the branch heads in such a vast and large library system?

The answer will be somewhat general. We are creating the NLL as a well-organized structure with a staff possessing exceptional human competencies capable of adopting the experience of the most advanced national memory institutions and incorporating universal strategic management models, which provide framework for building a "self-creating" sustainable library.

Could you describe your typical day at work? Is there ever a typical day at work?

No. There are no typical days in top management. Always **Expect the unexpected** and "always be ready for situational leadership and crisis management."

What scholarly and professional associations are you a part of, and how do they inform you in your work?

Advisory Board Member of the Knowledge Management Professional Society (KMPro), USA.
- Chairman of the Information for All Program of the National UNESCO Commission.
- Lithuanian representative at the UNESCO Information for All Program Council.
- Member of the IFLA Management and Marketing Committee.
- Chairman of the Lithuanian Libraries Council.

All these associations provide added value to my competences.

Who are the majority users of the National Library of Lithuania? That is, who comes to see you about your collections, programs, and services?

All groups of the society: children, students, academics, etc. In fact, any Lithuanian and foreign citizen is a potential client of information services provided by the Library including the growing E-services.

Could you give examples of types of new programs and services at the National Library of Lithuania, which you've found successful or innovative?

The project "Libraries for Innovation 2" financed by the Bill & Melinda Gates Foundation, which strengthens the potential of Lithuania's public libraries to meet the demands of the developing society and consolidates libraries as sustainable community institutions capable of improving the life of Lithuanian people.

Developing the contents of the data bank of the digital cultural heritage and integration of the digital content of the Lithuanian cultural heritage into a single European digital space.

Could you tell us more about the Epaveldas (Collection of Digitized Lithuanian Cultural Heritage)?

At the end of 2015, the Virtual Electronic Heritage System and the portal www.epaveldas.lt. containing 315,000 objects of digitized documents. The development of the portal www.epaveldas.lt underwent further expansion of electronic services for the users by presenting a larger number of diverse cultural heritage objects.

We continued the integration of Lithuania's digital cultural heritage into the Europeana web portal by exporting bibliographic records for books, periodicals and manuscript documents.

What's the role of technology and innovation at the National Library of Lithuania?

NLL, in compliance with its strategic goals and priorities and those on the national level, implements a project for creating the integrated Lithuania Integrated Library Information System, and is responsible for the computerization of the library and information processes within Lithuanian public libraries, and integration of the Lithuania information resources into the worldwide information system.

Our strategic priorities are ICT and innovations.

Which part(s) of your job as the Director do you find most rewarding? What is the most frustrating?

Most rewarding for me is modelling the vision, mission and management principles of NLL. It is a pity that a major part of competences of NLL staff members tend to be no longer adequate not only to the dynamic evolution of technologies, but also to radically changing situation in the information market. It is the most worrying issue.

8 Alberto Manguel

Director, National Library of Argentina

Introduction

Originally set up as a municipal library, the Biblioteca Pública de Buenos Aires was founded in September 1810 by decree of the First Assembly *(Primera Junta)* of the May Revolution. It was later converted into the Biblioteca Nacional de Argentina, when it redefined its mission as a national institution in 1884, and was renamed the Biblioteca Nacional Argentina Mariano Moreno in 2013. The Library's history is noted for mirroring the strokes that reflect the social and political life of the nation. Since the retirement of Horacio Gonzalez, multilingual Argentine-Canadian anthologist, translator, essayist, novelist, and editor Alberto Manguel has been serving as the Director of the National Library of Argentina since 2016. In the past 20 years, Manguel has authored and edited a great number of literary works, including *A History of Reading* and *The Library at Night*, the anthology *Black Water: The Book of Fantastic Literature,* and the novels *News from a Foreign Country Came* and *All Men Are Liars*. In the following interview, Manguel discusses his background as a literary scholar, and how it contributes to his current work as the Director.

Fig. 8.1: Director Manguel in his office next to a painting by Emilio Pettoruti titled Tres verticales, part of the library's collection (Photo: National Library of Argentina).

Fig. 8.2: The current building of the Biblioteca Nacional Argentina Mariano Moreno was designed by Italian-Argentinian architect Clorindo Testa. The imposing building provides a panoramic view of the city from the traditional neighborhood of Recoleta (Photo: National Library of Argentina).

Fig. 8.3: Displayed on the main wall of the exhibition Borges el mismo, otro, a timeline relates Jorge Luis Borges's readings with his literary work (Photo: National Library of Argentina).

Fig. 8.4: Artist's book recreating the unpublished Los naipes del tahúr c. 1921, part of the "Libros conjeturales" (Photo: National Library of Argentina).

Could we begin this interview by first introducing yourself, for example, your professional training and education background (e.g., which university did you attend and what did you study at university)? Could you also describe your current roles and scope of responsibilities as the Director of the National Library of Argentina?

My name is Alberto Manguel and I am the Director of the National Library of Argentina Mariano Moreno. I did not attend university. I graduated from the Colegio Nacional de Buenos Aires[1], and decided that after the excellent training at the Colegio the university would be a disappointment. My current job is to administrate the Library with a staff of over one thousand employees.

What did you study for your B.A., M.A. and Ph.D.?

As I said, I have none of these degrees. I have a high-school diploma, that´s all. (I have several honorary degrees, however.)

---

1 Colegio Nacional de Buenos Aires – Homepage. Available at: http://www.cnba.uba.ar

Have many different languages have you mastered?

I have mastered no languages, but I can read, write and converse in English, German, Spanish, French, Italian, and I have a smattering of Portuguese and Latin.

Have you always worked in libraries? Could you tell us more about your career path to becoming the Director of the National Library of Argentina?

I had never worked in a library before now. Throughout my life, I have collected books and my personal library, now in storage, holds approximately 35,000 books.

In December 2015, you were named the Director of the National Library in your native Argentina, replacing Horacio González. You became formally in charge of the National Library of Argentina in July 2016. Based on what criteria did the recruitment committee select you to take up such an important position at the National Library of Argentina?

I have no idea what the criteria was used that led the recruitment committee to select me for what you rightly call "an important position at the National Library of Argentina."

You are an author of a number of books on librarianship and also university lecturer in literature and philosophy. How do your previous experiences influence your thinking, management and leadership style about your current position as the director of a national library?

In addition, you are not a librarian by training. Instead, you have always been active as a writer and scholar – do you see this as an advantage when it comes to managing the National Library of Argentina?

An advantage, since it allows me to see the Library from the point of view of a reader. A disadvantage, since I know very little about the technical matters that are the heart of a library.

Throughout my life, books have been essential to me as a way of acquiring experience of the world, and they have led me to reflect on their identity and use. I hope that the experience of reading might inform my current position, and help me work in dialogue with the Library's staff.

Could you describe your management and leadership style? Mentorship is such an important theme in leadership – both mentoring and being mentored. Could you please tell us about your experiences about both? Do you still have mentors that you go to?

It is hard to describe what you call "management and leadership style." Yes, mentorship is essential, and I hope that I can identify people who wish to be mentored in the areas of library operations. My own mentoring has been haphazard and stemmed from all manner of encounters: teachers, writers, other librarians and even people not directly related to books. However, I find it impossible to identify particular traits that I might have picked up from them except encouragement of my curiosity, and confidence in my learning abilities. Jorge Luis Borges, who was perhaps this library's most famous director, mentored me (unintentionally, perhaps) teaching me that literature is a generous art, and is above all attempts to categorized or limit it. I feel that there are also influences from people I haven't met such as Aby Warburg and his notion of the "good neighbor" in terms of organizing books, and Callimachus assisting readers with his annotated catalogs.

Could you please provide a brief introduction about the National Library of Argentina?

The National Library of Argentina was founded 13 September 1810 by one of the national heroes of independence, Mariano Moreno, profound thinker and ideologue. From that day onward the Library struggled (as all libraries must) to both acquire books and organize them appropriately for its readers. Surviving the different regimes that governed Argentina, for the most part as dictatorships with a few democratic interludes, the Library that I have inherited and still suffer from both these problems. Its catalog is in the process of being completed so at present I can only say that its holdings surpass three million documents.

What is the current size of the National Library of Argentina's collections, including its special collections? Could you also describe what you deem are the highlights of the collection?

The highlights of the Library's holdings are its collection of colonial literature, its important periodical series, many manuscripts related to the history of Argentinian literature and twenty-one incunabula.

Does your Library work closely with other libraries across Argentina? What about the rest of the world? If so, could you tell us about such cross-national or global collaborative projects? What are some highlights?

My administration will try to work more closely with the provincial libraries of Argentina. At present not every province has its own library, and I intend to create them where they are lacking. However, there is a system of what is known as "popular libraries," the Comisión Nacional de Bibliotecas Populares (CONABIP)[2], with which we will be working, helping create new libraries across the country, and establishing scholarships for librarians and continue their training in Buenos Aires.

Also, we have a handful of agreements with libraries abroad (the National Library of Brazil, the British Library, the National Library of France), but little has been implemented until now. I intend to activate, and strengthen these links and create many more in order, not only to share experiences, but have a system of exchange whereby we will share exhibitions, digital collections, etc.

You are Canadian as well. How does your background as a Canadian and knowledge of its institutions influence or inform your work currently?

I believe that my experience as a Canadian might help bring a touch of logical efficiency to the bureaucratic methods in place in Argentina. Also, Canada's concern for its native populations might help me in my efforts to establish a center for native studies at the National Library of Argentina.

Your multi-cultural background and your extensive overseas experiences – have they in any way contributed to your current work as the Director of the National Library of Argentina?

Of course. Borges declared many years ago that Argentinians have the choice of being either a national caricature of themselves or being universal. I will try to help the National Library become as universal as possible while at the same time enhancing a clear Argentinian identity. This means extending the holdings and the internal department of scholarly investigations to areas such as China, India, the Arab world. I will be introducing scholars in these areas to enrich and explore the Library's holdings. In this regard, I will take advantage of current events, such as the arrival of 3,000 Syrian refugees to the country, to exhibit areas of our culture that remain little known, for instance the Syrio-Lebanese contribution to Argentinian history.

Please describe the staffing structure at the National Library of Argentina?

My main purpose at this point is restructuring the Library in order to rationalize the different sections and their relationship to one another.

---

[2] Comisión Nacional de Bibliotecas Populares (CONAPIB) – Homepage. Available at: http://www.conabip.gob.ar

Could you describe your typical day at work? Is there ever a typical day at work?

A typical day at work consists of my arrival at the Library at 7:00 in the morning, reading the reports that might have arrived as well as the morning news, and then having meetings with people in the different areas, as well as external visitors, until the late afternoon.

What scholarly and professional associations are you a part of, and how do they assist you or supplement your work?

I am a member of PEN, the Translators' Association of Canada, and several academic groups and I resort to their services whenever I need to.

Who are the majority users of the National Library of Argentina? That is, who comes to see you about your collections, programs, and services?

The majority of users of the Library are students who come and work at the Library, but not necessarily using the Library's holdings; that is to say, they bring their own books. My purpose is to acquire as much material as possible that might be of use to them and others since for the past fifteen years acquisitions have been inadequate and we need to try and fill huge gaps in the holdings. But we also of course receive local and international researchers who study our range of rare printed materials, periodicals, archives, images, audiovisual materials, etc. Visitors also come to see our exhibitions; for instance the one we just opened for the thirtieth anniversary of Borges's death, in which we exhibit sixteen of his manuscripts, is attracting a fair amount of people.

Which part(s) of your job as the General Director of the National Library of Argentina do you find most rewarding? What is the most frustrating?

The part of my job as library director that I find most rewarding is imagining the future. The most frustrating is dealing with the past.

"The part of my job as library director that I find most rewarding is imagining the future. The most frustrating is dealing with the past" – could you give any examples to illustrate your points?

Simply that I like imagining what this great institution can be, extending its services to the whole country, creating links with sister libraries throughout the world, increasing the holdings, perfecting its services to the readers. However, every change in vision means administrative change, which is always a great challenge.

You have always been active in different intellectual pursuits, e.g., being an anthologist, translator, essayist, novelist and editor, etc. After taking up the director position at such a major national library, do you sometimes lament the fact that you are unable to spend as much time and energy on the other intellectual endeavor as you used to?

When I took up the position as Director of the Library I knew I had to give up, at least for the time being, my activities as writer and become an administrator. I had thought that at sixty-eight I had reached the last chapter of what I considered a hugely entertaining novel. I didn't expect there to be a second volume like the one I have just started.

Nature versus Nurture – despite you never received any formal higher education, you have written a great number of novels, non-fiction books, as well as books on anthologies. Where did you acquire your skills and the internal drive for your literary and scholarly endeavor? Do you think it was a skill that has to to be taught? Or a talent that one has to be born with?

Neither: I think it's a skill that has to be earned, it can't be taught.

Throughout your life, you have received numerous awards for your literary and scholarly achievements. Despite of your achievements and successes, did you you ever have any regrets or second thoughts about your career choices, and/or your creative or scholarly outputs? Is there anything you might wish to have done differently if you were given the same opportunity again?

No, I would not have a changed a single thing. I've had a charmed life.

9 Jelena Djurovic

Director, National Library of Montenegro

Introduction

The National Library of Montenegro "Đurđe Crnojević" (NLM) is a public institution that preserves print materials and other media published in Montenegro, by Montenegrin people and about the country of Montenegro. The NLM has a long-standing tradition despite the fact that its continuity was interrupted on several occasions – mainly by historical events. The NLM "Đurđe Crnojević" was named after the 15th century ruler of Montenegro, who in 1493, established the first state printing house in Europe.

A graduate of the University of Belgrade and majoring in Italian Language and Literature, Jelena Djurovic has been serving as the Director of this historic national library since 2004. In the following interview, Djurovic discusses her unique transparent management style as well as how we could develop an understanding of the struggle for freedom, and the unique cultural/ethnic identity rooted in the Montenegrin people, by reviewing the publishing history and collections of the NLM.

Fig. 9.1: The NLM's director Jelena Đurović in her office (Photo: National Library of Montenegro).

Fig. 9.2: Main library hall (Photo: National Library of Montenegro).

Fig. 9.3: Researchers' reading room (Photo: National Library of Montenegro).

9.4: Home page of Digital collection "Petar II Petrović Njegoš" (Photo: National Library of Montenegro).

Could we begin this interview by first introducing yourself, for example, your training and background? Could you also describe your roles as Director of the National Library of Montenegro?

My name is Jelena Djurovic (Jelena Đurović), and I'm the Library Advisor and Director of the National Library of Montenegro (NLM)[1] since 2004. I graduated in Italian Language and Literature from the Faculty of Philology, University of Belgrade.[2] Soon after graduation, I started working in the National Library [of Montenegro], and from that day on, I've devoted my knowledge, time and energy to this institution. I've traveled all the way from a beginner, through a cataloger, indexer, chief of department, deputy director, to the director of my library.

---

1 National Library of Montenegro – Homepage. Available at: http://www.nb-cg.me
2 University of Belgrade – Homepage. Available at: http://www.bg.ac.rs/en/

Besides authoring numerous papers in the field of Library and Information Science (58 records in the national bibliographic database), I've participated in the development of the National Digitization Program of libraries, the latest Law on librarianship and a series of accompanying rulebooks. My professional years were, and still are, filled with giving presentations and participating in multiple international conferences as lecturer as well as regularly organizing educational programs, seminars and conferences for librarians in Montenegro.

I've been the President of the Montenegrin Commission for taking professional library exams, Committee member for the award of professional titles in librarianship, and currently am a member of the National Commission of Montenegro for UNESCO.[3]

As an author of various projects, such as the "Centre for Permanent Education of Librarians in Montenegro – Library In" and co-author of the project "Virtual Library of Montenegro," I've realized a very successful cooperation between my library and national libraries in the region in the field of continuous education of librarians, as well as with the Institute for Information Sciences (IZUM), Maribor, Slovenia during the second phase of regional COBISS.NET[4] development. It was then when we established the Centre for Library and Information Systems of Montenegro and the Centre for Microfilming and Digitization. Successful functioning of these two centers I consider my great accomplishments.

I'm a member of CENL (**C**onference of **E**uropean **N**ational **L**ibrarians)[5] and CDNL (**C**onference of **D**irectors of **N**ational **L**ibraries).[6] Through CENL, my library joined the TEL project, and we are currently on the move to Europeana, together with other European libraries of our kind. I've initiated or participated in various projects. I've been a member of the Governing Board of the ISSN Centre[7] in Paris for four years, too, and ISSN and ISBN National centers are seated in the National library.

I've initiated and supervised projects of architectural restoration in order to create optimal conditions for preservation and restoration of Library's collections

---

[3] National Commission for UNESCO of Montenegro – Homepage. http://mep.c-g.me/en/national-commission-unesco-montenegro-2015/
[4] COBISS.NET – Homepage. Available at: http://www.cobiss.net/
[5] Conference of European National Librarians (CENL) – Homepage. Available at: http://www.cenl.org/
[6] Conference of Directors of National Libraries (CDNL) – Homepage. Available at: http://www.cdnl.info/
[7] ISSN (International Standard Serial Number) Centre – Homepage. Available at: http://www.issn.org/

and rehabilitation of its facilities. I've provided and directed funds from multiple valuable donations in order to perform all the necessary adaptations (in total, over 1 million euros).

All this work has been awarded, too. Besides awards in the fields of librarianship (MLA's Award and Slovene Institute for Information Sciences' Award), there are recognitions in the broader field of culture (Award of the Montenegrin Royal Capital, city of Cetinje, and an award from the Italian Government).

All my efforts aimed at transforming my working environment, and the library as a whole into a modern cultural institution, promoting it and creating the library without walls by making its rich written cultural heritage accessible to broad audiences.

My vision of library development is: serving knowledge, education, memory and literacy; enabling general access to information as well as professional, educational and cultural contents; serving as a basis and an impetus for overall development, progress and strengthening of Montenegro; serving the purposes of and fostering research, learning, entertainment and creativity; serving all citizens of Montenegro without any distinctions and limitations.

My motto in the management of the Library is that we are only temporarily here, and we simply have to respect what the previous generations have left us as a legacy. Only by insisting on a commitment to the profession it is possible to leave a mark in time. We shall all serve to the Library in the noblest sense of the word.

Have you always worked in libraries? Could you tell us more about your path to becoming the Director of the National Library of Montenegro?

I'm always happy to remember the moment when I first came to work in the Library. I cannot exactly recollect what my expectations were. I was familiar with the library only as a library user. I didn't know what were supposed to be my responsibilities. That day, an old cataloging rulebook was waiting for me on the table. I took into my hands the reference book whose content I did not understand a little bit. The same thing repeated the next day. But then, I decided to put an effort and start learning step by step.

After finally mastering the rules, the next challenge was the Universal Decimal Classification. I gladly took over that job in order to convey my knowledge to others and form a systematic catalog. Guided by the tough experience of self-study, I introduced a mentor to help each novice in work with monographs.

Today, I also believe that access to education and good organization are important segments of getting capable librarians and for application of new standards. During my work in the Library, I've held many seminars and workshops for librarians in the library and librarians from the whole of Montenegro, mainly related to classification and cataloging.

Thanks to the application of information technology, I was also one of those who directed the procedures for a new way of creating the catalog, and on my initiative a new organization of work was implemented by linking two departments into one, more functional department in order to improve the economics of work and achieve better results. The idea was initially met with resistance, but proved to be justified and later many other regional libraries have accepted it.

I was a Deputy Director from 1995 to 2004. To sum up, stairways toward the position of Director of the National Library were long and difficult to pass. And this is my third term on this position.

Could you please provide a brief introduction about the National Library of Montenegro?

National Library of Montenegro "Đurđe Crnojević"[8] has a long-standing tradition despite the fact that its continuity was interrupted on several occasions, mainly by historical events. During the period of reign of Petar II Petrović Njegoš (Prince-Bishop of Montenegro, poet and philosopher), the secular books in Cetinje Monastery have been separated from church books. They've been acquired by him and his predecessor Petar I, and transferred to his residence Biljarda (1838). It is considered that Njegoš's library functioned as a state library.

The idea on establishing, that is restoring the state library at Cetinje was not launched again until 1893. Prince Nikola I Petrović decided, on the occasion of 400th anniversary of Crnojevic printing house, to establish a public library. The Law on Montenegrin Princedom Library enacted in December 1896 entrusted the library with gathering "all works, published in all languages, dealing with Montenegro," as well as the books of other South Slavic and Slavic nations. The Law also introduced the title of a State Librarian.

The Library holdings were increased both by purchase and gifts, and since 1905 also with the institute of legal deposit. It was in that year that by the Law on Printing in the Princedom of Montenegro, the Library gained the right to three obligatory copies of "each printed item" within the territory of Montenegro.

After World War II, with the act of the Ministry of Education of the Republic of Montenegro[9] from March 26th, 1946 the State Central Library was established

---

8 National Library of Montenegro "Đurđe Crnojević" – Homepage. Available at: http://www.cnb.me/index.php?lang=en

9 Ministry of Education of the Republic of Montenegro – Homepage. Available at: http://www.mpin.gov.me/en/ministry

in Cetinje. At first, it was located within the State Museum and subsequently was separated as an autonomous institution in late 1946.

The National Library of Montenegro "Đurđe Crnojević" (NLM), as one of those with the deepest roots among the national libraries in this part of Europe, is a real treasury of Montenegrin written heritage, intellectual memory of the nation and one of the symbols of culture in the country.

It preserves material evidences of Montenegrin cultural reality and the origin and identity of the people who live in this part of the Balkans for centuries. Its Conservation Laboratory takes care of damaged and endangered copies of documentary heritage and the Library itself takes part in programs of cultural heritage preservation in accordance with the Ministry of Culture. As a library with one of the richest and most diversified collections in the region, the NLM promotes Montenegrin written heritage and enriches the cultural life of citizens of Montenegro. Under the aegis of this mission, the Library preserves written and published (in all media) materials.

It also has a long-standing and well-developed publishing activities. The National Library publishes works of enduring value for Montenegrin culture, thematic and personal bibliographies and professional library and information (LIS) literature. It also publishes "Herald of the National Library of Montenegro."

It is the parent library to all libraries in Montenegro and the National Agency for the allocation of ISBN, ISSN, ISMN and other international bibliographic numbers, as well as for preparing Cataloging in Publication (CIP) for publishers in Montenegro. It maintains the national union catalog COBISS.CG and produces the National current bibliography (books in print).

What is the current size of the National Library of Montenegro's collections, including its special collections? Could you also describe what you deem are the highlights of the collection?

The library currently holds around two million units of various types of materials.

The Basic Fund consists of books, newspaper titles, serials, and other formats – European, world and Montenegrin. The National Collection, "Montenegrina," holds Montenegrin books and periodicals. Montenegrin Books consists of more than 45,000 bibliographic units, and books in foreign languages about Montenegro are of special significance in this collection. Montenegrin Periodicals holds magazines and newspapers – the total of 1,437 titles, and Old Montenegrin Periodicals contains 175 titles.

The Old and Rare Books Collection consists of old books, rare editions and miniatures. The oldest book in this collection is an incunable, "Noctes Atticae" by Aulus Gellius, printed in the printing shop of Andrija Paltašić from Kotor (Venice,

1477). The Manuscripts and Archival Records Collection keeps, stores and processes manuscripts from the Montenegrin past, extensive correspondence of notable figures in Montenegrin history, rich holdings of photographs, postcards, posters and other non-book materials.

The Cartographic Collection consists of more than 500 geographic atlases and 2,500 geographic maps. Among them is the atlas from 1764 "Carte de la Mediterranée" by famous French hydrographer Joseph Roux. The Collection of Printed Music and Audio-visual Material has about 27,000 library units, that is around 19,000 units of audio-visual material and 8,000 printed music (notes). The Art and Graphics Collection contains about 74,000 posters of all kinds, of which 17,000 Montenegrin – political, film, concert, exhibition, theatre, education, and tourism and commercial posters.

Except newspapers (daily or official) and magazines, the Serials Collection includes newsletters, yearbooks, almanacs, calendars, chronicles, proceedings (of companies, universities, institutes, academies), work reports, plans and work programs, information, reviews of university lectures, statistical yearbooks (of states and cities), school papers, annual reports, reports written in shorthand.

The National Library of Montenegro "Đurđe Crnojević" holds seven legacies, or seven separate personal libraries, which the prominent Montenegrin public figures donated to the National Library.

The Digital Library includes digitization and presentation of the most valuable collections of the National Library, such as manuscripts, books, newspapers and magazines, etc.

Given Montenegro's unique history and geographical location – being so close to Italy and Turkey – and having Serbia and Bosnia as neighbors, being part of Yugoslavia (during the Soviet Union era), also once ruled by the Ottoman Empire – how have all these shaped the literary developments and publishing industries of your country – as a results – how have the missions and policies of the National Library of Montenegro evolved in the past centuries – in order to deal with such major social, political and cultural changes? In addition, during the 1990s – when Yugoslavia, Croatia and Kosovo were at war – did it have any major impacts on the operations and long-lasting effects on the National Library of Montenegro?

The struggle for freedom and preservation of identity that lasted for centuries are deeply rooted in Montenegrin people and are part of its heroic ethical code. They have been transmitted and sublimed in the best way through books and literature.

In hard times of enemy aggressions when it was not possible to do it in Montenegro, our books have been printed abroad, while – lacking the munitions – metal types have been melted into lead bullets. However, over and over again, like a phoenix, the National Library has been reborn and rebuilt, and publishing has flourished.

Looking a few centuries back, as well as the recent history and the last war in the former Yugoslavia, the National Library has always managed to adapt to new circumstances and to pursue its mission. In the last ten years, in circumstances of creating a new – recreating the old state, and with a plethora of social changes, a fresh creative energy and enthusiasm have developed along with the conscience about the need of taking responsibility for our own cultural development. Thus, the Montenegrin publishing industry is rapidly developing to cover the diversity of academic and professional fields, and the National library – answering its legal depot obligation – does its best to keep pace with it. Besides, there are new forms of publishing, such as publishing on the web, and we are taking steps to build a comprehensive strategy of collecting, keeping and presenting this vast richness of sources, both traditional and new.

Do you also work closely with other libraries across Montenegro and Europe? Such as on cross-national or global collaborative projects? What are some highlights?

The Law on Librarianship says that NLM is a leading and parent for all libraries in Montenegro. Therefore, it developed a unique library information system and integrated bibliographic records into a single catalog: COBISS.CG. It is important to say that COBISS (Co-operative Online Bibliographic Systems and Services) is a model of a complex system that represents national library information systems in Slovenia, Serbia, Macedonia, Bosnia and Herzegovina, Montenegro, Bulgaria and Albania. All these systems are interconnected into the COBISS.Net regional network.

COBISS.Net is an established international development and cooperation project for the development of national library information systems and current research information systems. Linking between the two systems is crucial for managing researchers' bibliographies and evaluating research results.

The Library has participated in various European projects and initiatives: PULMAN, NAPLE, MANUBALK, SEEDI, Teca Mediterranean, within the Central European Initiative; and within JJI, ISBN, IFLA, OCLC.

In 2008, the National Library joined TEL (The European Library) project supported by CENL. National Library is a member of SEENL (South East European National Libraries) from its foundation four years ago. Our national catalog is available for searching via TEL through the unique interface for all participating European national libraries.

The National Library of Montenegro also has a rich and traditional international cooperation with more than 50 national libraries from around the world, including the US Library of Congress, national libraries of the United Kingdom, France, Italy, Russia, Czech Republic, and certainly with all the national libraries of Southeast Europe countries.

In 2012, the Central National Library of Montenegro "Đurđe Crnojević" was renamed the National Library of Montenegro "Đurđe Crnojević". Why was this done? What was the significance of this name change for you as Director?

Actually, the initiative for changing the name came from me, because the original form of the name in our language had the word "narodna," meaning "public." This obviously is neither the role nor the function of the library; I felt it was necessary to change it so that from its new name, it can be immediately clear what the role and function of the library is. Misunderstanding and confusion have often occurred, especially in international communication. I think that the title of "national" at the beginning of its name gives it a clear distinction and refers to its identity, especially in the new framework of Montenegro as an independent state. I'm very glad that my proposal has been met with the approval, and the new name has been very quickly adopted by all.

Reference service is slowly fading away. Some library schools don't even teach it anymore, or teach a different variation – such as Human Computer Interaction (HCI). What are your thoughts on reference services? Does the National Library of Montenegro offer it anymore?

I think that libraries, especially national, still have to offer this service. To be able to retrieve library holdings and to find the best and most relevant material, one has to be skilled in information literacy and it is often not the case with our users, or they don't have enough time to browse our vast collections. Besides, I believe that library needs to keep its human dimension and contact with people that ask our services. Our library offers this service, since it is necessary for fast and efficient finding of what our users need. Help in finding information is very important for users. This works very well in our library and users are truly satisfied. Also, there are lots of remote users, and we really care about responding to their demands and requests in due time.

Please describe the staffing structure at the National Library of Montenegro. For example, what are the working relationships between the various Heads of subject/cataloging departments and the branch heads in such a vast and large system?

When we talk about the facts, having in mind tasks and functions of the national library, the size of collections, programs and projects, I dare say that the total number of 85 employees is insufficient. On the other side, the fact is that Montenegro is a country with a total of less than 700,000 inhabitants, and Cetinje, where the library is located, is the city of some 15,000 inhabitants. The annual budget of the Library is compatible with all of these indicators. In such a structure, a maximum contribution of every individual has to be expected, even when it comes to heads of departments who beside managing and leading their staff, also have to take over some additional work. It is very difficult to make a good personnel structure because there is a high proportion of non-librarian staff. It is necessary that all employees specialize in multidisciplinary projects, not only for one type of work, so we can accomplish all of the tasks, strategies and visions of the National Library. We have to achieve all that every other national library has to, but with much less staff, which is difficult but at the same time challenging for the whole team.

Could you describe your typical day at work? Is there ever a typical day at work?

I can hardly describe any working day as a typical workday or classify it in the field of typology as something that has its own routine. I try to make important decisions at the right time and to give priority to large-scale tasks without neglecting smaller responsibilities. I think that the most important and least important form one harmonious whole and give the work a dynamic flow. There is no day without an event. Apart from the planned agenda for the day, there are always new and unexpected tasks, challenges, ideas, communications and contacts. From all this new projects are conceived. It altogether enriches every day and makes it completely filled with activities and responsibilities. Anyway, I'm the happiest when I can say at the end of the day: "It was difficult, but successful!"

What scholarly and professional associations are you a part of, and how do they inform you in your work?

I've been a member of the Montenegrin Library Association and its president for four years. The National Library of Montenegro "Đurđe Crnojević" is a member of and contributor to many international library associations and agencies, and very often, I am the Library representative in these bodies. We are a member of IFLA, ISSN (I'm currently a member of the Governing Board of the ISSN International Centre in Paris); ISBN, LIBER; CDNL; CENL; EUROPEANA (preparation phase); OCLC – Online Computer Library Center (signed agreement for the integration of electronic catalog of Montenegro in the World directory – WorldCat).

All these various instances, as you know, produce vast amounts of informational and working materials, apart from regular meetings. These are precious source of current information that help me to stay in touch with state-of-the-art in different sectors of library and information work. Because of chronic lack of time sometimes, it is hard to follow everything, but thanks to years of experience, I am usually able to quickly spot important things and then to follow them more extensively.

Who are the majority users of the National Library of Montenegro? That is, who comes to see you about your collections, programs, and services?

We have group and individual visits from all categories of citizens, school and university students, but mostly researchers of Montenegrin history and social issues visit us. Our cultural programs, exhibitions and events are not of interest for only citizens of Cetinje, but for people from the neighboring towns as well.

The average annual number of services at the spot is 14,000. Our union catalog and website has ca. 10,000 and 116,000 visits per annum, respectively. We design and organize some 15 bigger cultural events in the Library per annum with a total of 750 visitors.

Could you give examples of types of new programs and services at National Library of Montenegro which you've found successful or innovative?

Among numerous programs and projects in the last ten years, I consider the most important the Virtual library of Montenegro and establishing the COBISS Center in Montenegro. It significantly influenced the improvement of professional librarians work and enabled users to enjoy all advantages of union online catalog. It caused creation of COBISS network on the national level with 26 member libraries of all types. That way, the National Library didn't improve only itself, but other libraries and general users experience and access to information.

Another influential service that started as a project (named 'Half of a Millenium') is *Montenegrin Online Retrospective Bibliography*. The database is based on our printed bibliography of books and articles in 33 books with more than 200,000 bibliographic units that covers period from 1494 when the first book, *Octoechos the First Voice*, was printed in Cetinje, to 1994. From 1994 on, there is our Current Bibliography on Montenegro available to users online. The Retrospective Bibliography consists of records for works published in Montenegro, foreign works on Montenegro and Montenegrins, and works of people from Montenegro published elsewhere. This project enabled a new service to our users to browse almost all of the documentary materials on Montenegro from one point of access. I wish to say that we are very proud of it because we are the first to create such a database in the region, searchable through multiple access points. In that way, we created a model of best practice. Therefore it gained high praises at conferences where we presented it.

There is also the digital collection "Petar II Petrović Njegoš," who was the greatest Montenegrin prince-bishop, poet and philosopher, and he lived in the first half of the XIX century. During his short life (he died when he was 38), he left us a rich literary and philosophical heritage. Montenegrin culture still strongly relies on it. Our digital collection covers various documentary forms: books, letters, archive material, musical and theatrical adaptations, translations to many languages. It was highly evaluated at professional forum when we presented it because it consists of many formats: books, handwritings, discs, VHS tapes, posters, etc., and because it is a high quality didactical resource: Njegoš is not the subject only in our schools but in all Slavic departments all over the world.

The last practice I would like to highlight is the changing concept of cultural programs. I've introduced the concept of open and inviting library by creating programs of broader interest. Book promotions, public readings, exhibitions, concerts, theatrical performances, even fashion shows. All these are for one goal: to give audiences more reasons to come to the library in order to raise their number and widen the profile of visitors, and to give them any possible opportunity to learn about the significance of and the possibilities offered by the National Library.

The National Library of Montenegro is located at two sites in Cetinje, in two significant historical mansions built in 1910 for the Italian and French diplomacies in the Kingdom of Montenegro (1910–1918). In addition to preservation of its collections, what types of maintenance is needed for these two old and prestigious buildings more than a century old?

Cetinje is the Old Royal Capital of Montenegro and apart from the King Nikola's Palace and residences, which today are in the service of museums, its characteristic is the existence of various buildings of former embassies and legations, which foreign countries have built for practicing their diplomatic missions. Today, all those buildings are protected monuments of culture and our architectural heritage.

Due to their age and long periods of disinvestment, two old buildings, which are used today by the National Library, were in pretty bad shape, and therefore, it was necessary to renovate them in order to protect them as cultural monuments, to achieve their valorization and, of course, to preserve collections stored in them and create better conditions for users and employees.

Since 2006 until today, thanks to donor funding of over one million euros and funds by the Government of Montenegro, these buildings saw the most significant architectural conservation works – reconstruction of roofs, facades, interiors and new installations. Now the former Italian Embassy building is almost completely renovated, together with a huge park complex with an open-air reading space and tennis court.

Reconstruction of the former French Embassy building has been done in its basics – new roof and electric installations. The main Museum of Books and National Literature conceptual project has been developed. I expect the realization of this project to start in the following year, as it was included in the National Program of Culture Development 2016–2020. This will be novelty in the National Library and will enhance development of education, culture and science.

What's the role of technology and innovation at National Library of Montenegro?

I consider new technologies as a development that was inevitable and that was widely welcomed in libraries. They simply stick to libraries because librarianship is highly structured and standardized profession and it suits very well to computing logic and organization. New technologies not only changed the face of libraries, but contributed significantly to the increase of professional standards and demands. They also helped greatly to raise visibility and significance of libraries in the eyes of their founders and financers, and of the society as a whole.

For all those reasons, libraries are now, in the 21st century, again in the front lines of all cultural institutions by introducing and implementing heavily digital processes and products. My library, too, is at the very peak of interest in government projections, in the strategic document National Program of Culture Development 2016–2020, in the center of issues such as preservation and presentation of written cultural heritage, but also development of creative industries and culture of making, and contribution to the economy (e.g., through cultural tourism).

Could you describe your management and leadership style? Mentorship is such an important theme in leadership – both mentoring and being mentored. Could you please tell us about your experiences about both? Do you still have mentors that you go to?

I've always nourished self-responsibility, dedication and enthusiasm for the work and tried to communicate them to my associates. I believe that these elements define a personality of a manager and make him credible in the eyes of collaborators. I respect transparency in work and in making decisions. It adds up to mutual trust and confidence with employees of the Library. I'm not using authoritative models of management and prefer managing through competences and building connections and organizational patterns. Of course, there is always negotiation, too.

While I was a student, I envisaged myself as a professor. The library profession opened an opportunity for that. I constantly feel committed, able and willing to transfer to others everything I know and get to know. Librarianship is a vivid profession, always transforming and improving, and I have traveled with it. It keeps demanding new skills and competencies, and I had favorable conditions to master many of them. After that, I communicated them to others in a structured way. I was always fully aware that knowledge is a non-rival good and that it only has sense if it is shared with colleagues, within our institution and beyond its borders. It is the way for all of us to contribute to changes and development of the profession as a whole.

Therefore, I can't tell exactly how many seminars, workshops and continuous professional development and workplace learning programs I have initiated, designed and realized. Neither can I say how many Montenegrin and other librarians took part in them. Just as an illustration: one year of Library In, informal program of CPDWL (**C**ontinuous **E**ducation and **W**orkplace **L**earning), saw 183 participants and 150 hours of training, and it happened in a country with 500 librarians altogether.

I was also always very supportive to formal post-graduate studies for librarians and succeeded in realization of cooperative activity through the CEI (**C**entral **E**uropean **I**nitiative) program when a number of NLM's librarians obtained their MAs in neighboring Croatia and Slovenia.

Normally, I learn each and every day using the knowledge and experience of others to improve myself. I regularly take part in professional conferences and seminars. It is not always on strictly library subjects, but on management of institutions of culture, on managing projects from the concept to realization, on broad range of topics from the field of culture. Numerous international, regional and domestic conferences have always filled me with material and informed me on other colleagues' experiences, and it all has helped me to create my own ideas and to apply them within our local conditions.

Which part(s) of your job as the Director do you find most rewarding? What is the most frustrating?

My most precious reward is seeing results of my work and satisfaction of my collaborators and general public. The moment when my personal satisfaction becomes our common satisfaction is the highlight of my day at work. When I see others using and applying my designs and projects, in other communities, it gives me a great pleasure, too.

The most frustrating moments are those when I see young people lacking energy and enthusiasm. Young people who do not seek their place in profession and in life, a place that would fill them with satisfaction makes me sad. Then, something inside urges me to try to show them that our profession can offer them fulfilment of their aspirations, excitement and pleasure of working on the very edge of new technologies. All that is for good cause of serving people and the society they live in.

In the very end I would like to say that I completely found my place in this profession; it fulfils my aspirations and makes me content and happy.

10 Dr. Claudia Lux

Librarian, Project Director of the Qatar National Library in Doha
IFLA President 2007–2009

Introduction

The Qatar National Library (QNL) is a non-profit organization under the umbrella of the Qatar Foundation for Education, Science, and Community Development – established with the mission to spread knowledge, preserve the nation's heritage for the future, and, more importantly, support Qatar in its development from a carbon-based economy to a knowledge-based one by "Unlocking Human Potential." In the country of Qatar, Qatari nationals currently make up only 13% of the population, with the remaining population comprised of foreign workers – mainly from Asian or Arab countries – with diverse cultural and educational backgrounds. Although Arabic is the official language, English is widely spoken. On the whole, QNL combines three library functions in one: the national library, university and research library, and the central public library function.

In 2012, Dr. Claudia Lux was assigned by Her Highness Sheikha Moza bint Nasser, Chairperson of the Qatar Foundation, to become the Project Director of the QNL. Prior to joining QNL, Dr. Lux worked as a Sinologist at the State Library Berlin and was the Director of the Senate Library (Berlin). In 2007, she became the Director-General of the Central and Regional Library of Berlin (ZLB). Along with this, Dr. Lux served as the President of IFLA from 2007–2012, which represents 1,500 associations from about 150 countries. In the following interview, Dr. Lux discusses her unparalleled passion, her goal to impress upon politicians and the public the importance of libraries in the development of the information society, as well as QNL's contributions in "bridging with knowledge Qatar's heritage and future."

Fig. 10.1: Prof. Dr. Claudia Lux 2014 (Photo: Qatar National Library).

Fig. 10.2: The 45000 sqm Qatar National Library in Education City designed by renowned architect Rem Koolhaas (Photo: Qatar National Library).

Fig. 10.3: QNL: A view from the side tiers on the bridge, the heritage collection and the main collection tiers (Photo: Qatar National Library).

Fig. 10.4: On the bridge inside QNL there are multifunctional areas for reading, working, discussing and under the bridge the coffee shop, a theatre and a gaming area offers space for recreation (Photo: Qatar National Library).

Can we begin this interview by first introducing yourself – your education, professional training, and other professional affiliations?

My name is Claudia Lux, and I have a Master's degree in Social Science from Ruhr University Bochum[1], and I have also studied Chinese and have a Ph.D. in Chinese Studies, also from Ruhr University Bochum. I was always interested in the Chinese language and culture. I studied from the beginning in Berlin, Kansas, Beijing, and then finally at Ruhr University Bochum – the biggest East Asian Faculty in Germany. In addition, I could align this with my previous Social Science studies from the same university.

After obtaining my Ph.D. degree, I was admitted into a professional librarian program at the Berlin State Library[2], which brought me to undertake another Master's degree in Library and Information Science (MLIS). It was a two-year program with one year of internship – that is one year of practical work at the library and one year of academic studies at the University of Cologne.[3]

How did you begin your career as a librarian? In addition, what was your specialty, in terms of professional knowledge, skills and experiences?

That's because the Berlin State Library was looking for people with special language knowledge, to manage a very big collection under the East Asian Department, so I applied for the job. When I first arrived at the Berlin State Library, I was dealing mostly with modern Chinese materials. So, this is how I entered into the library profession.

In other words, you began at the State Library in Berlin, but what happened afterwards?

Yes, I was developing my professional knowledge and other technical skills in all respective areas, while using the Berlin State Library as a base. After spending a few years working at the Berlin State Library, the two Berlin State Libraries (one located on in the Kulturforum on Potsdamer Straße in West Berlin, and the original main building on Unter den Linden) – as a result of the German Unification, which took place in 1989. Then, I received some requests for going to some big public libraries in Western Germany to work. But, I wanted to stay in Berlin, so I applied for a job at the Berlin Senate Library – it was a special library for the

---

[1] Ruhr University Bochum – Homepage. Available at: http://www.ruhr-uni-bochum.de/index_en.htm
[2] Berlin State Library – Homepage. Available at: http://staatsbibliothek-berlin.de/en/
[3] University of Cologne – Homepage. Available at: http://www.portal.uni-koeln.de/uoc_home.html?L=1

supporting the overall administration in Berlin. The Berlin Senate Library is not a Parliamentary Library, but an administrative library for the Berlin Land and a special library on urban development.

Can you tell me your duties and responsibilities at the Berlin Senate Library, as well as what kinds of materials and collections you had to work with?

I was serving as the Director of the Berlin Senate Library. I had to change their whole operation system to a new one, that is from the previous manual-based operations to a completely new IT-based library. We set up the whole network infrastructure, including introducing a new automated library system that could support online cataloging. We also introduced email to and a website to the whole library organization, etc. With reference to the collection of the Berlin Senate Library, it was meant to support urban development issues throughout the whole country of Germany, and not only for Berlin alone. And this was a very pressing issue right after unification. One of the main roles of the Berlin Senate is to collect materials published from all the German cities – which are mostly official government publications and the grey publications. The grey literature was aligned with a research institute, Deutsches Insitutu fuer Urbanistik DIFU[4], which was not under the library but located right next to it. The research institute would place local publications in a database, and we would collect the material so that whenever somebody requested something out of this database, we would support this by direct loan.

How many people were working with you or under you at the Berlin Senate Library at that time?

When I first arrived at the Berlin Senate Library, there were only 27 or 28 people altogether. However, as we developed, the number of staff gradually increased to 36 over the years.

You began your career as a librarian around the same time as the 1989 German Unification – what kinds of impacts did such a major political and social change have on the overall developments of libraries and library projects in Germany at that time?

A big impact, for sure! In order to cope with such major sociocultural and political changes, we had to undertake as well as to provide a great deal of on-the-job training for the administration libraries in cities and ministerial libraries of

---

4 Deutsches Insitutu fuer Urbanistik (DIFU) – Homepage. Available at: https://difu.de/

Eastern Germany. We also had a lot of exchange of materials, and when libraries were closed, we acquired and took over their materials. There was quite a lot of cooperation between east and west at that time.

What was the biggest challenge caused by the 1989 German Unification? I suppose you would have to supervise library staff from the former Western and Eastern Germany – meaning that despite they both speak the same language, their mentalities, their working styles, their ways of communication would be drastically different from each other – is that correct?

Yes, I totally agree. But that was not so much when I first went to the Berlin Senate Library. In 1997, I became the Director-General of the new organization (Zentral und Landesbibliothek Berlin – ZLB – Central and Regional Library[5]), which was the foundation of the unification of the big central city libraries of both parts of Berlin.

Here I had to unify a total number of 300 People, 150 people from the City Library in the eastern part of Berlin and 150 from the American Memorial Library of West-Berlin.

What were the biggest challenges of bringing together people from two different cultural backgrounds?

They both spoke German, but they don't speak the "same" language! One example that I always talk about is the way you had a birthday celebration. At that time in the western part, at the American Memorial Library, people were very much influenced by the student movement in the 1960s, and they were more "leftist." On a birthday, they send special invitations to their group of people and not to everybody. Contrary in the East where everybody was invited to celebrate the birthday with coffee and cake.

But, when the library functions were united and a western group was placed next door to the eastern team, the following happened. A birthday celebration hosted by a member of the eastern group was on-going, and when they sat down to enjoy their cakes and their coffee, one said, "That is typical of the west! They're not coming to our birthday." The people from the west were staying in their room next door, then saying, "Typical of the east! They're not inviting us." Everything is the same, yet they could not be any more different. And we couldn't solve it immediately, as we need to talk and try to understand the issues in communication.

---

5 Zentral und Landesbibliothek Berlin (Central and Regional Library, Berlin) – Homepage. Available at: https://www.zlb.de/

To understand this unspoken background knowledge is really difficult. The most important thing is open communication. Only with good, open and frank communications can you solve those issues.

There were also different styles in life. I had lived in China, so I knew a lot of people who were not immediately saying what they think. If you ask them if it is okay, and they say nothing, it is like they are not agreeing with you. In West Germany, if you don't say anything, that means agreement. There were a lot of these underlying communication issues, but you have to understand, and I think I could understand a lot from living in different countries – especially living in Asia. I think that this was something that helped me a lot, and I could talk to different people in different ways. There were times that some of the librarians from the east were upset with some of the librarians from the west because of they were so outspoken, or speaking very aggressively, and too openly during a meeting. Some people were hurt because they felt that they were not being heard in the same way – they were not aggressive and not putting things on the table. Only afterwards, they came to tell me what they wanted. But, it is important for a manager to get all these different views.

How and where did you acquire the diplomacy skills that are comparable to a top-level ambassador to resolve such situations at work?

Well, you could also learn these diplomacy and communication skills at a university if you engage in courses or classes that are outside the regular curriculum. I think anyone can gain such experiences by working in any student associations or other associations in society or being a parent or teacher in a kindergarten or school, and that is why I often ask people, "What are you doing in your free time? Are you engaging yourself in any kind of volunteer work?" This is where you get these skills. I can tell you that I was always interested in meeting new people from different social and cultural backgrounds, and I have always worked voluntarily in all kinds of associations and societies or student or professional librarian groups, and so on. But, when I was doing my Ph.D. studies, I was fully drawn deep into my academic studies, so I also can understand the people who are like this.

How did you resolve the conflicts and disagreements in the workplace between the Eastern and Western German groups?

You have to smooth down these conflicts at workplace. Just like in the beginning, I had to make compromises to the different sides. For example, when I had to unify the classification systems between the two state libraries – it was apparent that we did not want to continue using the Soviet Union classification system. And we had the classification from the western part, which we decided to use for all. On the other side, we had more people from the Eastern part knowing how to manage the legal deposit that was now assigned to the Central and Regional Library. And they knew how you had to collect everything from the city and the Berlin State. So, I supported them. However, this was new to colleagues from the western part of the library – thus, they would say, "This is the material I don't like and don't want." But, with my own knowledge from the legal department's viewpoint and the grey material from the Senate Library, I knew how important this material is for the history of the city and the state. As the Director General of the Library, I had to educate both sides – informing them why they had to do this or that and why. I always tried to make the decisions sometimes according to the interests of the eastern part, and sometimes to the western part. I really tried to unite them (both spiritually and in working styles), and let them work together because by the time they actually started together, they did perform better and there was no more conflict at the end.

As a leader coming from the western side, how did you deal with the conflicts and disagreements between the two parties? How did you prove that you were fair to both parties?

Sometimes, people don't think you are fair even when you are fair. It is most important that you develop a team of staff that you have around you from both sides – who know the communication styles of each side, and would also support your vision. You also need to make clear to your staff that the library's vision is important. We tried to make some successes with the outside presses or media with the positive activities that we were doing. I think these were also very important to support the unification process. Then, we also recognized the history, which was a 100-year history of an important library. So we had all of these activities about the 100 years of the history of the library so we could recognize the work that the people have done during the time of the GDR (East Germany). I think that this was essential to recognize the work that they have done, that not everything they had done was wrong, or did not apply to the new setting. They did try, but they just didn't have the resources. So, it is very important that you acknowledge people in the way that they have done their work and build something positive upon that. Every side had their good and competent librarians, and that was the key element for me to be a successful director of the whole library system.

Would you say that the librarians from the former East Germany would be good at something while the ones from West Germany would be good at something else?

I think the difference went beyond the ways in which they worked. For example, there were librarians who lacked knowledge in the book market, or dealing with free access, but how could they know the book market when the books were coming from a one centralized organization? So there was some lacking in these areas, but mostly the basic library processes and operations on both sides were all the same. There were international standards on how to work in a library. In general, I think we could build on basic good professional practices. We did a lot of new training programs for the library systems, so this for sure was new to the East, but it was also new for the other side, the West side.

After Berlin, where did you go?

I was there for 15 years, and then I went to Qatar.

Would you like to tell me about your work as the President of IFLA?

During the time I was at the Central and Regional Library of Berlin, I also became the President of IFLA. For two years, I was the incoming President, the President-elect, and I eventually became the President of IFLA for another 2 years. During the time I was the IFLA President, I visited a lot of countries, and I was constantly looking for different kinds of changes that I could bring to the IFLA Association. When I was the IFLA President, I noticed that there was a great lack of advocacy for libraries in society – especially to the politicians – this was indeed a worldwide issue. Because many people from political levels would come up to me and said, "Now that everything is on the Internet, there will be no need for libraries in the future!" In some countries, there are politicians who are more supportive towards libraries. In other words, in terms of advocacy, the IFLA Association itself has important roles to play at many different levels, regionally, nationally and internationally, so I felt it was time to put "Libraries on the Agenda", on my presidential theme.

Why do you think some politicians choose not to support the libraries and librarians?

I always give this one example: when there is a person responsible for the culture in the city, he is sitting down in an evening event, and he sees somebody from the music school playing the violin. He says, "Wow! This is wonderful, and I will never learn and play at this level – it's so complicated." The next day, he goes to the library, and he sees somebody placing a book on the table, and giving it to somebody else. On the next table, he sees somebody showing something on a screen. So, he says, "Oh, my wife can do that." The difference is that our work is brainwork – something that they cannot see. If you cannot explain that, and that was also something I recommended to do, what is your work that you are structuring knowledge, in order to make it better accessible. If you cannot explain this, you are simply lost, and your work will not be recognized. I had one German university student who said, "I only understood what my mother, who was a librarian, was doing after I had started to study Library Science." I said, "This cannot be true! Your mother should be able to explain to you what she is doing." I think it's also a lack of training and competence to explain to the general public exactly what we are doing as librarians, and why it is relevant.

How would you go about advocating our work as librarians amongst the politicians?

First, you need to look at who is the right person to do this advocacy with. Not everybody is able to do it. I remember the colleagues of mine who went to a very nice exhibition. They went to the mayor directly and said, "We have problems with the rain, and you need to fix the roof." So they don't understand that the situation on the art exhibit is a nice event, where the mayor wanted to relax. Instead, they should have gone to him and said, "Oh, your speech was wonderful, and I really admire what you are doing." Then, later, they can say, "May I have a meeting with you?" After then, you can come up with your problems. What I saw were librarians going straight to their politicians and only complain about problems. This is not the way to do it. You just have to adjust to the situation, as advocacy is all about establishing long-term partnerships.

Did you recommend yourself to IFLA saying that you wanted to become the President? Or did they find you and elect you?

This goes through your own national library association and you have to work in several areas of IFLA, so people know you, to have a chance to be elected. When they start trusting you, they will say that you can become a candidate, and then for me, this was a direct election all over the world. IFLA had a new statute, so ten people could be elected worldwide. People would look at your CV or they knew you, and I gave lectures in many countries before I became the President. I worked with the Goethe Institute, providing training in different parts of the world, so people knew me in different countries. Through this and through the support of my library association in Germany, I was elected.

After you became the President of IFLA, what do you think was the most pressing agenda on the list?

One thing is to initiate this process of understanding of advocacy for libraries. I think that that was my main task. It was why I was traveling around and talking about libraries on the agenda, the role of libraries in society, what we can do if we are in a very diverse situation in a rural area or in the city, and also to try and find good examples. We had to activate people to focus less on the internal problems and focus on the external ones, looking how to work for advocacy, building funds for IFLA, as I built up the presidential meetings and the first grant from the Bill & Melinda Gates foundation for IFLA. There were some other activities that I introduced, and I know they are still doing the presidential meeting now. My main focus was to alert every library association to be active and do advocacy. One of the programs that came out of all of this was the Building Strong Library Association program.

When you were proposing new projects or programs for advocacy, would people sometimes say that it would only work for your country?

Yeah, I think that this is the wonderful thing about IFLA. We have all of these different areas, and you can see some people in certain remote areas who are more successful than somebody with a lot of funding in a city. Why? Because this depends on their activities. If you can show the impact of your library, then you can see that it's not just like your money makes everything. It's more like the energy of the librarians – how they work together, how they can influence a politician, makes all the difference. This is very often more important. It's not always easy, but with the training we are giving through the Building Strong Library Association program, everybody can achieve it. But, we know that there are some people out there who are more active or it's easier for them to talk with politicians and others who are too shy, or cannot find the right words. We need these people for different work that IFLA and the library associations are doing.

How long have you been working at the National Library of Qatar?

Four years, now.

When you were first offered the job, what was your initial reaction?

I was surprised and not really interested on first sight. Then it was a very long process. There were a lot of things to discuss, so it took maybe about one and a half years. Even after everything was completely finished, I still had to ask the mayor in Berlin – he was not so happy about it, so I had to convince them that it was right to go at that time.

Why were they not happy?

Because they just decided on a new library building in Berlin. However, I had told him that the new library would only be ready in 2023, and I'm already retired at that time. So, to get a new director now would be better for developing the new library and follow up the construction process.

Please tell me about your first day of work at the National Library of Qatar.

That was very interesting. I said hello to the staff, and held a short staff meeting, I said what kind of projects that I wanted to make happen because we were in the really early stages. There was also a meeting with all QF directorates and a presentation for me about the new building because the excavation for the building had just started, but there was nothing to see – at least the presentation showed some renderings of the project. This was the first time I saw in detail how the building would look like.

Are you the first head of the National Library of Qatar, or was there someone before you?

No, there were people before me at the Central Library, a director from the USA. But, they hadn't really started with the building construction at that time and parts of the budget were frozen. When I came, he was already gone. His deputy went off in November 2011 and I came in April 2012.

Why were they hiring foreigners to be the director of the National Library of Qatar instead of local people?

Qatar is building their workforce high speed and they have already developed quite a few. However, it is very often that they work with foreigners to build an institution up, and then later, replace the foreigner by a local person – this process of Qatarization is important. During these last four years, I am telling them that they need to have a Qatari in place as director for the opening of the National Library. And there is a foreigner who can support him or her. It is normal in the Gulf region, they rely on foreign competences in museums and other institutions, too, but in the meantime they are building their own workforce.

What are the advantages of having a foreigner there?

I think it has to do with having the international connections and the knowledge about the whole publishing situation, about licensing of databases, and to be able to convince local people that this is international standard what you are doing in libraries. When they set up the library, it was more based on foreigners, but we now have a good mixture of foreigners and Qatari as a team, and this mixture is of great value. Many Qatari get a lot out of this work in the library, as they go out to conferences, and they can see professional exhibitions and listen to professional talks from other libraries. In this way they can have the same experiences as people from Western countries. Foreigners might be important for education and also for international standards for a certain time. There are so many standards from IFLA, and there are so many international standards on libraries. For Qatar, they want to follow this, as they want to have a high professional and a most modern library. They don't want slow development or traditional libraries; their goal is to build the most advanced libraries of the world. And now as these young Qatari are doing their Master in Library and Information Science or even their Ph.D. – and this new group of young local library professionals are developing themselves as perfect leaders for the National Library in a very short time.

What are the skills that you have gained from the past have allowed you to contribute greatly to your current work?

One of the most important skills I learned from the past is flexibility combined with a clear vision and that you need to work with a team. I think there are different contributions. First of all, as Qatar is a small state, it was clear that the old Central Library concept had to be changed and the library could be a combined library of three functions: the national library function, academic library function and a central public library function. Then I analyzed what was the reason why the project stopped because it was a project where there was no building. So I invented to open the library as a digital library with databases giving access to e-books, articles, music, and videos and this was accompanied with a marketing campaign to get readers for these e-resources. I also had to analyze if the building structure and areas designed by the world renowned architect Rem Koolhaas would fit for a new National Library with three functions, and what needs to be changed from the central library concept (e.g. a bigger children library, a restaurant, etc.). And I developed the strategy, the business plan, the KPIs, the team and the procedures for this new entity. The other part was about the heritage collection – so, how to get more valuable materials for this collection. You need to have someone who really knows about the history of the Gulf and the Islamic world. As a librarian, you know that you have to acquire these materials, in order to make your collection complete, and you really have to strive for it. Last but not least, you have to decide the collection policy together with the staff, which books will be in the building and which books would be available electronically.

The history of Qatar is very brief in comparison to other countries like Iran, Iraq, or Saudi Arabia. So where would you go about to start building a library collection that would represent the local Qatari cultural heritage?

Yes. There are quite a few famous Sheikhs who had great collections in Qatar. One of those had started to collect heritage materials – especially manuscripts, early Arabic prints, and all of the travelogues from whoever traveled through this area. He started this collection in the 1970s and built it all through the 1980s and 1990s. So, there is a collection of about 50,000 books, which you can say is a really wonderful cultural heritage collection. This is one of the biggest on this topic – at least in the Gulf area. Sure, you cannot compare this with Egypt or Iran, but it is a different topic that Qatar is looking for. They were collecting Arab and Islamic science that influenced the Renaissance in Europe. They wanted to build on traditional and modern knowledge and become a knowledge society. The material we have in the heritage collection is starting somewhere in the 10th century with maps and manuscripts up to the 19th and 20th century when it comes to travelogues. The former owner also had the opportunity to buy many rare materials. For instance, in this heritage collection you find the first and second edition of the Napoleon's description de l'Egypte, which is a famous book documenting Egypt in the early 19th century. This heritage collection is really a cultural treasure of Qatar National Library. The new building will have an exclusive space to feature this great collection in a special designed area. It's in the center of the new building, and it looks like an excavation in the Arab desert. If you look at the pictures, you can see that it expresses the heart and the soul of the national library.

Are you able to find the people with the relevant professional experiences or library qualifications from the local people to process the collection?

We have hired quite a lot of foreigners in the beginning, and then we started to hire locals. There are many young, passionate, intelligent Qatari coming to us and wanting to work with us. We get them into the library, train them on the spot and after one or two years, and then we send them into a Master's degree in Library and Information Science degree program. They come with backgrounds in literature, English language, psychology, engineering, biology, and finance – so, whatever they have as a Bachelor's degree, many of them from a Western university, and we build on this and train them to achieve their Master's degrees.

Other Qatari librarians have often worked as school librarians in Qatar. Qatar has many school libraries and many school librarians. Some of them have done a really nice job teaching their students, and they were very creative in their work. We hired them as children librarians and some of them has previously worked as research librarians, as they know information literacy and cataloging, and the professional library work. Now, more and more of them are going to do their Master's degree, too.

Your task is to launch the Digital Library at the National Library, which is one of the largest online collections of historical records on Arab Gulf countries. Can you elaborate on that?

The Qatar Digital Library (www.qdl.qa) is, indeed, a very special project and will have more than 1.1 million pages on the history of the Arabian Gulf and on scientific manuscripts at the end of 2018, open for free to anybody in the world. In a project with the British Library, we have identified material in their Indian Office Archive about the history of the Gulf region, which are of high interest for scholars as for the general public. If you look at this source now, it is a beautiful digital library, which is heavily used by the region and all scholars of the history of the Gulf. And we will have more collections – digital and printed as stated in our collection policy. I think the mixture of a strong digital library and a modern high-tech library building is the best mixture for a strong national library in this century.

Together with the Qatar Foundation for Education, Research and Social Development, we have identified our stakeholders in our strategy and QNL is eager to serve them all. One of the main aspects for QNL is to serve education – especially higher education. The second is to support the research developments in Qatar, as there is a growing support of research by the Qatar national Research Fund. Last, but not least, the library will be open to the public, for everybody who is living in the country, which is a very diverse community. QNL will have a beautiful children's library and an exciting young adult library. We also will have materials in different languages of those nationalities working in Qatar, though our collection policy is mainly based on the main languages used in Qatar: Arabic and English. In the Education City, most of the universities are American, and most of the courses are taught in English and students and researchers are using study and research materials in English.

Why does the library not have three separate entities – a national library, a university library, and a metropolitan public library – rather than merging them into one building?

That is something I discussed, and I think I convinced the chairperson about this because when we started, it was built as a central university library of the Education City for all these different universities coming in from outside. You can imagine that we had to do some adjustments to really have it as a national library. It came up that there is no real functioning national library here. There was only a big public library that had some parts of the role of a national library. The chairperson asked us to really develop it into a national library. Now, we had two roles as a university library and a national library. The next question of the chairperson was that would it be open to everybody. I said that as Qatar is a small country, you should open it up to everybody because it would really be used. It's a big building – it's over 45,000 square meters. The population is only 2.5 million. That is also the reason why in addition to being a public library, we have unified all three different functions – that is being national library, a public library, and an academic library – all in one. We don't have branches yet, but we are working on this. To open the library to all is a very important step.

The techniques used for preserving and restoring the Qatari heritage collection, are they similar to the ones used for preserving Western books?

No, we have to have a specialist on Islamic manuscripts and restoration. There are significant differences to the way of binding. We have a team of four people dedicated to the restoration of these materials. It was a very important task for us when developing this collection.

What kinds of materials would the Islamic civilizations use for writing?

We do have rare manuscripts on Arabic paper. The material is stable in normal conditions, but often these manuscripts were exposed to heat, humidity, insects and other threats. So they need a good conservation program. Many famous works of Islamic and Arabic sciences were translated into Latin and were published as codices written on parchment.

How does the philosophy of the German National Library compare with the Qatar National Library?

The German National Library is concentrating on the legal deposit of Germany in print. But, this is a big task, as there are many publishers in German and it also includes collecting material from Switzerland and Austria. They are collecting digital material, too, and safe it for the future. But, it's not a university library as QNL is. They are not really extending their services outside so you have to go there. What we are doing is to serve all of the researchers in the country and all of the children with e-resources in Arabic and English. Adding a print collection is what we want to do when the library is open. We want them to do research in the library, meet up in the library, and we will invite them to many more activities. The library is also a meeting point – quite a difference than a normal national library elsewhere. In a way, it is comparable with Singapore, which is much more advanced, and they have really developed their collection and their activities and services. We are different from Singapore, as have all the materials available in one place, whether it is for the national library, the university library, or the public library. My idea is to put all related books together on one shelf, regardless they come from the national, the public or the academic library – so that people could decide for themselves what level of reading they want to have.

What are the Qatar National Library's collaborations with other national libraries in the Middle East as well as in Europe and the US?

We have two main partnerships until now. One is with the British Library and the other is the World Digital Library with the Library of Congress. The Library of

Congress' concept with the World Digital Library (www.wdl.org) is a partnership with UNESCO, and the concept of WDL is to place the most important material from each country of the world in the web, no matter where in the world it is kept. And it will be free for use by schools, students, and teachers as for research or individual use. WDL went around the world to collect these special materials, and Qatar has supported this project with UNESCO financially for quite a long time so that WDL could build the infrastructure. We also have a lot of our wonderful map collection about the Arabian Gulf. It is, in a way, something from each country represented there. This partnership is very special for QNL. We use it to develop digital competences in the Gulf region. We invite colleagues to a regional WDL conference and provide training on digitization, on metadata, and other aspects of active participation in the WDL.

With the British Library, it is a bit different. The British Library has the India Office Archive, which is a great source about 200 years when the British were in this area of the world. A lot of this material is especially from their political agency in Bushehr in Bahrain. It deals with all of the activities in the Gulf region. What we did is select with the British Library what we should digitize. Now, we have about 700,000 documents, and we are now in the second phase of our project. The first phase was for the first three years after we signed the contract. A key part of this project is that it is accessible worldwide free of charge. These documents are really excellent for knowing more about this topic and very important for all countries around the Arabian Gulf.

Can you describe the uniqueness of the architectural design of the Qatar National Library?

The physical building itself is exceptional, a diamond-shaped form, looking almost like a spaceship from a science fiction movie from the outside. When you enter through the main entrance, and the moment you open the door, you can nearly see the entire library collection. These are placed in terraces up on different areas. There is a big bridge in the middle of the area, and downstairs, you can see the excavation area where we have placed our heritage collection. From the architecture, you get the impression that you have boundless opportunities and limitless access to the knowledge of the world.

As the Project Director of the National Library of Qatar, which part of your job do you find the most gratifying?

The most satisfying feeling I have is seeing the development of the young Qatari in our library and their undying passion for using the library's collections, facilities and services, etc.

Why is it so important for a junior-level library manager to have professional exposures on an international level?

Based on my personal experiences, and many other seasoned LIS professionals would also tell you the same – that is people with international experience are more open to change – which I think is the most important part of our LIS profession. These people will handle problems and unsolved issues better than others. They know more libraries worldwide have the same challenges. They will be inspired by solutions their colleagues have found to solve those problems. For junior-level library manager I can only give one advice: to learn more about the international library world and learn from the experiences of your colleagues. This will be the richest knowledge for your carrier.

Further readings

About Qatar National Library – METLIB 2016 Qatar. Available at: http://www.metlib2016qatar.org/en/about-qnl

Claudia Lux, IFLA President 2007–2009. Available at: http://www.ifla.org/past-presidents/archive/lux

Did you know? Facts about Qatar National Library [YouTube]. Available at: https://www.youtube.com/watch?v=eM5MRTVkP9U

The Heritage of Ibn Al Haytham at Qatar National Library [YouTube]. Available at: https://www.youtube.com/watch?v=73xLhTiVJhA

IFLA World Library and Information Congress 2009 [YouTube]. Available at: https://www.youtube.com/watch?v=D9Nr_2M55-4&t=3s

Lux, Claudia. (2014). Qatar National Library – Architecture as innovation in the Arab world *IFLA Journal*, Vol. 40(3), pp. 174–181. Available at: http://journals.sagepub.com/doi/pdf/10.1177/0340035214546984

OMA to Design "Iconic" Qatar National Library. Available at: http://www.archdaily.com/300508/oma-to-design-iconic-qatar-national-library

Prof. Dr. Claudia Lux – DAAD. Available at: https://www.daad.de/der-daad/unsere-aufgaben/alumniarbeit/alumni-galerie/portraits/en/39347-prof-dr-claudia-lux/

Qatar National Library – 50 years Anniversary Film [YouTube]. Available at: https://www.youtube.com/watch?v=uvCvJQASPdI&t=72s

Qatar National Library – About the Library. Available at: http://qnl.qa/about-the-library/learn-more-about-the-library/about-the-library

Qatar National Library – Meet the Team. Available at: http://qnl.qa/about-the-library/learn-more-about-the-library/meet-the-team

QNL on Qatar Television [YouTube]. Available at: https://www.youtube.com/watch?v=A4Fe7d_coP4

11 Oren Weinberg

Director, National Library of Israel

Introduction

Founded in 1892, the National Library of Israel, formerly the Jewish National and University Library, is dedicated to collecting the cultural treasures of Israel and of Jewish heritage in all formats. The Library currently holds over five million books, and it is located on the Givat Ram campus of the Hebrew University of Jerusalem. The Library was also established with the mission to acquire all publications on the subject of Israel, the Land of Israel, and Judaism published in any language, as well as all materials published in Hebrew or any of the languages of the Jewish diaspora (such as Yiddish and Ladino). The Library is known for having the world's largest collections of Hebraica and Judaica, as well as one of the world's foremost collections on Islam and the Middle East.

Managing a team of over 350 staff is Oren Weinberg, the current Director of the National Library of Israel. While earning his Bachelor's degree in Art History from the University of Haifa, Weinberg began his lifelong career in librarianship shelving books at the same university over 20 years ago. In the following interview, Weinberg shares with the readers his take on the history and future of the National Library of Israel, as well as his unique perspective on the future face-to-face reference services – an information landscape that is increasingly media-rich, socially connected, and brilliantly chaotic.

Fig. 11.1: Oren Weinberg, Director of the National Library of Israel (Photo: Hanan Cohen, National Library of Israel).

Fig. 11.2: The National Library of Israel, Lady Davis Building (Photo: Assaf Pinchuk).

Fig. 11.3: Mordecai Ardon Windows (Photo: Assaf Pinchuk).

Fig. 11.4: General Humanities Reading Room (Photo: Assaf Pinchuk).

Could we begin this interview by first introducing yourself, for example, your training and education background? Could you also describe your role as Director of the National Library of Israel?

My name is Oren Weinberg, and I have been the Director General of the National Library of Israel (NLI)[1] in Jerusalem since 2010. Prior to that, I was the Director of the University of Haifa Library[2] from 2004 to 2010. I earned a BA in Art History and General Studies from the University of Haifa in 1993, certification in Library Studies from the University of Haifa in 1997, and an MA in Library and Information Studies (LIS) from Bar-Ilan University[3] in 2005.

Have you always worked in libraries? Could you tell us more about your path to becoming the Director of the National Library of Israel?

I worked my way up through the ranks in the University of Haifa Library, starting with a student job shelving books. I steadily moved into different positions with

---

1 National Library of Israel – Homepage. Available at: http://web.nli.org.il/sites/nli/english/Pages/default.aspx
2 University of Haifa Library – Homepage. Available at: http://lib.haifa.ac.il/index.php/en
3 Bar-Ilan University – Homepage. Available at: http://www1.biu.ac.il/indexE.php

increasing responsibilities – Manager of Reserve Services (1993–1996), Manager of Circulation Services (1996–2000), and then Manager of the Library Information Systems Team (2000–2004), and I was appointed Director in 2004.

The backdrop for my entire professional development has been libraries of Israel, primarily the University of Haifa Library, and it has been an excellent education and the best preparation I could wish for to now serving as the Director of the National Library of Israel. The path that I took means that I understand the operations of a library from within, and intimately know the different parts that make the whole library as an organization to come alive.

Could you please provide a brief introduction about the National Library of Israel? Given the unique history, political situations and cultural climate of Israel – could you tell me how the missions of the National Library of Israel have evolved over the last decades or centuries? Grateful if you could give detailed examples in this regard.

The National Library was founded in 1892, prior to the establishment of the State of Israel, as a modest yet ambitious center for the preservation of books relating to Jewish thought, religion, and culture worldwide. In 1925, with the founding of the Hebrew University of Jerusalem,[4] the newly termed "Jewish National and University Library" assumed the additional functions of a general university library and broadly expanded its collections. Following the 1948 War of Independence and establishment of the State of Israel, and the consequent evacuation of Hebrew University's original Mt. Scopus campus, the Library moved among several temporary locations in West Jerusalem during the 1950s. In 1960, Hebrew University opened the new Library facility as the centerpiece of the recently built Givat Ram campus, which has functioned as our building until the present day.

While the building served scholars and students very well during that time, the Library's location became less "logical" following the return of the Humanities and Social Sciences departments to the original Mt. Scopus campus, and the establishment of Givat Ram as the science campus in the late 1970s. The somewhat secluded location of the Library in a gated university campus also hindered awareness and access for non-university users. At the end of the 20th century, as national libraries throughout the world began to redefine their roles as central cultural institutions, and places in which technological tools enabled broad engagement with content, it became clear that the Jewish National and University

---

[4] Hebrew University of Jerusalem – Homepage. Available at: http://new.huji.ac.il/en

Library, in its current configuration and location, was not in the best position to meet the challenges of the digital and open-access age.

Beginning in the 1990s, a group of private, university and governmental stakeholders joined together to re-envision the Library. This informal consortium instigated an open dialogue about the future of our Library, first with a set of high-profile international advisors in 1998, and then with a national committee in 2004 – and recommended that the Library be separated from the Hebrew University and be reborn.

Following the recommendations of these committees, the Israeli Knesset enacted the National Library Law in 2007, providing for the change in status of the Library from part of the Hebrew University to an independent, not-for-profit institution. The Knesset's mandate charged the National Library "to collect, preserve, cultivate and endow treasures of knowledge, heritage and culture, with an emphasis on the Land of Israel, the State of Israel, and the Jewish people around the world." The Law also established the Library as the custodian of the nation's main research collections in the Humanities – in particular, in Judaic studies, Israel studies, Islamic studies and the Cultures of the Middle East.

In 2008, in accordance with statutory provisions, the newly renamed "National Library of Israel" was established under the joint ownership of the State of Israel (50%), Hebrew University (25%) and additional public bodies (25%). Between 2008 and 2011, the National Library reached agreements with primary stakeholders and began to operate independently, leading to the official launch of our renewal project in March 2011.

The National Library of Israel (NLI), presently undergoing a process of comprehensive renewal, is a unique institution among the great libraries of the world. The Library is charged with a dual mandate: it is the prime institution of national memory both for the State of Israel and for the Jewish People, historically and globally. The NLI has and will build collections that embody this broad cultural, geographical, and historical range, and will preserve its core collections for perpetuity. In addition to acquisition and preservation, we seek to become the country's flagship for information technology, offering open, democratic access to the vast world of physical and digital resources, tools, and services, not only those based on our own holdings and trained personnel but also the almost limitless resources available through collaborative arrangements with other libraries and repositories of knowledge.

Moreover, the NLI is committed to the active dissemination of knowledge and to fostering an informed and pluralistic society through educational and cultural activities. We aim to serve as broad and diverse a population of users as possible, both in Israel, with our inherently heterogeneous society, and throughout the world. In order to assume our role as the leading cultural institution in the State of Israel, the National Library requires: a facility that will enable wide and open access to the greatest number of users; secure and sustainable environmental conditions that will ensure preservation of the collections; technological infrastructure that facilitates global access to digital collections; and multiple venues for cultural and educational programming. Our new building complex, for which construction has recently begun (see details below), has been designed to meet these requirements, and more.

In a move not directly linked to the renewal process, in 2013 the Central Archives for the History of the Jewish People (CAHJP) and the National Library of Israel signed an agreement to implement a merger between the Archives and the Library. The CAHJP was established in 1939 and holds the archives of hundreds of Jewish communities, as well as of local, national and international Jewish organizations, and private collections of many outstanding Jewish personalities. The Archives contain the most extensive collection of documents, *pinkasim* (registers), and other records of Jewish history from the Middle Ages to the present day.

By joining the Library, the Archives now avail themselves of the Library's resources and facilities to gain greater access to repositories of Jewish archival material, and are able to make the contents of their vast holdings available to a wider audience, which, as detailed above, is a or the main goal of our renewal.

What is the current size of the National Library of Israel's collections, including its special collections? Could you also describe what you deem are the highlights of the collection?

The National Library of Israel holds the largest collection of printed Judaica ever amassed, as well as the world's largest collections of Jewish and Israeli music and ancient maps of the Holy Land. A consistent stream of material is added to our holdings by way of mandated legal deposit in accordance with Israel's Books Law (2000), under which the National Library is the legal deposit library for any work (including audio and digital) published in over 50 copies in Israel. We also actively expand our acquisitions in traditional and in creative ways from month to month.

Some highlights from our collections include Maimonides' *Commentary on the Mishnah* written in his own hand, the collection of Sir Isaac Newton's theological writing which was recently included in the UNESCO Memory of the World Register,[5] exquisite Islamic and Persian manuscripts dating back to the ninth

---

[5] UNESCO Memory of the World Register – Homepage. Available at: http://www.unesco.org/new/en/communication-and-information/memory-of-the-world/register/

century, and personal archives and archival materials of leading cultural and intellectual figures including Martin Buber, Stefan Zweig, and Naomi Shemer. The Gershom Scholem Library is the world's preeminent collection of works relating to Jewish mysticism and Kabbala. Large-scale digitization efforts already underway aim to offer access to treasures from NLI collections and partner institutions around the globe. Some statistics related to the collections:
- 4 core collections: Judaica; Israel; Islam and the Middle East; the Humanities;
- Nearly 4 million bound volumes;
- 24,000,000 digital objects;
- 1,000 individual archives of leading Jewish and Israeli figures;
- 10,000 Hebrew letter manuscripts, representing the greatest concentration in the world;
- 74,000 microfilmed manuscripts, comprising 90% of Hebrew manuscripts in the world;
- 2,500 Arabic letter manuscripts;
- 6,000 ancient maps of Jerusalem and the Holy Land and 2,000 modern maps;
- 35,000 hours of digitized music and sound recordings of songs, prayers, and more;
- 1,500,000 digitized pages of historic Jewish press, spanning two centuries and over 100 different titles in eight languages;
- 150,000 digitized Israeli ephemera items from 50 different archives and collections partnering in the Time Travel Project;
- 60,000,000 pages in the Central Archives for the History of the Jewish People from Jewish communities and organizations across the world;
- 20,000 electronic periodicals;
- 29,000 e-books;
- 73,000 theses/dissertations;
- 40,200 works of printed music;
- 370 incunabula.

In 2014, the project for a new home of the Library in Jerusalem was unveiled. The complex, designed by the Swiss firm Herzog & de Meuron, is scheduled for full completion in 2021. Could you tell us about the progress of this project and your plans for the new Library?

In 2020, our new National Library of Israel complex, designed by renowned Swiss firm Herzog & de Meuron, will open its doors. The new building, adjacent to the Knesset in Jerusalem's National District, will reflect the central values of democratizing knowledge and opening the National Library's world-class collections and resources to as broad and diverse an audience as possible. Within its 45,000 square meters of space, it will provide venues for exhibitions as well as cultural and educational programming in a secure, sustainable and state-of-the-art environment. The lead partners in the building renewal project are the Government of Israel, Yad Hanadiv (Rothschild Foundation in Israel), and the David S. and Ruth L. Gottesman Family of New York.

The official "Cornerstone Ceremony" took place in April 2016, followed by the beginning of excavations in preparation for construction.

The new National Library complex aims to serve a variety of central functions within one interconnected, harmonious structure. The building and grounds will incorporate areas for:

- Independent (i.e., quiet) research and study, among the collections;
- Public spaces for interactions and collaboration between users;
- Cultural and educational spaces for visitors, including a Children and Youth Area, exhibition halls, and a Visitors Centre;
- Library operations, including office space for staff;
- Preservation facilities, including stacks and storage areas.

The concepts that we have designated as "core values" are helping to guide us in the design and construction process:

Openness and accessibility: As opposed to the Library's present building, which is located within a university campus – suggesting that perhaps the knowledge housed in libraries is intended primarily as the province of scholar – the Library's new building will reflect the aim of democratizing knowledge and opening the Library's collections and resources to as broad and diverse a population as possible.

The symbolic openness to all layers of Israeli society, from any and all backgrounds, and to users from the entire world will also be evident in physical details of the design, for example, through the use of natural light, through an emphasis on the Jerusalem view, and through a connection to other important national sites in the vicinity. Furthermore, the wish for maximum accessibility of the Library will be part of the general conception of the building – not only the obvious need to provide appropriate accommodation for people with disabilities, but the desire to give all users, visitors, and employees a feeling of easy access to the building and what lies within it, and to offer a taste of the rich cultural holdings that the Library houses.

Pleasant, inviting spaces that encourage lengthy visits and frequent use: The population that the Library aims to attract is diverse in terms of age, religious and national affiliation, educational and income level, etc. It is therefore desirable that its design will appeal to as wide a common denominator as possible and convey a message of multiculturalism. Moreover, even though silence will be maintained in many of the research and study areas in order to facilitate concentration, it is important that the Library as a whole gives an impression of being a place that is vibrant and teeming with activity.

A space that encourages human interaction: The design of the areas intended for users and visitors, including outdoor areas, should facilitate and encourage communication between people. Interaction opportunities are particularly important for creating communities of frequent users, drawn to the Library not only because of the resources it offers, but also for the possibility of dividing time between working alone and enjoying an exchange of ideas with others. The Library as a meeting place between intellectuals is an essential concept for realizing the goal of turning it into a major, influential cultural institution.

Art and exhibitions: A variety of works of art will be integrated throughout the building and in outdoor areas, including commissioned sculptures. In addition, the Library will include a distinctive museum component, i.e., exhibition spaces, that will house both permanent and temporary exhibitions highlighting treasures from the Library collections.

Integrating technology: Given the dominant role of information technology in the activity of libraries, both in terms of user resources and library processes, the manner of integrating technology comprises a major element in the conception of our new building. Moreover, the design takes into consideration that technology is developing at a very rapid pace, and our building is therefore planned with built-in flexibility to accommodate future developments in the ways information is produced, distributed, consumed, and preserved.

Preserving the Library's collections: The National Library, as mandated in its mission, is entrusted with the weighty responsibility of preserving the spiritual and cultural treasures in its collections for the sake of future generations. The new building will follow strict maintenance of suitable and stable environmental conditions in accordance with international standards. In addition, advanced security and control systems will protect the collections against theft, vandalism, or illegal use.

Sustainability and maintainability: The new building will adopt principles of sustainable ("green") building and will comply with relevant Israeli and international standards. The planning aims to optimize savings in energy and water and strive for maximum utilization of natural resources. Moreover, the design of the building will take into account its future operation and maintenance.

After 1948, the libraries of a number of Palestinians who fled the country as well as of other well-to-do Palestinians were transferred to the National Library. According to some sources, about 6,000 of these books are in the Library today indexed with the label "Abandoned Property." Could you comment on what the Library's plans are for this collection? Would you catalog and open it up for public access one day?

The National Library has on deposit a collection of books, periodicals and manuscripts that were collected from empty Arab Palestinian homes during the 1948 war and were later transferred to the Library. The Custodian for Absentee Property of the Israeli government has instructed the Library to preserve these materials and make them available for research purposes. The materials have been cataloged and are publicly accessible through the Library's electronic catalog for use within the Library building. This collection has been and continues to be used by a broad spectrum of researchers, including Palestinian researchers.

Our Library is keenly aware of the historical importance and sensitivity of these materials and has maintained the AP collection as a separate collection, with a distinct call number, and not part of the Library's own collections.

Does your Library work closely with other libraries across Israel? What about the rest of the world, including the Jewish Diaspora? If so, could you tell us about such cross-national or global collaborative projects? What are some highlights?

Our work with other libraries across Israel and throughout the world is essential in the work that we do. On the most basic level of services, the National Library of Israel has interlibrary loans to and from other libraries and also facilitates two-way *international* library loans between institutions in Israel and abroad. The NLI permits access and free circulation rights to students of many academic institutions in Israel and visiting scholars from abroad and is a participant, and often leader, in countrywide discussions of the inter-university library groups. The National Library holds conferences and on-the-job training courses for librarians, hosts the national union catalogs, and is in charge of the National Name & Subject Authority Files projects.

As the national library for both the State of Israel and the Jewish people throughout the world, the National Library of Israel is committed to opening access to the cultural, intellectual and spiritual treasures central to its mission, whether those treasures are physically housed in the National Library in Jerusalem or not. As such, we have initiated and shepherded a range of local and international collaborations, particularly in the digital realm. The following are some leading projects we have undertaken in partnership with libraries, archives, and institutions in Israel and across the globe:

JPRESS: The Historic Jewish Press Project – JPRESS presents a digital gateway to Jewish newspapers and journals across continents and generations. Using advanced digitization technology, periodicals are viewable in their original layout and are fully searchable. Spanning two centuries, eight languages, and 15 countries, the platform currently provides access to nearly 100 titles, 150,000 issues, and 1,500,000 scanned pages. The National Library is working to steadily expand this invaluable resource. The project is undertaken in partnership with Tel Aviv University,[6] and other project partners include the National Library of Poland,[7] the Harvard University Library,[8] New York University (NYU),[9] Columbia University,[10] the New York Public Library,[11] and more.

Ktiv: The International Collection of Digitized Hebrew Manuscripts – The NLI's Institute of Microfilmed Hebrew Manuscripts (IMHM), envisioned by Israel's first Prime Minister, David Ben-Gurion, in 1950, is a collection of all extant Hebrew manuscripts, whether privately owned or housed in public collections. It provides researchers and the public with access to nearly 80,000 manuscripts, comprising some 90% of known Hebrew manuscripts worldwide. With rapid advances in technology that significantly expand options for preservation, presentation and access to digital content, the National Library recently launched Ktiv, undertaken in partnership with the Friedberg Jewish Manuscript Society (FJMS) and the Israeli Ministry of Jerusalem and Heritage's Landmarks project, which will enable global centralized digital access to the complete corpus of existing Hebrew manuscripts. The images will be preserved long-term using state-of-the-art technology, and the collection will be accessible, using innovative research and discovery tools, to international communities of researchers and other users. Leading institutions that have already committed to partner in this initiative include the Vatican, the British Library, the National Library of Russia, the German National Library, the Bibliothèque Nationale de France, the Palatina Library in Parma, the Jewish Theological Seminary, Bibliotheek Ets Haim in Amsterdam, the Austrian National Library, and others.

At the Source, professional training course for European librarians and archivists that work with Jewish collections – Last year the National Library's **Gesher L'Europa** (Bridge to Europe) program, funded by the Rothschild Foundation (Hanadiv) Europe, brought select participants from across Europe to the Library for an intensive three-week course to develop library and archive skills, intended to assist in enhancing the preservation and accessibility of the Jewish collections held in the participants' home institutions. In addition to learning important skills through their participation in "At the Source," participants formed strategic connections with National Library colleagues and

---

6 Tel Aviv University – Homepage. Available at: https://english.tau.ac.il/
7 National Library of Poland – Homepage. Available at: http://bn.org.pl/en/
8 Harvard Library – Harvard University – Homepage. Available at: http://library.harvard.edu/
9 New York University (NYU) – Homepage. Available at: http://www.nyu.edu/
10 Columbia University – Homepage. Available at: http://www.columbia.edu/
11 New York Public Library – Homepage. Available at: https://www.nypl.org/

with each other that will support them through their future careers as the custodians of significant and sometimes endangered Jewish archives and libraries throughout Europe. Fifteen participants total from ten countries took part in two separate courses. Participants came from institutions including the National Library of Ukraine, the Museum of the History of Polish Jews, the Jewish Museum in Prague, and the University of Amsterdam's Bibliotheca Rosenthaliana, among others.

The Israel Archives Network (IAN) – IAN will, for the first time ever, connect archives from across Israel in a single, searchable, state-of-the-art website, providing access to invaluable materials that chronicle the history of the country, its communities, organizations, and leading figures. Materials that were previously difficult if not impossible to access will be made available to the public, enabling users from across the globe to search all participating archives at once, and ensuring long-term preservation of archival materials in digital format. IAN is part of the Ministry of Jerusalem and Heritage's Land Marks initiative and is being undertaken in collaboration with the Israel State Archives.

Time Travel Israeli Ephemera Project – Developed in conjunction with UCLA and the Arcadia Fund, this project has entailed collecting, scanning and making digitally accessible 150,000 ephemera items in a range of languages from NLI collections and from over 50 private archives and collections throughout Israel, including kibbutzim, Arab and Druze communities in Israel, Israeli corporations, leading cultural institutions, and more. A crowdsourcing initiative to promote the collection and gather additional descriptive information about the items in it was also recently launched.

Judaica Collection Curators Conferences – This bi-annual conference, organized by and hosted at the National Library of Israel, brings together Judaica collection curators from across the world. For the most recent conference, held in July 2016, approximately 80 curators and professionals from libraries and other institutions with significant Judaica collections worldwide gathered to discuss "Material Books and Virtual Collections," focusing on the added value that digitization brings to manuscript, book, and archival collections, as well as the continued necessity for physical materials in libraries and in the world, even with digitization.

Reference service is slowly fading away. Some library schools don't even teach it anymore, or teach a different variation – such as Human Computer Interaction (HCI). What are your thoughts on reference services? Does the National Library of Israel offer it anymore?

Reference services have changed over the years but are definitely *not* fading away at the National Library of Israel. Altogether we have seen an increase in the number of applications for information, but the balance has changed in that today there are more questions that come through digital channels and fewer that are face-to-face. That said, every day and all day we field questions at the various reference desks at the Library and over the phone. Human Computer Interaction is not a substitute for library reference services or information literacy education. Knowing how to use a computer or to search the web is important for day-to-day life, but a different set of skills is needed for academic research. This includes skills for working with non-academic materials such as primary sources, daily newspapers, manuscripts, visual objects, and musical recordings and scores. Also, with the many different databases, catalogs, digital collections and projects, services, materials, etc. that the Library has and is involved with, it seems that the more we have to offer, the more questions we receive.

In parallel to the above, the Library receives dozens of questions by email and online chat on a daily basis, and the staff work in shifts to provide the best answers possible. A few months ago we initiated a WhatsApp reference service via smartphone, and we now answer (short) questions over WhatsApp.

As a National Library that serves the entire public from school children to internationally acclaimed professors, some may be able to use our systems with relatively little assistance whilst others need much more. Finally, we find that while our users are more capable at independently finding the answers to basic questions, the need for in-depth reference (also known as "needle in the haystack") is on the rise, in many fields. For that reason we are enlarging our subject-specialist reference, to cope with this growing need.

Please describe the staffing structure at the National Library of Israel. For example, what are the working relationships between the various heads of the subject or cataloging departments and the branch heads in such a vast and large system?

I sit at the head of the organization, together with our Chairman of the Board. We are accountable to a National Library Council and Board of Directors, an internal auditor, and a company secretary. The Library is divided according to function area into Departments, each led by a Department Head – Culture & Education, Digital Accessibility, Logistics and Operations, Public Services, Technical Services, Information Systems, Logistics and Operations, Finance, and Collections, as well as Human Resources and Resource Development and External Relations. Each of the four main collections of the Library – Israel, Judaica, Islam and the Middle East, and the Humanities – has its own curator. All Department heads report to me and prepare reports for our Board of Directors on a regular basis, work in cooperation with one another, and oversee the people who work in their function area.

Could you describe your typical day at work? Is there ever a typical day at work?

No day is ever exactly the same, but the work that I do on a typical day in the Library is divided primarily along three general lines:
1. Many, many meetings covering the regular operations of the Library – including budget, work plans, acquisitions for our collections, and more.
2. Strategic and practical planning for our *new* National Library of Israel complex (described in detail above). The ground-breaking was in the spring of 2016, and we hope to open our new building in 2021. This will understandably be a major focus of my work over the next few years.
3. Working to advance cooperative efforts with partners in Israel and all over the world, whether it be other libraries, current or potential donors to the Library, universities and research bodies, or the general public. I also dedicate a great amount of time to hosting VIP visitors to the Library, exposing them to the richness and the treasures of the National Library of Israel.

What scholarly and professional associations are you a part of, and how do they inform you in your work?

In Israel, I am part of a forum of Directors of University Libraries. We are a small country, so it is especially important that those of us in the field maintain an ongoing and open dialogue with everyone, and everything connected to our world of libraries, books, and archives. I am also part of the Higher Council of Archives, an Israeli governmental body.

On an international level, I am a member of CDNL, the Conference of Directors of National Libraries, and take part in the annual conference, which is a great opportunity for networking with library leadership from across the globe. In general, in my daily work, I am in contact with professionals in national, university, and all other types of libraries around the world. At any given time the National Library of Israel runs programs and initiatives in collaborations with numerous libraries in numerous fields, and I view the maintenance and promotion of these professional associations to be an integral and essential part of my job.

Who are the majority users of the National Library of Israel? That is, who comes to see you about your collections, programs, and services?

While the Library has been open to the general public almost since its inception, the majority of users of the National Library were traditionally academics and other researchers in the humanities, especially Judaica and Israel studies. However, over time, in particular over the last decade, the Library has become a focal point for users with varying interests and needs, and has opened its doors to an ever-broadening body of patrons, from high school students researching term papers through retirees researching genealogy, to "Wikipedians" and music lovers. Users of the NLI with academic pursuits have also diversified, including large numbers of undergraduate students from smaller colleges, teachers in training, and tour guides. Aside from offering unique services to assist these patrons who often cannot find appropriate materials in local libraries, the Library actively reaches out to the wider public through cultural events, educational programs, and a wide array of lectures and courses.

Could you give examples of types of new programs and services at the National Library of Israel, which you have found successful or innovative?

Many such programs and services have been mentioned throughout this interview, but I will briefly recap and highlight a few. What is important to note is that successful and innovative programs and services can be quite small-scale or very comprehensive, and on either scale can have a significant impact. Many of our more recent innovations have been in the digital realm, but many also are in the personal interaction realm, and of course, there are more often than not these days overlaps between these areas. Off the top of my head, a few examples of exciting and recent innovations are:

- The Gesher L'Europa (Bridge to Europe) **Jewish European Ephemera Project** – the NLI has installed collection boxes in strategic Jewish communal locations across Europe into which everyday people deposit everyday items (largely posters, postcards, advertisements), giving an interesting mosaic of Jewish Europe, providing materials for future scholarship, and engaging members of Jewish communities. A few thousand items have already been collected and will be sorted and cataloged at the NLI.
- **The House of Hebrew Songs (*Bayit Lazemer Haivri*) and the Piyut and Prayer websites** – bring Israeli musical history and treasures to the general public through innovative websites initiated and maintained by the NLI.
- **Reference Department services through WhatsApp**, and real-time engaging and interactive updates to friends of the NLI through our **English and Hebrew Facebook pages and NLI blogs**.
- **Cultural programs** for the public – the National Library initiates and hosts an ongoing array of cultural programs for the general public including concerts, lectures, exhibits and more. This week, the NLI is hosting Docu.Text – a documentary film festival – and every screening is filled to overflowing. This area of programming for the NLI is a way to open access to the Library, an excellent PR tool, and a central means for engaging the general public in the National Library, who we are, and what we do.

- **Ruach Tzeira ("Young Spirit") Humanities Program for Gifted Students** – In collaboration with the Jerusalem education system and the Hebrew University, this enriched matriculation course for high school honors students provides an unprecedented opportunity to study the humanities at an advanced level. There are three classes (10th, 11th, and 12th grades) concurrently studying in the program at the National Library of Israel.

What is the role of technology and innovation at the National Library of Israel?

Technology and innovation play a very central role in the National Library of Israel, and I think are central to any library, big or small, trying to navigate its way through the 21st century. A main aspect of what we are trying to achieve through our renewal process is to transform the Library into a cutting-edge global center at the forefront of knowledge dissemination and cultural creativity. One of the driving principles behind this is the principle of open access – which is taking place in the physical realm, with the construction of our new landmark facility, and in the realm of content with a wide range of cultural, educational, and technological initiatives already underway.

In order to make the holdings of our National Library available to all, we are investing tremendous resources into digitizing materials in all areas – not just books but also periodicals, rare manuscripts and maps, ephemera, and music are main areas in which we have invested or will invest in digitization. The fruits of these processes are evident, for example, in two websites recently launched by the Library, one for Jewish religious and liturgical music (Piyut and Prayer website), and one for Ottoman and Mandate-era Palestinian Arabic newspapers (Jrayed).

In cultural and educational areas we always aim to expose the treasures of the NLI to the outside world, and in these areas we excel at innovation. Some examples are the revival and performance of an all but forgotten Israeli opera of a past era, and an educational program, online, in which educators present an item of their choosing from the Library's collections, and then integrate the item into a lesson plan for teaching the young generation. These lesson plans are available to other educators in Israel and around the world.

Mentorship is such an important theme in leadership – both mentoring and being mentored. Could you please tell us about your experiences about both? Do you still have mentors that you go to?

I had the privilege of being able to learn very much under the wings of the two Directors of the University of Haifa Library who preceded me. One, like me, came up through the ranks in the field of library science, while the other was an academic, in the field of geography, with excellent managerial skills. I learned tremendously from these mentors, both of whom gave me great support in my professional development. I don't see myself as a mentor, per se, but I believe that those who work with me learn from me, and I continually learn from them.

Which part(s) of your job as the Director do you find most rewarding? What is the most frustrating?

Every single day I get to see the realization of big ideas and "vision" take place. This is expressed, albeit sometimes in small ways, on an on-going basis, and it is extremely rewarding. It is very satisfying to see my staff, who work in a variety of areas and with a variety of projects, enjoying their work, being inspired by what they do, and cooperating together to achieve our goals. Especially moving is how our team is rallying together in a huge joint effort to make our renewal process goals – in content, physical, and digital areas – a reality.

What is frustrating is when we have these big goals, together with very capable professionals and wonderful intentions, and yet – sometimes things move slowly, sometimes important and timely processes are delayed by external factors beyond our control.

For further information

Education in the National Library [YouTube]. Available at:https://www.youtube.com/watch?v=XQ6u_k0BtsI
National Library: the Next Chapter Begins [YouTube]. Available at:https://www.youtube.com/watch?v=pJX3Uej-l6s
National Library Cornerstone Ceremony [YouTube]. Available at:https://www.youtube.com/watch?v=O8UvLHrEX6I
National Library of Israel Renewal [YouTube]. Available at: https://www.youtube.com/watch?v=GE_y-ZTB47o

12 Dr. Ismail Serageldin

Director, The Library of Alexandria (Egypt)

Introduction

The Bibliotheca Alexandrina (Library of Alexandria) is a major library and cultural center situated on the shore of the Mediterranean Sea in the Egyptian city of Alexandria. It is a commemoration of the Ancient Library of Alexandria in an attempt to revive the old library, which was burnt down by Julius Caesar in 48 B.C. and suffered further attacks by Aurelian in the 270s, A.D. The Library of Alexandria is a trilingual library – containing books in Arabic, English and French.

An Egyptian national, Ismail Serageldin has been serving as the Director of the Library of Alexandria since 2001. In addition to his role as Director of the Library, Serageldin also serves as the Chairman of the Boards of its 13 affiliated research institutes and four affiliated museums; Ambassador of the United Nations Alliance of Civilizations; Chairman of the Executive Council of the World Digital Library (WDL); Chair and Member of Boards of Directors and advisory committees for academic, research, scientific and international institutions and civil society efforts. In the following interview, Serageldin discusses his unparalleled time management skills that allow for prioritization and participation in so many different national and international professional engagements at the highest levels.

Fig. 12.1: Dr. Ismail Serageldin, the Founding Director of the New Library of Alexandria, with the charming exterior view of the Library at the Background (Photo: Library of Alexandria).

Fig. 12.2: A magnificent arial view of the Library of Alexandria (Photo: Library of Alexandria).

Fig. 12.3: The glorious artificial lake infront of the Library of Alexandria (Photo: Library of Alexandria).

Fig. 12.4: A magnificent view of the cascading levels and open shelves at the Main Reading Hall (Photo: Library of Alexandria).

Could we begin this interview by first introducing yourself, for example, your training and background? For example, what did you study at university? Could you also describe your current role and areas of responsibility as the Director of the New Library of Alexandria in Egypt?

My training and background are in the field of architecture. I hold a B.Sc. in Architecture from Cairo University[1] in 1964, and a Master's degree in City and Regional Planning Economics from Harvard University's Graduate School of Design[2] in 1968. I then continued my studies towards a Ph.D. degree in City and Regional Planning Economics and Development, and received the degree from Harvard University's Graduate School of Arts and Sciences[3] in 1972.

---

1 Cairo University – Homepage. Available at: http://cu.edu.eg/Home
2 Graduate School of Design, Harvard University – Homepage. Available at: http://www.gsd.harvard.edu/
3 Graduate School of Arts and Sciences, Harvard University – Homepage. Available at: https://gsas.harvard.edu/

After obtaining my Ph.D., I went on to work in the World Bank[4] in Washington DC, and years later, I moved back to Egypt to assume the role of Founding Director of the Bibliotheca Alexandrina (BA)[5], the new Library of Alexandria inaugurated in 2002.

As Director, I have had to set up the whole administrative structure of the new institution, hire the staff, and write the statutes for the management of the Library. I have also created the many research centers affiliated to the BA, and established the museums in the premises. In addition to all that, I formulated the work program of the new institution, set our work priorities and have personally trained the staff working on all our diverse programs.

Moreover, in my capacity as Director of the Library, I represent it at all international meetings and committees. Thus, I serve as chair or member of a number of advisory committees for academic and scientific research and international institutions, including as co-Chair of the Nizami Ganjavi International Center[6], the Advisory Committee of the World Social Science Report for 2013 and 2016, as well as the UNESCO-supported World Water Scenarios, the Executive Council of the Encyclopedia of Life and as Chair of the Executive Council of the World Digital Library.[7] I am also a member in the National Academy of Sciences (NAS)[8], and the National Academy of Medicine's (NAM)[9] Committee for Human Gene Editing: Scientific, Medical and Ethical Considerations. Furthermore, as Director of the Library, I do a lot of negotiating with donors for funds to support and implement many projects in the BA.

Could you tell us more about your path to becoming the Director of the Library of Alexandria? You are not a librarian by training in traditional sense. Why do you think you have been selected to serve as Director of the New Library of Alexandria?

Libraries, books, knowledge and culture have always been an integral part of my life. For as long as I can remember, my life has been centered around books and knowledge, and my interests in several areas has increased over the years. A very good example of this is my specialization in architecture, which led me into city and regional planning, then from this I got interested in how regions actually

---

4 World Bank – Homepage. Available at: http://www.worldbank.org/en/about
5 Bibliotheca Alexandrina – Homepage. Available at: http://www.bibalex.org/en/default
6 Nizami Ganjavi International Center – Homepage. Available at: http://nizamiganjavi-ic.org/
7 World Digital Library – Homepage. Available at: https://www.wdl.org/en/
8 National Academy of Sciences – Homepage. Available at: http://www.nasonline.org/?referrer=https://www.google.co.jp/
9 National Academy of Medicine – Homepage. Available at: https://nam.edu/

grow, which brought me to the field of economics and national development policies. In pretty much the same way, I have taken my interests further into financial policies, literature, history, culture, language, scientific research and the latest technological developments.

True, I am not trained as a librarian, but my extensive knowledge in many fields, plus my several and diverse publications, my international participation in several committees and boards, as well as my international reputation have all contributed to my selection as the Founding Director of the New Library of Alexandria.

You are currently serving as advisor to the Egyptian Prime Minister in matters concerning culture, science and museums, that is including Chairman of the Boards of the thirteen affiliated research institutes and the four affiliated museums, Ambassador of the [United Nations] Alliance of Civilizations[10], Chairman of the Executive Council of the World Digital Library (WDL), Chair and Member of a number of Boards of Directors and advisory committees for academic, research, scientific and international institutions and civil society efforts, etc. How do you work and your participation in these areas contribute to your current work as the Director of the Library of Alexandria?

A most interesting question. Yes, I am the advisor of the Prime Minister for culture, science and museums, and I chair all the boards of the scientific and academic research centers of the Bibliotheca Alexandrina (BA), as well as serve on many committees and boards. As such, I am constantly busy with planning, supervising and organizing work programs within the BA centers as well as attending international meetings and committees. This constant contact with international organizations has had a positive impact on the BA work programs. Many of my colleagues in the library have direct contact with important executives and committee members of international organizations, and have had the opportunity to work on various projects with them thus, increasing the visibility of the BA on the international scene.

Some examples of this are our work with the Smithsonian on the Encyclopedia of Life, our development of the Research Methods Library and the Science Supercourse – which contain over 170,000 PowerPoint lectures online and available to researchers everywhere. Another very successful project is our engagement in the edX platform for online learning, and our establishment of the African Networks program, which serves African researchers in several areas. Consequently, my presence on the international scene has helped the BA become more engaged with other renowned institutions.

---

10 United Nations, Alliance of Civilizations – Homepage. Available at: http://www.unaoc.org/

You are an author of a number of books on biotechnology, rural development, sustainability, and the value of science to society. How does your scholarship shape and inform your thinking about your current position as Director?

Indeed, my interest in science, technology and development has informed my outlook of how the Library should function. I made it a point to host many scientific conferences in these areas, and I have encouraged my colleagues to work on joint projects with national and international entities in the areas of science, technology and development. In addition, and in my capacity as Director of the Library, I have initiated the founding of several research centers that work in these specific areas like the Center for Special Studies and Programs (CSSP),[11] which encourages young researchers through giving research grants and by acting as the secretariat of a number of international and regional scientific entities, as well as through hosting the biannual Biovision conference. I have also established the International School of Information Science (ISIS),[12] which is a research center that acts as an incubator for digital and technological projects, and the Center for Environmental Studies (CES),[13] which is working towards becoming a leading national and international center engaged in high-quality, cutting-edge, and policy-relevant research.

Could you please provide a brief introduction about the Library of Alexandria?

More than 2,000 years ago, the city of Alexandria was founded, and in it, the Ancient Library embraced the best creations of the human mind, and it became the beacon of knowledge. Although it was destroyed around 1,600 years ago, its memory continued to be a source of inspiration, and it was a model of knowledge and excellence to scientists, intellectuals and researchers from all over the world.

The New Bibliotheca Alexandrina was inaugurated in 2002 to become a center of excellence for the production and dissemination of knowledge and to be a place of dialogue and understanding between cultures and peoples. Today, The Bibliotheca Alexandrina receives more than one million visitors and holds more than 700 events every year.

It is a huge cultural complex that serves as a hub for leading scientists, thinkers, intellectuals, academics and artists. The library houses more than 8 million books in

---

[11] Center for Special Studies and Programs – Homepage. Available at: https://www.bibalex.org/cssp/
[12] International School of Information Science – Homepage. Available at: http://www.bibalex.org/isis/frontend/home/home.aspx
[13] Center for Environmental Studies – Homepage. Available at: https://ces.williams.edu/

all fields of knowledge in print and electronic forms. It has a main library that has the biggest reading area in the world, with a number of specialized libraries that include:
- The Arts and Multimedia Library
- The Taha Hussein Library, for the visually impaired, with the latest innovations to enable the visually impaired to read, write and use the Internet,
- The Children's Library, targeting ages from 6 to 11, and providing them with diverse activities to enhance education.
- The Young People's Library, targeting ages from 12 to 16.
- The Maps Library, which houses Atlases, modern maps and historical maps.
- The Francophone Library

The New Library of Alexandria is a leading institution of the digital age, that has:
- The Internet Archive: A complete collection of all the web pages of all websites since 1996,
- Culturama; An attractive patented, interactive show with 9 digital screens that are the first of their kind in the world, and a tool for presenting the only opera in ancient Egyptian language, and the winner of international awards.
- Virtual Immersive Science and Technology Applications (VISTA); 3D simulation models to aid help researchers,
- A Supercomputer with specialized scientific applications that open new horizons of innovation and scientific research,
- The Espresso Book Machine that can print and cover books up to 50,000 pages in minutes, and
- The ICT Exhibition for ICT applications.

The Library is a leader in several digital projects, including:
- The first Arabic digital library in the world,
- The "Eternal Egypt" website: An impressive project for the documentation of locations, heritage and Egyptian cultural history,
- The "Memory of Modern Egypt" website, with tens of thousands of documents, images, maps, and audio-visual recordings.
- The first DVD for of the "Description of Egypt" catalog.

To recapture the spirit of the ancient Library of Alexandria, the Bibliotheca Alexandrina established a number of research and cultural centers, including:
- Alex-Med: A center dedicated to researching and documenting the tangible and intangible heritage of Alexandria and Mediterranean countries;
- The Hellenistic Center: Concerned with studies of the Hellenistic period;
- The Arts Center: A center that supports contemporary arts and acts as a forum for artistic techniques of all types, nurturing and developing children's and young people's talents;

- The Writing & Scripts Center: Dedicated to studying and researching scripts and writings from all over the world, through different historical periods.
- The Center for Special Studies and Programs: A place that provides young scholars with programs and grants.
- The Center for the Documentation of Cultural and Natural Heritage: A center that employs state-of-the-art technologies and innovations for the documentation, dissemination and preservation of Egyptian cultural and natural heritage,
- The Manuscripts Center, dedicated to the preservation, restoration, and digitization of manuscripts and publishing them for review, study and research,
- The Center for Democracy and Social Peace Studies that conducts research, training and supports the culture of peace and democracy, as well as develops the capabilities of women and youth,
- The Center for Development Studies, primarily concerned with research in the area of development,
- An International School of Information Science; with a leading role in technological and digital projects.
- The Center for Coptic Studies, to study and disseminate "Coptic Heritage for all Egyptians",
- The Center for Islamic Civilization & Modern Islamic Thought, dedicated to the study of Arab and Islamic scientific heritage and Islamic intellectual and cultural productions,
- The Center for Environmental Studies that aims to play a pivotal role in researching and promoting environmental issues in Egypt.

To consolidate the role of science in society and support the spirit of discovery and research, the Planetarium Science Center was established to provide diverse scientific activities, and events with the purpose of encouraging the love of science, discovery and innovation. The PSC has also successfully produced the first Arabic film specifically for planetariums.

The Bibliotheca Alexandrina has a conference center with the state-of-the-art equipment, which holds events ranging from international conferences and meetings to exhibitions, concerts and theatrical performances. The role of the library is not limited to the dissemination of sciences, for it is also concerned with arts.

The library also has temporary and permanent exhibitions, and special art collections as well as four museums:
1. The Antiquities Museum,
2. The Manuscripts Museum and its Rare Collections Section,
3. The Sadat Museum, and
4. The History of Science Museum.

In the end, the Library of Alexandria seeks to contribute to the advancement of human knowledge, from visual arts to information revolution, and from the documentation of heritage to the dissemination of peace, and has tried, through being this comprehensive cultural complex, to be worthy of its legacy.

What is the current size of the Library of Alexandria's collections, including its special collections? Could you also describe what you deem are the highlights of the collection as well as services?

The BA has a collection of diverse subjects ranging from the Arts to Zoology. The collection policy aims to contain a variety of intellectual wealth while, simultaneously, meeting the specific needs of its patrons; in order to do that, BA has developed a collection development policy that specifies the levels of importance in collecting library materials. The policy lays the principles that govern the selection and retention of the library holdings, as well as the acquisition priorities.

Most books found in the main reading hall fall within the ten general subjects defined by the Dewey Decimal Classification System. The general collection includes printed materials of all types, books, periodicals, conference proceedings, maps, and reference materials.

The special libraries and special collections include multimedia materials, depository documents, university dissertations, in addition to the standard printed materials. The BA also provides access to many valuable electronic resources.

In addition to the general collection, the library has extensive holdings in closed stacks. These items are not directly accessible by the public and may have various restrictions on use for a variety of reasons or other criteria set by the BA librarians. The BA collection as of June 2016 reached 2,286,067 books.

The Rare Books and Special Collection section provides research services to university students from Egypt and abroad, allowing them to search databases of the BA and other online libraries, and access rare books (in physical and digital formats). We serve more than 2,000 researchers a year.

The Rare Books collections have over 15,000 books in different languages. The oldest one is the epigrams of Martialis, printed in Venice in 1482, and it is one of five incunabula the BA holds. We also have a collection of the early printed books in Arabic, which were printed in the Bulaq Press in the early 19th century.

The Special collections has 26 collections that were donated by private individuals and institutions. The most important ones are the collections of the late president Anwar Sadat, His Majesty Sultan Qabus of Oman, Dr. Boutros Ghaly, the former secretary general of the UN, Dr. Abdel Razzak al-Sanhoury, the famous Egyptian jurist, Nour al-Sherif, an Egyptian actor, and a number of other university professors and Egyptian artists. The books of those collections exceed 70,000 and 40,000 periodical issues. Some of the books are signed by their owners or their authors. Some are special and valuable editions, like the second edition of *La description de l'Egypte*, printed by Panckoucke between the years 1821 and 1830 (24 volumes of text and 11 volumes of plates). We also have facsimiles of valuable books, like a facsimile of the Gutenberg Bible, a facsimile of the Codex Vaticanus B, which is one of the oldest extant manuscripts of the Greek Bible, written on parchment in 1,536 pages, and a facsimile of the second edition of *Don Quixote*.

Does your Library work closely with other libraries across Egypt? What about the rest of the world? If so, could you tell us about such cross-national or global collaborative projects? What are some highlights?

Yes, the library does work closely with international libraries. We work with the Library of Congress[14], the BNF (National Library of France)[15], and the BA is the Chair of the World Digital Library. On the national level, we have collaborated with several national libraries, and we also have nineteen Embassies of Knowledge situated in Universities and Research Centers across Egypt, and these provide remote access to residents and students to BA services and events.

What is the role of technology and innovation at the Library of Alexandria?

The Bibliotheca Alexandrina was born digital! It is the child of this century, and as such, we embraced the new digital technology from the beginning, recognizing that this will give this new version of the great library its edge. So, from the start, we made sure that it would function in "Hybrid" mode and that it will have physical as well as electronic books and databases and other electronic resources.

Over 3,300 computers are spread throughout its halls and offices, and, as mentioned above, it has the Culturama, VISTA, a Supercomputer and the only copy of the Internet Archive outside California, plus the many important technology-based projects and research the library is engaged with. We are also very much involved with thinking through technology issues, and are part of the major decision making processes in areas of technology innovation.

Please describe the staffing structure at the Library of Alexandria.

The Director is the Head, and presently there is a Deputy Director and nine Sector Heads each supervising a sector, namely: Central Projects and Services, Library,

---

14 Library of Congress – Homepage. Available at: https://www.loc.gov/
15 BNF (National Library of France) – Homepage. Available at: http://www.bnf.fr/en/tools/a.welcome_to_the_bnf.html

Cultural Outreach, Academic Research, Finance and Administration, Security, ICT and External Relations. Under these sectors, there are Departments/Centers with sub divisions (Sections and Units) as required.

Could you describe your management and leadership style? Mentorship is such an important theme in leadership – both mentoring and being mentored. Could you please tell us about your experiences about both? Do you still have mentors that you go to?

My management style is participatory. I always make it a point to discuss all work related and crucial matters with my senior staff with whom I meet regularly. In their turn, they transfer the discussions, lessons and decisions to their staff, and we all work together to manage this diverse institution.

True, leadership is mentoring, and that is what I believe in very much. As such, I take the time to listen, discuss and guide my staff whenever necessary, and always give them a chance to take decisions, even make mistakes, and help them learn through responsibility and careful monitoring.

Could you describe your typical day at work? Is there ever a typical day at work? We all have 24 hours per day. In order to achieve so much as you do, and to be able to take part in so many professional engagements at both national and international levels, would you say you are a master of time management?

Ah! If there were only more hours in the day! That is my favorite statement. As you can see, I have so much to do, and thus find it rather bothersome not to be able to have more hours to finish all that needs to be done. However, I work rigorously from morning till evening, and I do not believe in set working hours and thus, I often stay late in the office and most of the time I work on weekends as well. Also, the fact that I have good, trained senior managers allows me to travel often and leave them to take care of administrative matters, and, recently, with the appointment of a Deputy Director, I feel more at ease attending international meetings knowing that my deputy is capable of taking care of matters inside the BA.

Who are the majority users of the Library of Alexandria? That is, who comes to see you about your collections, programs, and services?

The library offers customized services to all its users such as students, researchers, disabled people, and the general public. The majority of users are university students, graduates, researchers and scholars. In addition, school children are constant visitors to the Children and Young people's libraries, and many of them are also permanent visitors of the Alexploratoriam and Science Clubs.

The library also has special programs that involve patrons of all ages and with all interests, as well as art performances and specialized training in many areas.

The library has held a variety of symposiums in 2011 in support of the Egyptian community and emphasising the 2011 Egyptian Revolution, the Egyptian Constitution and Democratic Government in Arab nations. Could you tell us your role and how the library has changed along with Egypt since 2011?

Our vision for the new library is to recapture the spirit that characterized the Ancient Library; a spirit of openness, dialogue and rationality. Since its inauguration, it has stood out as a space for dialogue, freedom of speech and a venue for reform ideas. And because I always maintain that the BA has a neutral position from partisanship in political affairs, our main focus was on living up to our reputation as a center for learning and dialogue. As such, our main focus was always on encouraging educational curricula reform, promoting serious scientific research and offering the country, and its people, a venue to discuss, innovate and promote reform.

Following the 2011 Revolution, the library has held many events to discuss relevant and timely issues such as the new constitution, the formation and role of political parties, but most importantly, we aim to have a lasting effect on the cultural and educational scene in Egypt and the Arab world. Consequently, our major role is to continue to invest in youth and encourage cultural and educational activities.

One of our main concerns since the revolution, is to combat extremism and xenophobia, and so we have created a full educational, cultural and scientific program to promote tolerance, proper understanding of religion and moderate thought. To promote education, the BA has become a partner in the edX online learning platform and we are offering free online courses to the public to enhance culture and learning. Indeed, our very own Embassies of Knowledge project is in itself a vehicle for the promotion and dissemination of knowledge across the country.

Which part(s) of your job as the librarian do you find most rewarding? What is the most frustrating?

The most gratifying and rewarding part of my job is to work with excellent colleagues and to mentor highly promising young people. It is also the ability to look beyond the horizon and define the new domains which we should be involved with and plan our path accordingly.

The least satisfying (most frustrating) part of my job is that I have to deal with the government bureaucracy with its arcane and ossified conceptions of reporting and decision-making. Luckily, the BA has received support to lead in the domain of being a 100% digital public institution, which should minimise these frustrating aspects in the near future.

The New Library of Alexandria has consistently been voted as one of the most beautiful libraries in the world – as the General Director – would you like to say something to respond to this?

It indeed is. The New Library is truly a beautiful building that expresses much about its very role. Located on a superb site on the historic eastern habor of Alexandria, almost exactly where the old library and the royal palace of the Ptolemies once stood. The setting for the New Library of Alexandria, the beautiful new building, with its distinctive granite wall covered by letters of all the world's alphabets, is today a recognisable landmark of the new Alexandria. The scheme lays out the main circular building in connection with the smaller sphere of the planetarium and allows the existing conference center to act as a counterpoint in the overall massing. The plaza that connects them all is open and inviting, with olive trees providing a powerful symbol of the Bibliotheca Alexandrina (BA) underlying premise of peace, openness to the other, dialogue, rationality and understanding. The complex is trans-pierced by an arrow: a slim, elegant pedestrian bridge at the second floor level, crossing from the university campus in the southeast towards the sea on the northwest.

The southern part of the main building (from the Port Said street side) is elevated to allow an unimpeded view of the planetarium and the sea right across the project. The planetarium is a floating sphere with blue ribbons of light at night to highlight the special character of this major component of the composition.

From the plaza, there are three entrances to the complex: one for the Conference Center, which houses the great Auditorium (around 1,350 seats) and three smaller auditoriums below with a capacity of some 300 seats each, and two large exhibition areas and several cafeterias and other ancillary meeting rooms and spaces. It is connected to the rest of the complex under the plaza. The plaza was an existing building and its architecture is very different from the new design, which enveloped it and integrated its functions into its interconnected space.

The second entrance is down to the planetarium – a floating ball connected to the main plaza by four connecting "tunnels" or bridges. Around at the second level below the plaza is the space devoted to the science museum and next to it are exhibition areas and the science exploratorium for children.

The third entrance is to the library proper, the main new building in the complex to which much of this essay is devoted.

The plaza itself has works of art and statuary. A soaring statue of "Prometheus bearing fire" is standing amidst the olive trees.

Inside the vast circular structure, one can read the building fairly easily. A spine separates the vast reading space and library functions on one side from the administrative and research functions on the other.

The scale of the building is impressive. It is about 160 m in circumference and 11 stories high, except that by slicing it across the top in a slant and burying four floors underground, the mass of the building is largely unnoticed. It is deceptively small on the outside, and invitingly human in scale when you approach it.

The role of water is pervasive. Water surrounds the whole building and provides both a reflecting motif from various angles and a reflecting and separating medium for the main complex, creating a unique separateness and a hint of "floating" the building out of reach of the surrounding, other than the plaza entrance.

Further readings

Burning of the Library of Alexandria [YouTube]. Available at: https://www.youtube.com/watch?v=fPufdlOiQlk

Carl Sagan introduces the library of Alexandria [YouTube]. Available at: https://www.youtube.com/watch?v=OLlVnKOb4Mk

Carl Sagan on The Library of Alexandria and Hypatia [YouTube]. Available at: https://www.youtube.com/watch?v=nRkReKGFqHY

Dr Ismail Serageldin lecture at the British Academy about the Bibliotheca Alexandrina May 28th 2013 [YouTube]. Available at: https://www.youtube.com/watch?v=d1YXP0VBq-Q

The Hidden Library of Alexandria - Ancient Mystery Documentaries [YouTube]. Available at: https://www.youtube.com/watch?v=06PgcVX9tsM

Interview with Ismail Serageldin [YouTube]. Available at: https://www.youtube.com/watch?v=bbfwHZAbPo8

Ismail Serageldin – Homepage. *Available at:* http://www.serageldin.com/Home/Index.aspx

Legendary Library of Alexandria - National Geographic [YouTube]. Available at: https://www.youtube.com/watch?v=HCbiUP2C0D8

Mystery of Ancient Egypt's - The Royal Library of Alexandria (Documentary) [YouTube]. Available at: https://www.youtube.com/watch?v=fRmS_37lMUk

Public and city libraries

13 Pam Sandlian Smith

Director, Anythink Libraries, Adams County (Colorado)

Introduction

In September 2009, the Rangeview Library District in Adams County, Colorado, just north of Denver, changed the name of its community libraries to Anythink Libraries, as part of the district's new branding efforts.

Pam Sandlian Smith is the current Director of Anythink Libraries. Prior to her role at Anythink, Sandlian Smith was the Director of the West Palm Beach Public Library and held a variety of leadership roles at the Denver Public Library. Through Sandlian Smith's extraordinary leadership and commitment, the public library system went from being the most poorly-funded system in the state of Colorado to one of the most recognized library brands nationwide. Via this new "Anythink" model, the system has reinvented itself as a library focused on participatory learning, community engagement and shifting perceptions of the role of libraries. Highlights of Anythink's new services include: a fine-free policy for overdue items, and using locally developed word-based classification system to replace the Dewey Decimal Classification, and many others. Furthermore, Anythink was awarded the 2010 National Medal for Museum and Library Service, the 2011 John Cotton Dana Award for Outstanding Public Relations, etc. In the following interview, Sandlian Smith shares with us her unparalleled passion and unrelenting efforts in serving the communities of Adams County.

Fig. 13.1: Pam Sandlian Smith, Director, Anythink Libraries (Photo: Anythink Libraries).

Fig. 13.2: Anythink Libraries (Photo: Anythink Libraries).

Fig. 13.3: Minecraft (Photo: Anythink Libraries).

Fig. 13.4: Creating space to interact with information at Anythink Brighton (Photo: Anythink Libraries).

Could we begin this interview by first introducing yourself, for example, your professional training and education background? For example, what did you study at university? Do you come from a family of librarians? Choosing a career in public librarianship – was it a calling for you?

You might call me an accidental librarian. My original goal was to be a writer. My undergraduate degree is English Literature and liberal arts degrees can be some of the most fulfilling intellectually, yet challenging when finding direct correlations to the working world. I started my career in libraries as a clerk typist for the Denver Public Library.[1] I originally intended for this to be a short-term position while I found another path with my writing. I was not the best typist and found the work to be quite tedious, so eagerly promoted to a library assistant working under the tutelage of a very traditional and wonderful children's librarian. I found my world in children's literature, programming and marketing the library for children and families. Initially, I learned the craft of librarianship by working with tremendous mentors at the Cherry Creek branch of the Denver Public Library.

---

1 Denver Public Library – Homepage. Available at: https://www.denverlibrary.org/

Hospitality, generosity, collection development, community engagement were critical components to our branch library service. Those were the days of filing catalog cards every Saturday morning, then finalizing the book purchases for the week in an editorial style team meeting. I fell in love with the work, and began my lifelong pursuit of turning static, somewhat boring and beige libraries into catalysts for ideas and creativity. After working in libraries for approximately ten years, I completed my MLS (Master of Library & Information Science) with the distance education program through Emporia State University.[2]

Have you always worked in libraries? Could you tell us more about your path to becoming the Director of Anything Libraries? Could you also describe your current role and areas of responsibility as the Director of Anything Libraries?

I worked my way through school by waiting tables, and working as a nanny. I was the Manager of Children's Services at the Denver Public Library during the years that we were building the new Central Library with the Michael Graves[3] architectural firm. This experience was critical in creating a path of designing library experiences that are filled with adventure and delight. Seeking a new challenge, I was the Director for the West Palm Beach Public Library[4] for ten years. This was a library that came close to being closed due to funding issues. My job was to bring it back to life. My brilliant team exploded the idea of a boring, stale, quiet library by renovating the library and creating life-like literature experiences from *The Polar Express*, *The Chocolate Factory* and *Harry Potter*. In 2007, I became the Library Director for the Rangeview Library District, which has created the Anythink brand, as we are known today. As Director of Anythink[5], I am responsible for leading the team that manages our library district in Adams County, Colorado. Anythink has seven branches providing services to a rapidly growing population currently at 498,187. This county borders Denver to the north and extends to the eastern plains of Colorado.

From 1987 to 1997, you worked as the Manager of Children's Service the Denver Public Library. Do you understand why school librarians and children's services librarians are often unvalued and underappreciated. For school librarians and

---

2 Emporia State University – Homepage. Available at: http://www.emporia.edu/
3 Michael Graves – Architecture & Design – Homepage. Available at: http://michaelgraves.com/
4 City of West Palm Beach Public Library – Homepage. Available at: http://www.wpb.org/Departments/Library/Overview
5 Anythink Libraries – Homepage. Available at: https://www.anythinklibraries.org/

children's services librarians who feel stuck in their jobs, and not being appreciated/valued by their co-workers, what would you like to say to them?

In some cultures, children and professionals who work with children may not be given the respect that they deserve. As Manager of Children's Services, I took my responsibility in instilling seriousness and respect into the position, particularly finding resources necessary for success in the role. Tenacity and creativity are hallmark traits of children's librarians, which is why I encourage them to see themselves as leaders. Because children's librarians must be politically savvy, persuasive, resourceful, creative and community connectors, they make excellent candidates for upper management. I encourage children's librarians to become Library Directors, which allows them to create systems that value children and families and the ability to allocate resources to support this work.

Could you please provide a brief introduction of the Anythink Libraries and its associate system?

Just a few short years back, Adams County libraries were some of the worst-funded libraries in Colorado. While the staff did their best to make the most of limited resources, and our customers felt a sense of loyalty to their libraries, the fact was that the Rangeview Library District needed help.

Across the world, funding decisions were forcing some libraries to close or reduce services. In November 2006, our community voted to increase library funding, which has provided the resources to create a fresh start for our libraries. Because of this support, Rangeview Library District was able to transform into Anythink and reinvent its library services.

Building the Anythink brand started before we even began thinking about a new logo. The district's leadership built four new libraries and renovated three buildings under a premise of designing libraries for people, not books. At the heart of this philosophy is our decision to create an experience model, which means everything we do at Anythink is based on creating amazing experiences for our customers. This influences the way our spaces are designed, our interactive programming, our decision to go fine-free, and our move away from the Dewey Decimal System to WordThink, our staffing model and the Anythink brand itself.

The Anythink staff manifesto anchors the inspiration of the brand: "You are not just an employee, volunteer or board member. You do not merely catalog books, organize periodicals and manage resources. You are the gateway into the mind of the idea people who come to our facilities to find or fuel a spark. Part wizard, part genius, part explorer. It is your calling to trespass into the unknown and come back with a concrete piece someone can hold onto, turn over, and use to fuel their mind and soul."

Please describe the staffing structure at Anythink Libraries?

I would describe our staffing structure as minimalist. We were very leanly staffed before the operating funds were increased through the ballot initiative in 2006. As we began to examine our staffing needs, we looked at our existing job descriptions, which were outdated and did not adequately describe our work. We created three key positions for front line staff: Wranglers or Materials Handlers, Concierges and Guides. Each of our seven branches has a staffing allocation with all three of these positions. The numbers for each position correlate to the hours of the library, the circulation, the programming and community needs. Our concierges are hired based upon their hospitality skills, their ability to connect with people, their love of ideas, books, music and movies. We look for people who are generous and welcoming, caring and passionate about people, their colleagues and our product.

We changed the name of our librarians as a shift from the traditional keeper of the collection to a person who guides a customers through their learning quest. Our Guides work to create experiences, programs and informal learning opportunities for our community based on age levels and interests. We have children's, teen, adult, technology and studio Guides.

Last year, I accidentally stumbled onto a YouTube video, featuring you as a keynote speaker of TEDxMileHigh. I was so touched and inspired by your story about this little boy requesting for a space to set up his own puppet show inside your library. What you said in this open lecture was so meaningful, and is also one of the reasons I said to myself, I have to do an interview with you, and include it as one of the book chapters. I wonder if you could share the same story with the readers one more time? Or I could transcribe what you said from this YouTube video – in order to save your time. And also the story about the sheep...

When I was Manager of Children's Services at the Denver Public Library, a young boy who was about 8 years old asked if he could use a room that was the story hour space for the week. There was an old puppet theatre folded in the corner and he wanted to write and produce a puppet show to deliver later in the week. We weren't using the space over the week. I quickly worked through the request, thinking through any obstacles that might be reasons to deny the request. In a sense, the young man was asking to check out a room for the week instead of checking out a book. My governing response is always try to get to yes if it is possible. It was easy to say yes with a couple of caveats; he needed to check-in with the staff and clean the space every day.

He came back every day, working industriously, and on Friday afternoon, as promised, he put signs up around the library promoting his puppet show. He delivered a fun presentation for an audience of 20 to 30 children. As promised, he put everything back in order, thanked the staff and left a very happy young man.

We didn't see him for a couple of months, but one Saturday afternoon, he came in the library with his dad. He came to the desk announcing that it was his birthday and the one thing he wanted to do was come to the library on his birthday. He also told us that he wanted to say goodbye. His dad had gotten a job; they were getting an apartment and moving out of the homeless shelter. Their new home was too far to be able to visit the library.

Little did I know how important that week was for the young man. I had no idea how much he needed space and support. We never know what is going to be asked of us in public libraries, but that experience reinforced how critical it is to try to say yes.

Goats have become one of the Anythink icons. Our facilities manager suggested we hire goats to mow our prairie grass. Of course, I thought, what could go wrong if we had goats on the property? We worked through the zoning issues with the Planning Department and they looked at this as an experiment. So one day 300 goats arrived, complete with the goat herders, who herded the goats into a fenced space and the goats began to eat every piece of grass and weed. Almost immediately, children and their families gathered around and started asking questions, "What do goats eat? What does their stomach look like? Can I feed the goats?" The goat herders turned into reference librarians. Over the next couple of days, we had crowds of people stopping to watch the goats and feed them. They even went home to pick grass and weeds and brought them to the library to feed the goats. We had no idea that hiring goats for sustainability would turn into a learning experience. At Anythink, we are continually surprising our community and ourselves. Now we bring goats to our libraries every year to give people a chance to pet the goats.

Could you describe your typical day at work? Is there ever a typical day at work?

I don't know that there is such a thing as a typical workday. Right now, we are engaged in reinventing our library, or creating Anythink 2.0. Our Board of Trustees has asked the management team to look to the future and develop the next iteration of Anythink. My time is divided between meetings with community agencies and partners, collaborating with my Anythink team in setting and implementing project goals, coaching and mentoring staff, working with the administrative directors as we solve problems. One of my favorite roles is that of editor, challenging the team to push for the best, most creative solution.

What scholarly and professional associations are you a part of, and how do they inform you in your work? I am an active member of the American Library Association and the Public Library Association. I am PLA President – 2017–18. Working with PLA gives me an opportunity to collaborate with some of the most thoughtful leaders in the public library profession. I am a member of the Aspen Institute Dialogue on Public Libraries working group. This affiliation has elevated my thinking to include opportunities to influence policy discussions regarding public libraries at the national level. I recently have presented at IFLA and find the international conversation on public libraries to be some of the most progressive.

Could you describe your management and leadership style? Mentorship is such an important theme in leadership – both mentoring and being mentored. Could you please tell us about your experiences about both? Do you have any mentor or role model yourself?

My management style is collaborative. One of my favorite books on leadership is *Leadership is an Art* by Max DuPree, CEO of Herman Miller. Two quotes from his book:

> The first responsibility of a leader is to define reality. The last is to say thank you. In between the two, the leader must become a servant and a debtor. That sums up the progress of an artful leader.
>
> Only a group of people who share a body of knowledge and continually learn together can stay vital and viable.
> — **Max DePree**, *Leadership Is an Art*

I enjoy setting the bar high, and encouraging the most innovative, creative solutions to solve our challenges. I am also a big fan of Simon Sinek, and his concept – Start with Why. I encourage our team to create the vision together, and then support them as they find their own way to accomplish our vision. I would say that I am an aspirational leader.

Some of my most important mentors were generous, kind librarians that I worked with early in my career. I have also enjoyed learning from architects, designers, and creatives outside of the library profession.

I am not a formal mentor, but rather an informal mentor. I especially enjoy planting challenges for people or creating opportunities that might seem untenable, and then supporting people to accomplish goals that seem insurmountable.

Anythink Libraries do not charge fines for late materials. Library users receive notification of overdue items and are billed for replacement and processing after 25 days overdue. Does this policy still apply today? What are the users' reactions and attitudes towards this no-fine-charged policy for late-returned materials?

Anythink has been fine-free since 2009. This policy has changed the landscape of our work. Our staff now have time to enjoy connecting customers with ideas, programs, etc. instead of having to be in a disciplinary role of having to say no. Unfortunately, you may not check out materials, use the computer, etc., until you pay your fine. People enjoy this sense of trust and are grateful to have an organization that understands their busy lives and gives an extended grace period for people to return their materials.

WordThink – a word-based classification system developed by Anythink Libraries to replace the Dewey Decimal Classification (DDC), patterned after the BISAC Subject Heading. WordThink organizes materials according to 45 different categories with additional subcategories. Materials are then arranged alphabetically by title – what are the advantages of switching to the WordThink system? Were there many oppositions from the users (general public) and reluctance amongst the library staff when the WordThink system was first implemented?

What a terrific question. I have always been enchanted with the idea of organizing materials bookstore style after talking with so many people who are frustrated that they cannot figure out our classification system. A team of five staff visited the Maricopa County Public Library in 2008. This public library had converted a number of their branches to the Book Industry Subject and Category system.

After talking with the team in Arizona, our staff returned enthusiastic to try this idea at Anythink. They set a goal of converting all of our collections to BISAC within one year and they accomplished their goal. The team designed a conversion process, and everyone on staff helped to convert our collection. This engagement helped us all to understand how the new system works. Our team has named our system, WordThink, which uses BISAC as the base model, but allows us to modify language to meet user's local needs as well as establishing neighborhoods of associated materials that fit the natural searching habits of our community. The community has transitioned easily to this system.

It is very straightforward to describe and once users have a short briefing, they have mastered the concept and find using the library less of a chore and more like a discovery. Their relationship to the library is impacted positively because they are less dependent upon staff to help them decipher the classification code. One gentleman's retort when we tried our first reorganization at a small branch library, "What took you so long?" When I asked an 8 year old boy what he loved about the library, he said, "Because you organize the books so I can find them." Early research in school libraries that have moved to BISAC indicate students check out four to five times more books than libraries that remain with the Dewey classification. This idea has moved from heresy to one that many libraries are considering.

All Anythink locations set up unique "experience zones" throughout the year. Experience zones are areas created by Anythink staff that allow for interactive experiences in the library. These zones use a hands-on approach to make information and learning more interactive within the library setting – could you talk more about this "experiences zones" and its latest developments?

In 2008, our board of directors supported the idea of becoming an "experience library." That concept focuses our work on the customer's experience. This shifts our resources to creating informal learning opportunities. This can be as simple as a book display marketing a genre or topic to a participatory, museum quality exhibit encouraging people to learn and interact with a topic such as music, art, or photography.

Currently, we are working on developing a structure within our library system that supports informal learning at all levels including a mastery or virtuoso learning experience that results in creating content. This shifts the idea of the library as a place to check out a book to a place that supports learning initiated by the individual. We are inspired by Nina Simon's concept from the *Participatory Museum*. She defines a "participatory cultural institution as a place where visitors can create, share and connect with each other around content."

Based on what I read on the Internet, there are so many exciting and innovative activities being launched by Anythink Libraries – which I have never heard of, e.g.: (1) mySummer, (2) The Studio, (3) Explore Outdoors, (3) Anythink Grows – could you tell me how Anythink Libraries managed to come up with such interesting and unconventional programs. In addition, what are the reactions and level of participation amongst the users?

When we were inventing our library, we worked with the creative director of Ricochet Ideas, John Bellina. He hosted a number of workshops for the staff and guided us through a series of disruptive thinking exercises. Out of this process, the staff initiated the idea of disrupting summer reading and "other" programs. We established criteria for our programs that include a level of interaction and participation in most of our programs. This moves our programming from passive to a level of engagement.

We are learning a great deal from work that is happening in museums around the concept of informal learning and focusing on the user experience. The experience in the library is a continuum and people choose their level of engagement. Sometimes it is at the transaction level, simply checking out a book, or sitting quietly reading or working independently.

Sometimes the experience rises to a much higher level of participation or engagement, which involves collaborating in groups and working with local experts or artists in residence to produce a product. One example is a group of teens working afterschool for a number of weeks. They wrote their own music lyrics, created the music, and produced a CD. They even performed a small concert for their peers and our board of directors.

Over the past month, as part of the Outside the Lines: Reintroducing Libraries initiative, Anythink hosted block parties in seven of our neighborhoods. The goals were to build community, reach new residents and to listen to our community and gather their stories. Over the course of a week, our team held a tailgate party with our community watching a local football game in a local park, hosted a dog party Sunday brunch for a new neighborhood complete with dog biscuits, dog portraits and dog art projects and an outdoor neighborhood market fiesta. By reaching out into the community, we created opportunities for people to connect with each other and the library in unexpected conversations, to see the library as a builder and a connector. We are impressed by the engagement of our community and their thirst for opportunities to connect.

Which part(s) of your job as the Director do you find most rewarding? What is the most frustrating?

While I stumbled into this career, I cannot imagine a better life. Working in public libraries has provided limitless opportunities to invent library programs and services that connect people with their community and information. Watching the community engage with each other, with ideas and information is always joyful. Public libraries are places that support culture, imagination and creativity. They are places of optimism and hope. Working in this arena, always moving to empower and connect our community is work that is a comfort to the soul. Watching my staff invent ideas and projects that create joyful experiences for our customers provides a sense of continuity and remarkable accomplishment.

Anythink was awarded the 2010 National Medal for Museum and Library Service, the 2011 John Cotton Dana Award for Outstanding Public Relations, 2011 Library Journal Landmark Libraries award – what are the driving forces behind the successes of Anythink Libraries and their services?

Since our library was one of the worst funded libraries until we achieved additional funding in 2007, we not only had a bad image, but we had numerous problems to solve to become a library that merited the support of our community. Our organization was an underdog, with a drive to prove our worth. Since we had an opportunity to invent a new library in a cohesive, structural, systematic way, we were open to taking risks to make a library that really worked for our community. Perhaps we are a group of dreamers who are inspired to create libraries that are not hindered by processes that no longer work. We give ourselves permission to design libraries that work for people. We also raise the bar high, and then continually push each other to meet and exceed our expectations.

Anythink Libraries – in what ways would you want Anythink Libraries to make a positive difference in the lives of everyone in the community?

My ultimate goal is for people to see the library as a partner in creating a successful and inspiring life for them, however they define success. If you can dream it, the library can help you achieve those dreams.

If a young person is inspired to become a librarian as a career, and comes to you for advice, what would you say to him or her?

I would tell them that being a librarian is not just a career; it is a calling. I would ask them about their aspirations and expectations to make sure that their perceptions of libraries are close to the reality of today's library work. Today's librarians need to be people who are relationship- and community-builders. We need creative, innovators who enjoy working with people.

Any other exciting stories that you would like to share with the readers?

Yesterday, we hosted a community conversation with the Aspen Institute Citizenship and American Identity Program[6] and supported by Rocky Mountain PBS.[7] The project convenes a conversation with community members around their What Every American Should Know program. http://www.whateveryamericanshouldknow.org

Over 60 people joined the conversation, bringing their list of ten things that they think fellow Americans should know to be culturally and civically literate. After an evening of conversation, people did not want to leave the library. They

---

6 Citizenship and American Identity Program - The Aspen Institute – Homepage. Available at: https://www.aspeninstitute.org/programs/citizenship-and-american-identity-program/
7 Rocky Mountain PBS – Homepage. Available at: http://www.rmpbs.org/home/

were so engaged in their discussions, they huddled in groups until after the library closed. This is an example of the library being that safe space where people are willing to listen and have their ideas be heard. Creating opportunities for civic and cultural conversation on what it means to be an American and the common knowledge that we should share as citizens was an extraordinary opportunity.

Do you have any strategic plans worked out for developing your Library for 2017?

Our community is growing rapidly and we will be working in 2017 to develop a common strategic vision for expanding our service, followed hopefully by a funding initiative in years to come.

As my Public Library Association (PLA)[8] President's term begins midyear, I will be working with PLA and the Legacy Partners to create a closer learning environment amongst public libraries throughout the world. Your book will be a very good way to integrate into this conversation. The Gates Global Library program is closing its doors at the end of 2018. Global Libraries have been working with PLA, IFLA and TASCHA (University of Washington[9]) to partner over the next years to create a leadership role for public libraries between the US and IFLA.[10] Right now, the three partners are working on their goals for the next year or two.

Further readings

Anythink Branding [YouTube]. Available at: https://www.youtube.com/watch?v=Z7sUV4du674
A Day in the Life of an Anythink Library [YouTube]. Available at: https://www.youtube.com/watch?v=VLUFz5aGFQc
Interview with Pam Sandlian Smith, Director, Rangeview Library Director. Available at: http://www.tnla.org/?403
Pam Sandlian Smith - American Library Association. Available at: http://www.ala.org/pla/about/election/sandlian-smith
Pam Sandlian Smith - AnyThink Libraries – Director. Available at: http://csreports.aspeninstitute.org/Dialogue-on-Public-Libraries/2014/participants/details/215/Pam-Sandlian-Smith
Pam Sandlian-Smith on "Creating Experience Libraries" [YouTube]. Available at: https://www.youtube.com/watch?v=21dD0eG0vrQ

---

8 Public Library Association (PLA), a division of ALA, American Library Association, our professional membership association in the US. Public Library Association – Homepage. Available at: http://www.ala.org/pla/
9 University of Washington – Homepage. Available at: https://www.washington.edu/
10 International Federation of Library Associations (IFLA) – Homepage. Available at: http://www.ifla.org/

Pam Sandlian Smith's Page – Library. Available at: 2.0http://www.library20.com/profile/PamSandlianSmith

What to expect from libraries in the 21st century: Pam Sandlian Smith at TEDxMileHigh [YouTube]. Available at: https://www.youtube.com/watch?v=fa6ERdxyYdo

14 Christopher Platt

Chief Branch Library Officer, New York Public Library

Introduction

Situated at 42nd St. and Fifth Avenue in Manhattan, the New York Public Library's Beaux-Arts style architecture has frequently appeared or has been referenced in many different forms of contemporary cultural and artistic expressions. Over time, this Library has become an icon, as well as one of the most popular tourist attractions in New York City. In fact, the NYPL's building has been featured in a large number of Hollywood blockbuster films such as *Ghostbusters* (1984), *The Day After Tomorrow* (2004), *Sex and the City* (2008), and *The Adjustment Bureau* (2011), etc. In addition to this building, NYPL has 91 other locations, including 88 branch circulating libraries throughout the Bronx, Manhattan, and Staten Island in New York City.

Overseeing the largest single circulating library system in the US as well as the Customer Experience, Adult Education, and Youth Education services and programming divisions is Christopher Platt – Chief Branch Library Officer of the NYPL. In the following interview, Platt discusses the challenges and strategies that the NYPL faces in providing information and other services for one of the most important centers for performing arts, education, and culture in the world.

Fig. 14.1: Christopher Platt, Chief Branch Library Officer, New York Public Library (Photo: New York Public Library).

DOI 10.1515/9783110533347-015

Fig. 14.2: Stephen A. Schwarzman Building, New York Public Library, Manhattan, New York City (Photo: New York Public Library).

Fig. 14.3: Rose Main Reading Room, Stephen A. Schwarzman Building, New York Public Library (Photo: New York Public Library).

Fig. 14.4: Kingsbridge Branch of the New York Public Library, the Bronx, New York City (Photo: New York Public Library).

Fig. 14.5: Chatham Square Branch of the New York Public Library, Manhattan, New York City (Photo: New York Public Library).

Could we begin this interview by first introducing yourself, for example, your training and background? What did you study at university? Do you come from a family of librarians?

Apart from a brief period in a bookstore, I have worked in or with libraries my entire career. I do not come from a family of librarians, but I do come from a family of avid readers who read recreationally, to expand our horizons, and to follow our curiosity.

I have a Bachelor's degree in French (with an emphasis in literature) from the University of California at Santa Barbara[1] and a Masters in Library Science from the University of Washington at Seattle.[2]

As part of your career as a librarian, you spent many years working for Baker & Taylor[3] a worldwide distributor of books – could you tell us how experiences in this area contribute to your current work as a public librarian?

This was one of the most interesting periods of my professional career. I joined – and later managed – a team of expert collection development librarians, who worked with libraries big and small across the United States to help curate opening day collections for new or renovated libraries, and provide ongoing curated collection recommendations to help libraries regularly acquire the books and media they needed to best satisfy their local communities.

Our clients were primarily public libraries, and I was able to meet and learn from many wonderful librarians across the U.S. It also helped me understand and hone skills necessary to profile communities and collections so that the latter is best serving the needs of the former.

I was also able to meet and work with many dedicated people in the ecosystem of books and reading – my work colleagues, publishers, authors, and the like – all of whom believed passionately in the value of the written word, and the role libraries play in fostering a literate and informed society. By and large, it is a very mission-driven ecosystem.

One of the most important things I came to understand, and which stays with me everyday in my work, is that communities of all sizes and socio-economic backgrounds place great value in their local library. It is not just a source of information, it is a vital community center, a place of respite, an institution that reflects connections across generations current and past, and a source of pride.

---

1 University of California, Santa Barbara – Homepage. Available at: http://www.ucsb.edu/
2 University of Washington, Seattle – Homepage. Available at: http://www.washington.edu/
3 Baker & Taylor – Homepage. Available at: http://www.btol.com/

There are approximately 9,000 public libraries in the U.S., I worked with a diverse assortment of them in this role. It is a great statement about our society that we invest in these institutions, because the best of them curate collections and expertise that would allow any community member to walk in and learn what they need to start a revolution. In this respect, the local public library is an example of how courageous this society is in freely placing resources at the fingertips of its communities.

Starting in 2005, you spent two years working at the Queens Library[4] – Queens Library versus the New York Public Library[5] – could you tell us what are the major differences in terms of the user profiles (users' needs and expectations) between these two major city libraries?

New York City is comprised of five boroughs, with three public libraries serving them: New York Public Library's branches serve the Bronx, Manhattan and Staten Island. Brooklyn Public Library[6] serves Brooklyn. Queens Library serves Queens. Any New Yorker can use any or all of these 3 library systems.

NYPL and Queens have more in common than actual differences. We both serve remarkably diverse and demanding communities. Queens Library has a rich history leading library best practices in serving immigrant communities through its New Americans Program.[7] During my time there, I enjoyed learning the nuances of collection development and services in world languages that I had not understood before.

NYPL is unique in that it is larger in numbers of branches and geographic service area. It also has incredible scholarly research centers and collections that all New Yorkers and visitors are welcome to use.

Could you please provide a brief introduction about the NYPL?

The New York Public Library has been an essential provider of free books, information, ideas, and education for all New Yorkers for more than 100 years. Founded in 1895, the NYPL is the nation's largest public library system, featuring a unique combination of 88 neighborhood branches and four scholarly research

---

4 Queens Library – Homepage. Available at: http://www.queenslibrary.org/
5 New York Public Library – Homepage. Available at: https://www.nypl.org/
6 Brooklyn Public Library – Homepage. Available at: https://www.bklynlibrary.org/
7 New Americans Program – Queens Library – Homepage. Available at: http://www.queenslibrary.org/services/new-americans-program

centers, bringing together an extraordinary richness of resources and opportunities available to all.

NYPL's neighborhood libraries in the Bronx, Manhattan, and Staten Island – many of which date to Andrew Carnegie's visionary philanthropy at the turn of the 20th century – are being transformed into true centers of educational innovation and service, vital community hubs that provide far more than just free books and materials. Our local libraries play a key role in closing the digital divide, especially for the one in three New Yorkers who don't have Internet access at home. New York City public school students rely on their local branches for homework help. The city's immigrant communities count on NYPL's English language and literacy classes. Job seekers depend on our comprehensive job search resources. Altogether, the Library offers 93,000 free programs annually, serving everyone from toddlers to teens to seniors.

In the always expanding digital realm, The New York Public Library provides patrons worldwide with powerful online tools to help them discover its extensive resources and services. On nypl.org visitors can browse the Library's immense collections, download e-books, and view more than 800,000 items from our award-winning Digital Gallery.[8] Our recently-launched SimplyE[9] e-book application provides patrons with rapid access to over 300,000 e-books. Through Ask NYPL our librarians are available to answer patron questions on any topic at any time.

The USA is not a developing country, is there a reason WHY one in three New Yorkers who don't have Internet access at home?

Cost and motivation. The costs are both on the personal level – for instance the south Bronx has the poorest congressional district in the United States with 38% of households living below the poverty line. For them, having a device and access to broadband, Wi-Fi, etc. is a very real challenge. There are also larger municipal costs – we are a city of complex infrastructure and government, and communities have made it a priority to increase the level of broadband access to underserved areas, but we still have a long way to go. Motivation is also key, in households who may have enough money to cover the cost, but would weigh that cost against other things they need or want to pay for on an ongoing basis, it may not be apparent to them why swapping out those other things for an Internet connection

---

[8] NYPL Digital Gallery – Homepage. Available at: https://www.nypl.org/collections/articles-databases/nypl-digital-gallery

[9] SimplyE – The New York Public Library – Homepage. Available at: http://gethelp.nypl.org/customer/portal/topics/864414

is worth it, especially if they are unfamiliar with the devices and the extent of opportunity available to them on the Internet. This is a key area in which libraries can play a role.

For these people who do not have access to the Internet, what kind of social or economic backgrounds do they come from? Are they mostly new immigrants?

It is a mix of multi-generational New Yorkers who are stuck in a cycle of poverty and low education, and new immigrants who arrive with few resources of their own. Helping these New Yorkers gain skills and education to break out of that cycle is a factor in deciding and implementing new strategic priorities.

Could you also describe your roles and responsibilities as the Chief Branch Library Officer at the NYPL?

My role is responsible for the programmatic operations of the largest single circulating library system in the U.S. made up of 88 branch libraries, including the Andrew Heiskell Braille and Talking Book Library[10] which is one New York state's two regional libraries of the National Library Service for the Blind and Physically Handicapped[11] of the Library of Congress. I oversee our Customer Experience units, which are comprised of Circulation and Access Services, our system-wide volunteers program, our AskNYPL[12] virtual reference service and Reader Services, which coordinates and promotes our recommendations services. I also oversee the education and program units that coordinate the curriculum and programming offerings for children, teens and adults, and I have administrative oversight of BookOps,[13] the shared technical services collaboration between NYPL and Brooklyn Public Library.

A colleague, William Kelly is the Andrew W. Mellon Director of the Research Libraries[14] and has oversight of the four scholarly research centers: the Stephen A. Schwarzman Building's humanities and social sciences collections, the Library

---

[10] Andrew Heiskell Braille and Talking Book Library, NYPL – Homepage. Available at: https://www.nypl.org/locations/heiskell
[11] National Library Service for the Blind and Physically Handicapped – Homepage. Available at: https://www.loc.gov/nls/
[12] AskNYPL – Homepage. Available at: https://www.nypl.org/ask-nypl
[13] BookOps – Homepage. Available at: https://sites.google.com/a/nypl.org/bookops/
[14] William Kelly – Homepage. Available at: https://www.nypl.org/press/press-release/december-14-2015/william-p-kelly-named-new-york-public-library%E2%80%99s-andrew-w-mellon

for the Performing Arts at Lincoln Center,[15] the Schomburg Center for Research in Black Culture,[16] and the Science, Industry and Business Library.[17]

What is the current size of the NYPL's collections, including its special collections? Could you also describe what you deem are the highlights of the collection and services?

Serving more than 17 million patrons a year, and millions more online, the Library holds more than 51 million items, from books, e-books, and DVDs to renowned research collections used by scholars from around the world. Housed in the iconic 42nd Street library and three other research centers, NYPL's historical collections hold such treasures as Columbus's 1493 letter announcing his discovery of the New World, George Washington's original Farewell Address, and John Coltrane's handwritten score of "Lover Man."

What's the role of technology and innovation at the NYPL?

NYPL is a leader in innovative library technology, as well as innovative approaches to service improvements and program development.

As one of the earliest adopters of circulating e-books, today we have one of the largest and most diverse e-content collections of any public library. We helped lead the ReadersFirst[18] movement to create principles around library patrons experience with using e-content in the context of libraries and we are especially proud our new SimplyE e-book reader app, developed with the support of IMLS (Institute of Museum and Library Services)[19] and many library partners in the U.S. to make the process of discovering and downloading an e-book from the local library as easy as possible.

As one of the leaders who helped create, and subsequently lead, the BookOps shared technical services collaboration between NYPL and Brooklyn Public Library, I point to this as a tremendous example of innovative service improvement in public libraries. Collectively, the two library systems spend over $30M annually on

---

15 Library for the Performing Arts at Lincoln Center (NYPL) – Homepage. Available at: https://www.nypl.org/events/programs/lpa
16 Schomburg Center for Research in Black Culture (NYPL) – Homepage. Available at: https://www.nypl.org/about/locations/schomburg
17 Science, Industry and Business Library (NYPL) – Homepage. Available at: https://www.nypl.org/about/locations/sibl
18 ReadersFirst – Homepage. Available at: http://www.readersfirst.org/
19 IMLS (Institute of Museum and Library Services) – Homepage. Available at: https://www.imls.gov/

materials, all of which must be selected, purchased, cataloged, processed, shipped and shelved in library collections across 4 city boroughs and storage facilities.

We also encourage staff-led innovation at the branch level through two new programs. Our Innovation Awards program is as process in which frontline staff are encouraged to submit proposals for new innovative programs or services that are selected and implemented as pilots based on a vote by their colleagues. In each of the past two years we have awarded $100,000 in the form of mini-grants in the $2,000–$5,000 range for the staff to then implement and pilot their proposal. Some pilots such as robotics programming and museum passes have been selected for system-wide expansion. Others such as a book-cycle on Staten Island have created new ways for local libraries to reach out into their communities. Our Innovation Communities program brings together a small group of staff from across the organization to lead a project that answers a system-wide service improvement question. One example is "How can we get books placed on hold by patrons into their hands easier and quicker?" That team spent more than six months identifying key areas to add efficiency and improvements to the process that will speed the process up by an average of more than two days and free up over 14,000 yearly hours of staff effort system-wide that can be redirected to other patron service. For a library of our size and scale, these innovations are important.

In 2014, you helped launch NYPL's new Customer Service Experience and Reader Services department. Can you tell us more about it?

In that year NYPL was implementing a strategic planning process and one of the early issues we understood was a need to better develop, direct and coordinate services that impact any patron's experience at any of our locations or online. We now have a Director of Customer Experience who in addition to overseeing services that help define that experience (Circulation and Access Services, AskNYPL, etc.) also works with staff and our Learning and Development Team to develop standards, testing, and training for new products and services.

As part of our re-affirmation of reading as a core strategic pillar of the library, and its importance in building out a stronger, more informed and more empathetic society, Reader Services is a small department created to help promote two things, our circulating collections, and our staff expertise in recommending good books and materials from those collections. NYPL's greatest asset is its staff, which is wonderfully diverse and literate. I strongly believe expert librarians are vital in connecting good books to good readers, especially as other outlets for book browsing and discovery diminish over time. We have far more libraries in our service area than bookstores. Reader Services creates mechanisms for that local expertise to be harvested for all New Yorkers and beyond, through staff picks shelf cards, reading recommendation social media streams and interactive Twitter and Facebook events, blogging, "best of" lists, read-alike lists, and the very successful "The Librarian is In" podcast.[20] Collectively, these efforts ensure that today the readers advisory expertise of NYPL staff is more broadly shared than ever before.

Please describe the staffing structure at the NYPL.

Most branches are managed by a Library Manager, supported by librarians, children's librarians, young adult librarians, information assistants, clerical staff, and pages – the latter must be enrolled in high school or college or vocational school. We have an additional program staff such as school outreach and early literacy specialists, technology trainers, and out-of-school time educators who also deliver program in the branches and at schools, daycares, and other community partners, etc.

87 of the branches are divided into seven networks, each managed by an Associate Director, who report to either the Borough Director of the Bronx, or the Borough Director of Manhattan and Staten Island, who report directly to me. 1 location, the Mid-Manhattan Library serves as our central circulating library and the Director of that library reports to me.

The programmatic departments cited earlier provide central direction, coordination and support of the branch work.

At NYPL, we are also supported by many operational divisions such as separate departments for Digital Services (led by a Chief Digital Officer), IT, Development (fundraising), Government Relations, Communications and Marketing, Capital Planning, BookOps (technical services), Security, Facilities, Legal Services, Budget, and Human Resources, etc. All units report up to one of six chief officers, who in turn report to the President and the Chief Executive Officer.

As the Chief Branch Library Officer at NYPL, could you describe your typical day at work? Is there ever a typical day at work?

As with most public service organizations, there is never a typical day, which is what keeps the work fresh. On any given day, I may be in meetings with my staff and colleagues assessing and planning programs and services, I may be in meetings with government officials, community organizations, or funders to discuss

---

[20] The Librarian is in Podcast (NYPL) – Homepage. Available at: https://www.nypl.org/voices/blogs/blog-channels/librarian-is-in

new program opportunities. I may leading the programmatic input to branch renovations, participating in community conversations to gain input on community needs, or working with our human resources department to help develop new training and professional development opportunities. Of course, my favorite days are those when I get to visit branches. Talking with frontline staff, and witnessing New Yorkers participate in our programs, check out our materials, or use our technology to apply for jobs, learn a new skill, or just do email is always an important opportunity for me to refocus on what the daily impact of a community library looks like and reprioritize efforts to improve the services and resources we offer to staff and the public. In a library of our size, the leadership by necessity talks of our impact in terms of large metrics such as circulation, visits or program attendance, however I am keenly aware that behind every tally count is as individual who chose to use our library in a way personally meaningful to them, and every day I spend at work is spent living up to that meaning.

Who are the majority users of the NYPL? That is, who comes to see you about your collections, programs, and services?

Our libraries are open for anyone to enter and use onsite. Services that require a library card, such as checking out materials or using a PC or laptop, are open to anyone who lives, works, or goes to school in New York State. In this sense, the majority of users at the NYPL as a whole are a mirror reflection of New York City itself, including tourists and visiting scholars who visit our more iconic locations.

We do know quite a bit about users of each of our branches, reflecting how unique each community is. For instance of our users with high education levels beyond high school, 95% of them are in neighborhoods served by libraries that demonstrate high rates of circulation. Whereas 77% of our users with low education levels are in neighborhoods served by libraries that have lower rates of circulation but higher rates of educational programming, PC/laptop use, and similar services. These latter neighborhoods also show higher rates of linguistic and ethnic diversity, and more poverty than those served by libraries that demonstrate higher rates of circulation. All of these factors and more guide us in shaping collections, educational and cultural programming, and services such as access to technology that will best meet the needs and demands of local communities.

Mentorship is such an important theme in leadership – both mentoring and being mentored. Could you please tell us about your experiences about both? Do you still have mentors that you go to?

Opportunities for mentorship are important, and in my own experience vary from individual to individual. I have participated in group leadership programs and individual mentorship & coaching programs. The formal programs I have gained the most from are the group programs, because I feel most successful when collaborating with colleagues to achieve outcomes. Individual mentors of mine from which I have gained the most and still maintain contact with are among my former supervisors and colleagues from whom I learn standards of behaviour, thoughtful ways to consider issues and address problems, professional development advice, and the importance of respectful relationships, etc.

At the library, I place importance on fostering opportunities for staff to come together to share experiences and best practices, and form the important collegial bonds that lead to peer-to-peer mentoring. We do create versions of formal mentorship through our library trainee program, staff sharing, and other professional development programs, but effective leaders I know often have strong informal peer-to-peer networks they have leveraged to help them advance their knowledge and experience.

NYC is one of the oldest cities in the United States, and continues to be an important center for performing arts, education and culture (both popular and high cultures). In addition, many renowned and highly ranked universities in the world are located in the NYC area. In this context, what roles does the NYPL play in the local community?

NYPL is one of the most important educational and cultural institutions in New York City. Not only do we partner with other renowned cultural, arts and educational organizations to offer world-class programs and exhibitions, we utilize our own collections and expertise to contribute to the cultural conversation of the city. These contributions at a high level include our Live at NYPL series of conversations with major authors and exhibitions such as NYPL's Library for the Performing Arts 'Curtain Up: Celebrating the Last 40 Years of Theatre in New York and London.' At a local level we have invested in our role as a learning institution in our communities launching industry-leading after-school programming and early literacy initiatives, expanding our Adult Literacy Center work to become the third largest provider of English as a second language instruction to immigrants in New York, and worked with our partner libraries in Brooklyn and Queens to launch the largest of its kind partnership with the New York City Department of Education[21] called MyLibraryNYC[22] which provides fine free student library cards, teacher professional development, and class sets of books to participating schools across the city.

---

21 New York City, Department of Education – Homepage. Available at: http://schools.nyc.gov/default.htm
22 MyLibraryNYC – Homepage. Available at: http://www.mylibrarynyc.org/

We also fully embrace the reality that the term 'local community' now encompasses users who interact with us online. We had more than 30 million visits to our online properties last year ranging from use of our expanding digital collections to placing holds on books in our catalog to searching for events to attend in our branches to listening to our expert podcasts. Our social media presence is also extensive covering multiple platforms with a greater emphasis on video and live interactive experiences such as our popular weekly book recommendation chats on Facebook and Twitter.

The NYPL – in what ways would you want the NYPL to make a positive difference in the lives of everyone in the community?

Under the leadership of our President Tony Marx,[23] we are committed to expanding and cementing our role as a trusted learning institution in our communities, not just to provide access to technology and information, but to emphasise and offer opportunities and encouragement to our users around the importance of reading, learning and creating. Taken together, the programs and services that promote access, reading, learning, and creating tell the story of how a patron can individually benefit from their local library to become a more informed, empathetic, engaged, and contributing member of a society, which makes the fabric of this city that much stronger.

To give examples: we want parents and caregivers to read more to and with their children. We want children to read at grade level by the time they enter 3rd grade, which we know is an indicator of later success. We want young adults to gain experience teaching younger children how to read and do homework. We want to help more young adults learn how to use technology and coding in innovative ways that help lead them to higher education or career opportunities. We want more foreign-born New Yorkers to know how to read and converse in English so they can navigate the city better, have broader employment opportunities, and feel less isolated. We want communities to come together to discuss important issues of the day or contribute directly to the growing historical knowledge-base of New York City through our oral history project, and much, much more. Our investment in programs and services in recent years reflects these aims.

The Metropolitan Opera, the NYPL are two of the most prominent arts and cultural institutions located in NYC. Joseph Volpe, former General Manager of the

---

[23] Tony Marx – President and CEO of NYPL – Homepage. Available at: https://www.nypl.org/help/about-nypl/president-and-leadership

Metropolitan Opera once described his work as, "The toughest job on earth..." Whereas for you, how would you describe your work as the Chief Branch Library Officer of the NYPL?

I would describe my job as one of the most humbling jobs one can hold. It can be easy to be caught up in the high profile of this institution, which is justifiably a world-renown brand. I have the privilege of meeting and working with amazing talent and influential individuals, and I never participate in a meeting in which I don't learn something new, which for a curious mind like mine is a reward. But the most amazing, and most humbling aspect of this role is when I hear from or talk with a library patron, who tells me how their local librarian helped make a difference in their life, whether it was learning to read, finding a job, helping their child succeed at school, or just be welcoming place to visit and connect with others. New York City is for many people a hard place to live, and 37% of residents are foreign-born, meaning for most of them it's even harder because they are learning a new culture and language. Everyday I get to do work that helps foster and support vibrant, knowledgeable, and engaged communities in this incredibly diverse city.

Which part(s) of your job as the Librarian do you find most rewarding? What is the most frustrating?

Opportunities to see our dedicated staff share their knowledge, expertise and talent are tremendously rewarding. For many people who use libraries their whole lives, the local librarian they have is an influential and important person. A five-year-old child using their library today will in decades time be a 70 year old grandparent telling their grandkids about the librarian who helped them develop a curious mind and a love of reading. That 70 year old will not know who Christopher Platt was, nor should they. My role is behind the scenes, helping foster that important bond between patron and librarian by supporting the staff in doing their job to the best of their ability. It is immensely rewarding.

Conversely, the most frustrating aspect is anything that gets in the way of that effort. Usually it comes down to money. In New York City, the public libraries have to advocate for funding every year from the City and other funders. While we are by and large successful at it, it can create apprehension and at times limit our ability to expand the good work that we do to more New Yorkers.

If a young person is aspired to become librarian, comes to ask you for advice for their choice of career in librarianship – what would you say to him or her?

Living in this information age makes it one of the most exciting times to enter the profession. Lately, as elections and politics are beginning to reshape our nation's direction and our fundamental understanding of each other, libraries as information navigators, and community engagement centers where people can come to understand each other better, have an opportunity to play a role in a more empathetic citizenry.

Would you like to say something inspiring and encouraging for our readers – as a nice way to conclude this interview?

When presented with the opportunity, try to say "Yes" more than you say "No." When you do, life and career adventures will present themselves.

Further readings

Christopher Platt [YouTube]. Available at: https://www.youtube.com/watch?v=8nHNvihMf4g
Christopher Platt – Chief Branch Library Officer. Available at: https://www.nypl.org/help/about-nypl/president-and-leadership
Christopher Platt, Director of BookOps. Available at: http://www.iop.pitt.edu/libraries/Powerpoints/Chris%20PlattPittsburgh%20BookOps%20PPT.pdf
Posts by Christopher Platt – New York Public Library. Available at: https://www.nypl.org/blog/author/1163

15 John F. Szabo

City Librarian, Los Angeles Public Library

Introduction

As City Librarian, John F. Szabo oversees the Central Library, its 72 branch libraries and the Los Angeles Public Library's (LAPL) $162 million budget. Under Szabo's leadership, the Library's major initiatives include immigrant integration and citizenship, financial literacy, health programs as well as online educational services, e-media resources, and new technologies while also expanding the Library's reach into the city's ethnic communities through local partnerships with community-based and nonprofit organizations. The library system for the City of Los Angeles manages nearly seven million physical and digital items for the four million city residents who speak more 220 languages in a 468 square mile geographic area. By any measure – creativity, impact, magnitude, and results – the Library succeeds in empowering individuals, delivering innovative services, and engaging all ages in lifelong learning for the largest and most diverse urban population of any public library in the United States. In 2015, the Library received the nation's highest honor for library service, the National Medal for Museum and Library Service, for its success in meeting the needs of Angelenos and providing a level of social, educational and cultural services unmatched by any other public institution in the city.

Fig. 15.1: City Librarian John F. Szabo (Photo: LA Public Library).

DOI 10.1515/9783110533347-016

Fig. 15.2: City Librarian John F. Szabo, Children's Librarian Ednita Kelly and Los Angeles Mayor Eric Garcetti gather with the LAPL Book Bike at a recent Downtown event (Photo: LA Public Library).

Fig. 15.3: Children's Citizenship Ceremony (Photo: LA Public Library).

Fig. 15.4 + 15.5: Summer Reading Club Lunch Program (Photo: LA Public Library).

Can we begin this interview by introducing yourself – for example, your background, training, what did you study in university?

Certainly. My name is John Szabo, and my degree is from the University of Alabama.[1] I was a Telecommunications and Film major, so I studied television as well as film – primarily documentary film – as an undergraduate. I also had a minor in Physical Geography.

I began working in libraries when I was 16 years old and continued in part-time, paraprofessional support positions in both the university library at the University of Alabama, and at the public library there. It was through that work that I developed a love for libraries and determined that rather than go into television, I would go into the library profession. I applied and, ultimately, went to the University of Michigan for a Library and Information Studies (LIS) degree.

Was it the place or the people that you loved the most from the library? Or was it a combination of both of these things?

When I went to get my library degree, one of the reasons I chose the University of Michigan was because they had a fellowship program where the dormitories or residence halls actually had very tiny libraries inside of them. I had the opportunity to be the head librarian, while I went to school, of a tiny library within a dormitory. When I went to the university on my first day, if you had asked me what my career goals were, I would have said I wanted to be an interlibrary loan librarian at a college library. That was because when I was at the University of Alabama, I actually worked in the interlibrary loan office.

---

[1] University of Alabama – Homepage. Available at: https://www.ua.edu/

The idea of borrowing materials from all over the world to help researchers was really exciting, and I loved my work in that office. I found it interesting, I thought I was good at it, and I loved searching for things. It was working in that residence hall with that fellowship that gave me the initial taste of the public library, and I have since been in public libraries for my entire career.

Could you describe the library system back in your hometown in the 1980s? Can you describe the circulation system, the atmosphere, the design, or the collections?

The public library in Montgomery had a fairly large central library in the downtown area, and I think there were branch libraries – maybe nine or ten. It was not a well-funded public library system, but it had a very automated circulation system. It had an online catalog; there were reference librarians; there were all the things you would expect in a public library. The building was built in the 1960s, so it was maybe 20 years old. It was an ethnically integrated public library at that time, and I worked with a diverse staff. The librarians who worked there, and this is true for libraries throughout all geographies I've worked in, were always excited when a young person was pondering a career in libraries and were eager to give advice. They wanted to fertilize the flower so that it would blossom.

Based on your experiences, could you describe the cultural and social functions that the public library is expected to perform in American society?

I think those expectations have changed over the course of my career – the last 20-plus years as a librarian. I think today, public libraries are more relevant than ever. In the United States and in North America, people are beginning to understand the value that the public library can provide, because not only can the public library provide physical materials, but they know the technology we have provided over the years. Also, we are in every community – there are branch libraries in every neighborhood.

We are a very trusted organization – we have a positive impression in virtually every community around the country. That is something to be leveraged with a great amount of care. The public library can make a difference in the issues within the community. That's why you see public libraries in the United States engaged in matters such as public health, immigrant integration, helping people become citizens, financial literacy, helping the homeless – we welcome everybody and provide services equitably. We truly believe in treating our mayor in the same way we treat a poor person who comes in off the streets. The public library is also willing to and eager to change, whether that means the format of the materials and information or the services we provide.

How do public libraries in the U.S. complement the services provided by centers with staff who are trained professionals in things like public health advocacy or with immigrants?

There are other non-profit and community organizations that work in citizenship and immigration services, for example, what the public library offers is place, information, and trust. We have seen that non-profits cannot address all of those needs themselves, so it is strategically important for the library to help meet those needs because we serve everyone. In many cases, immigrant communities may not be familiar with the tradition of free public library services in the U.S. So being able to provide information on a path to U.S. citizenship or provide health resources and programs is a way of getting people in the door. It is certainly our job to provide information assistance, and important to provide core library services.

Can you tell us about your general path to becoming the director of the Los Angeles Public Library[2]?

Going back to 1991 to 1992 when I was at the University of Michigan I had that fellowship, I was managing an annual budget of around $25,000. I was also managing 12 staff members – maybe working ten to 12 hours per week in the library. We really just needed one staff member in the library at a time – it was very small, just one room. But, that gave me the experience of management, and I helped do the cataloging, I did reference work, etc.

When I graduated, I applied for – not thinking I would get the job – a director job at a small public library in a rural area in Illinois. It was a town of about 8,000 people, and there was a single library – a wonderful library – and I was hired.

At the age of 24, I was a library director. I was there for three and a half years, and then I went to Palm Harbor, Florida, where I was the director there for another three and a half years. Then, I went to Clearwater for about six and a half years. It was there that I got management experience with running a library system – multiple branches, a large staff, a larger budget, and the construction of new library buildings. Then, I went to Atlanta in 2005 to be the director of that public library system. There, we served a population of about 1.2 million people, and we had a staff of about 525 people, 35 libraries, and served a very diverse community with multiple issues and needs. Atlanta is an Olympic city like Los Angeles. It was a great library system, and I led it for more than seven years. And now I have been here in Los Angeles for four years.

---

2 Los Angeles Public Library – Homepage. Available at: https://www.lapl.org/

What are the biggest challenges of being the director – overseeing such a large non-profit organization compared with a for-profit one?

We are working on improving how we measure our impact because I think that impact is huge. When you help someone find a job and it changes their life for the next 20 years, that is a tremendous accomplishment and a tremendous deliverable to the community at large, but it is hard to quantify.

There are certainly many challenges, and each day brings a new one. But, in a city as huge as Los Angeles – we serve more than 4 million people – I am constantly thinking about and making certain that the services we provide are tailored to each neighborhood and community. We are not a "cookie cutter" library system; so in one library, the services, collections, and skills of the staff are not exactly the same as a library in another part of the city. While they look different, and maybe the services are a little bit different, there are core services that are consistent throughout the library system. I want to make sure they are equitable – that we are providing the same quality service to each community.

How does your library market itself?

In a market like Los Angeles, we employ a variety of strategies to share the good work of the library. We have a Public Relations & Marketing team that is charged with increasing awareness of our programs and services. For example, we work with the bus and train system with some advertising, and we have banners downtown. We also have two full-time social media librarians. For example, just this morning, I did a Snapchat video talking about the free lunches that we provide to young people in 14 of our libraries. Schools provide free summer lunches in the United States. However, since school is not in session during the summer months, many students will not get the same nutrition as they would get during the year. So, we are serving more than 15,000 free lunches to children in our libraries. At the same time, when they come in for a free lunch, we are showing them library services, they're checking our books, they're getting story time, they're attending puppet shows, etc.

Can you give a brief introduction of the Los Angeles Public Library and its system as well as the highlights of its collections and services?

The Los Angeles Public Library serves the largest population of any public library in the United States. We have 73 libraries – that is, a central library and 72 branches. We have a collection of more than six million books and other materials. We have more than 3.4 million photographs in a very special photograph collection and a special photo curator on staff. We also have a vast map collection – one of the largest in the western United States. Other highlights in the collection include restaurant menus – we have a splendid collection of more than 15,000 restaurant menus, a sizeable collection of Hollywood material, Hollywood scripts, posters, other materials related to the film and television industry, and many other collections in a music library, an art library. All of those special collections are located here in our central library. The total number of individuals on our staff – many who work full-time – is a little more than 1,700 employees. Our budget in the current fiscal year is $162 million. We serve a physical area that is more than 400 square miles (1,036 square kilometers) – a large area with great diversity of services.

You mentioned having a collection of restaurant menus. Can you tell us your purpose in setting up a collection for them?

University libraries in the United States are very purposeful in their collecting around specific subjects. In public libraries, we focus our collecting around local history and things relating to our region. But, over the years, we find ourselves acquiring interesting and sometimes odd collections because people will donate their collections. The menu collection is interesting because there were two librarians in the 1970s who felt that it was really important – they had an interest in culinary history. There was an organization for them called the Culinary Historians of Southern California.[3] They began this mission to continue this collection, and it has grown and grown. Most of the menus are from restaurants here in southern California, but there are also menus from various other places around the United States and around the world. Researchers studying the culinary history of southern California or the graphic design or artwork in menus use that collection.

Can you describe more of the hierarchy and staffing structure of your Library?

Out of the 1,700 staff employees throughout the system, about 450 are degreed librarians. The rest are support staff or professionals in other areas. For example, we have a Human Resources department and a Finance department that manage the system. I, as the city librarian, have two assistant-city librarians or assistant managers. Generally, one focuses on administration and behind-the-scenes work at the library. The other focuses more on public services of the library.

Below that, we have the director of branch libraries – someone who is in charge of our 72 branch libraries. We also have someone else at the same level,

---

[3] Culinary Historians of Southern California – Los Angeles Public Library – Homepage. Available at: http://www.lapl.org/whats-on/events/culinary-historians-southern-california

who is the director of the central library. We also have a director of emerging technologies and collections and a director of engagement and learning – who is in charge of programs for youth, health, financial literacy, immigrant integration, and those social inclusion and social services areas. Then we have directors of finance, personnel, human resources, and public relations and marketing. Within branch services, under the director of branch services, we have an assistant director, and because we have so many branch libraries, we divide them into six geographic regions. There is an area manager in each of those regions, and each of them manages about 13 libraries.

How would you describe your typical day at work? Is there ever a typical day?

No day is the same. Most days, I am here in the office, but I am often off-site at City Hall meeting with elected officials and heads of other city departments. At my office, I frequently meet with representatives of non-profit organizations or with individuals or businesses who are donors to the library. We have a very large non-profit that exists solely to support the institution, but they are organizationally separate from the library. On a given day, of course I handle email and paperwork, but individually, I also work with social media and promoting the library and talking about library services. I also deal with budget, personnel, advocating for the library to policy makers, and also, a big part of my job is sharing the message of the library and speaking to the broader community about the value of the library: why the public library is important, the kinds of things we are doing, how we are being innovative, and how the library is a very relevant and current organization. We like to be the "test case" or "trial balloon;" we start something in L.A. that can succeed and then be replicated in Iowa or Mississippi or New York or elsewhere.

Could you describe your leadership and management style?

I have a very open-door style of management. I like being on the front lines, and I like interacting with staff at all levels. In a system as large as ours, I can't always directly affect the services provided at one of our branch libraries – I have to rely on others, so I want our staff to feel empowered to serve people. I said something during my first week here that has been repeated back to me many times now, and I believe it was to a group of children's librarians. I told them that I want them to be as innovative as they can. They take advantage of that! I really want them to be creative and try new ideas.

What are your views on diversity – especially with Los Angeles having communities with a lot of diversity and cultural groups with different needs? Also, is your team of staff very diverse in terms of ethnic backgrounds, cultural backgrounds, and also language abilities? How do you lead a library with inclusiveness in mind?

That's all incredibly important. We are always endeavoring for the library staff to reflect the community that we serve – broadly and also in particular neighborhoods. In L.A., we have large Latino populations coming from Mexico, Central America and South America as well. We also have tremendous populations from around the world and native populations who are Armenian, Korean, Chinese, Japanese, Filipino, and various growing African and Caribbean populations.

We are always ensuring that our collections reflect those cultures and that the staff do as well. Cultural competency is very important – being aware of various community needs. There is also a certain cultural competency in working with teens – and for our staff working with the LGBT community. We recently formed an LGBTQ (Lesbian, Gay, Bisexual, Transgender and Queer) library staff committee that is charged not only with outreach to that community, but with looking internally at our collections and services and providing training for our staff.

The senior leadership team is diverse in all respects. Within our personnel department, we are looking at how our staff population is representative of the population at large – we are looking at areas where we may be underrepresented. We are very fortunate in L.A. that we have such a large and diverse population, and it makes it easier to have a diverse staff.

What are the general expectations of the local community towards your library?

Given the library's history, there are great expectations. There are people in the community who expect the library to do all of the traditional things that we have always been doing, and certainly we will continue to provide those traditional services. But, I think that increasingly, as we step into new spaces like health and financial literacy, people will realize that the library is doing good work in that space and that the library is a good partner. People and organizations are increasingly asking us to do more. I also believe that there are still areas where we want their expectations to be even higher for us.

Can you talk about the awards that you received for your library? For example, the National Medal for Museum and Library Services, which is the highest honor given to museums and libraries for services to the community. You were personally awarded this at the White House last May. Can you comment on that?

We were incredibly honored in 2015 to be one of five libraries in the United States to receive the National Medal for Museum and Library Services. There were five libraries that win this medal and five museums. It was not based on size – there were small libraries that win, so the fact that we are so large was not a factor. The award is for libraries and the impact that they have on the communities they serve, which made it particularly special. The award was presented at the White House in a ceremony with the First Lady, and so we got the opportunity to meet her and receive the award directly from her. It was wonderful to bring it back to Los Angeles. We had a huge celebration here in the Central Library for all of the staff and their families because it is truly our staff who are responsible for delivering those services and are deserving of the award.

Can you tell us about a particular service provided by the library that has become a signature service?

Three years ago we launched "Your Path to Citizenship Begins at the Los Angeles Public Library." It is a partnership with the federal agency in the United States government that oversees the naturalization process. We established "Citizenship Corners" in all 73 libraries. That program has evolved into something much broader for immigrants – documented or undocumented – including giving them the information that they need and helping them with citizenship and English language classes. That has really become a signature program. When we went to Washington to receive the award, the White House asked us to bring one person in our community – just one user of our library.

Of course, in Los Angeles, that was incredibly challenging. We actually selected someone who became a United States citizen through the Los Angeles Public Library. He was a Mexican immigrant named Sergio Sanchez. His wife also became a citizen through the library's program. He was with me in the White House and was able to meet the First Lady. It was a very special and beautiful experience to have this immigrant, who made use of his local public library travel to Washington D.C. for the first time and get to meet the First Lady. It was a wonderful moment, and he couldn't have been a better spokesperson for the library.

What is the driving success behind the Los Angeles Public Library system?

It's the years and years of consistently outstanding service to the public through various services and the support from the community after having developed a relationship over all of those years. In the United States, just like when we vote for the President of the United States or mayor of a city, we sometimes go to the voters with a question: "Do you want to pay this much extra money for a service or a construction project or something for the library?" We have to ask them for funds. When the Los Angeles Public Library has gone to the voters, they have said a resounding yes. That has resulted in the funding that we need, and it has been an endorsement of the library as a public institution and an endorsement of the services we provide. That is not something that has happened within a year or two or because of an award. It is because of decades of consistent service and making certain that those services are tailored to those various communities. The library's mission drives success because it brings different cultures and communities together in dialogue, community, and enrichment programs.

What are your views on the impact of modern technology to your management of the Los Angeles Public Library system and the services provided by it?

I think that they're dramatically changing how we provide services, how we communicate with people through digital sign-in, how we provide e-content for individuals. I have found that in Asia, libraries are so much further along in doing outreach in e-content. We are creating an e-media kiosk in the Los Angeles Airport so that individuals can download e-books, stream movies, and use audiobooks from the Los Angeles Public Library while they are at the airport. We are also putting one in a train station and a recreation center. So, technology is allowing us to reach people in new ways.

We are also increasingly not only being a repository of content, but being a place where people can contribute their content. We have a digitization lab here where we are scanning the library's special collections content. We are creating metadata associated with that content as well, and then we are uploading it not only to our own discovery layer platform, but we are also a national platform called the Digital Public Library of America[4] so people can discover the special collections content we've digitized here in the library.

What about the huge photo and map collection? How do you see that contributing to the research and social capital of the community?

Much of what we have been digitizing has been those photographic images. They are almost all entirely about Los Angeles and the southern California region. It is a real treasure trove of LA history, and that LA history is hidden until we take them and digitize them, provide metadata, and allow them to be discovered. We do exhibits, we publish books on various topics: such as the

---

4 Digital Public Library of America – Homepage. Available at: https://dp.la/

history of women in the San Fernando Valley or African American leaders in south LA.

The Feathers Map Collection is something that has actually come to us since I was the city librarian. It was from a gentleman who had spent his entire life and all of his disposable income on maps and atlases. His home was filled with them, and when he passed away, some people who knew him reached out to the library and said that they were going to throw them away and asked if we wanted them. We said that we would take everything, and our maps librarian has been going through that collection and adding items to our already outstanding map collection. Our map collection is used by researchers, publishers, television and film, etc. We recently made all of those collections available to be used. We actually generate a small revenue stream through our photos in publishing, film, and television.

If there is a young person aspiring to become a librarian, what kind of advice would you give?

I would first say to go into the library, spend time there and get to know what the environment is like. Also, seek out and learn what libraries really are like versus what your perceptions of them are. Really get to know what libraries are doing today, and it is the most fabulous profession ever. It is an incredible way to have an impact on people – libraries truly make an impact. I think that for people interested in changing the world, having an impact on young people's lives, improving their community, and doing something really interesting and meaningful – this would be a fantastic position to hold.

What part of your job do you find most rewarding and most frustrating?

The part that is most rewarding is when I am actually able to see the work that we are doing – to see young people at a story time, or a homeless adult preparing for a job interview or someone who tells me their personal library story – what the library means to them or how the library change their life. I never tire of hearing stories like that.

I think that the most frustrating part is working in a very large organization where there can be certain constraints that relate to hiring, financial matters, and procurement. When the mission and desire to do good are so important, I want to be able to give staff the resources they need in order for those things to happen – whether that's a repair to a building, a contract for books that need to be ordered, policy change, the hiring of an important staff member, I want that to happen immediately, but sometimes it can take a little time. When necessary, I try and eliminate those barriers.

Could you describe some of the successful and popular outreach initiatives launched by the LAPL under your direction?

The LAPL Book Bike is a librarian powered mobile outreach machine used to take the library to the streets and meet people where they are. When Angelenos see the Book Bike, they can get a free book and learn about all of the free resources the LA Public Library card affords them. They can even sign up for a library card on the spot! The Book Bike has been seen at schools, farmers markets, community events, parades, and even at the laundromat! After the success of the first Book Bike, the library has added a second one, and a third Book Bike is in the works. Since 2014, the Book Bike program has met with more than 23,000 people, given away 15,258 books, and processed close to 600 Library cards!

Do you have anything you want to say to conclude our interview?

Anytime you are in a position like mine, to be able to talk about our library system, it is always a joy. As a city librarian, a lot of people ask, "You must not like being asked difficult questions about your budget from elected officials, right?" People assume that I do not like that, but I actually love it! Anytime people are asking questions, it's an opportunity to educate and let them know the truth and share something they may not have known about the library. If someone is going to be a librarian, they have to be ready to be a cheerleader and an advocate for the library.

In the photo attached, I as the City Librarian and the Children's Librarian Ednita Kelly and Los Angeles Mayor Eric Garcetti gather with the LAPL Book Bike at a recent Downtown Los Angeles CicLAVia event where streets are closed off to cars for people to connect on foot, bicycle, etc.

Another photo attached is from our Children's Citizenship Ceremony last month. Caption: Mayor Eric Garcetti and City Librarian John F. Szabo celebrate with nearly 80 children who became U.S. citizens on September 16 during a U.S. Citizenship and Immigration ceremony at the Central Library in downtown Los Angeles.

In this interview, I also talked about the library's Summer Lunch program. I am attaching two photos from that as well. In one, I am serving lunch, and in another, I am participating in a puppet theater presentation with two of the children who just finished eating.

Further readings

The City Library – Los Angeles Public Library. Available at: https://www.lapl.org/about-lapl/city-librarian

First Wednesday Breakfast with our City Librarian John Szabo [YouTube]. Available at: https://www.youtube.com/watch?v=AN0OtfiTwKI

John F. Szabo – OCLC. Available at: https://www.oclc.org/about/leadership/members/szabo-john.en.html

John Szabo, New City Librarian – Library Foundation of Los Angeles. Available at: http://lfla.org/welcome-john-szabo-new-city-librarian/

John Szabo – Los Angeles Public Library - City Librarian. Available at: http://csreports.aspeninstitute.org/Dialogue-on-Public-Libraries/2014/participants/details/218/John-Szabo

Living History: The John Feathers Map Collection [YouTube]. Available at: https://www.youtube.com/watch?v=ulAt-TpRms8

Los Angeles Public Library – JK Adventures [YouTube]. Available at: https://www.youtube.com/watch?v=S_BdpRrQWRs

Los Angeles Public Library Receiving the 2015 National Medal for Museum and Library [YouTube]. Available at: https://www.youtube.com/watch?v=xW4ltow6JVs

Your Path to Citizenship Starts at the Los Angeles Public Library [YouTube]. Available at: https://www.youtube.com/watch?v=_qq5c8VLXAg

16 David Leonard

President, Boston Public Library

Introduction

Established in 1848 and situated in the heart of a major international center of higher education (including law, medicine, engineering, business, and performing and visual arts), the Boston Public Library (BPL) is pronounced as being one of the largest public libraries in terms of its collection size.

In addition to its wide-ranging and valuable collections, BPL also hosts thousands of free public educational, arts and cultural programs each year, including author talks, local and family history lectures, the Lowell Lecture Series, Concerts in the Courtyard, and numerous art and history exhibitions, etc. Furthermore, BPL offers a wide variety of daily events for children, teens, adults, and seniors, including story times, book discussions, film showings, ESL conversation groups, research and technology classes, etc.

Overseeing this gigantic public library system is David Leonard, the current President of the Boston Public Library, who has spent many years working in the business sector before landing a career in public librarianship. In the following interview, Leonard discusses how his previous professional experiences, including in business development contribute to his current work as the President of one of the largest public library systems in the United States.

Fig. 16.1: Boston Public Library President David Leonard reads inside the new Teen Central at the Central Library, which opened in February 2015 (Photo: Boston Public Library).

Fig. 16.2: An exterior photo of the renovated Central Library's Johnson building (Photo: Boston Public Library).

Fig. 16.3: The Central Library Renovation of the Johnson building, which opened to the public in July 2016, features warm and welcoming spaces (Photo: Boston Public Library).

Fig. 16.4: Bates Hall in the Central Library's McKim building (Photo: Boston Public Library).

Could we begin this interview by first introducing yourself – your professional training and background and what did you study at your university?

My undergraduate work was actually in Philosophy and Mathematics with (the U.S. equivalent of) a minor in Psychology. I then did graduate work – also in Philosophy, but rather than pursue the academic path I had started down, I moved to the non-profit and then business technology worlds, and ultimately gained some professional certifications in the technology space over the course of my career.

My first position here at the Boston Public Library (BPL)[1] was that of Chief Technology Officer. From there, I was promoted to what was essentially a Deputy Director role, and then, as of June of this year, officially made President of the library. At the moment, I am also pursuing a Ph.D. in Library Information Science.

At what point did you decide to pursue a graduate degree in Library and Information Science? In the U.S., is it mandatory for practicing librarians to hold graduate degrees in Library and Information Science?

There are statutory rules on this; normally yes, but the Chief Executive role here at BPL does not require it absolutely, but, when the head of the library is

---

1 Boston Public Library – Homepage. Available at: http://www.bpl.org/

not a librarian, then we have to appoint a Chief Librarian to a senior leadership role. So, the rules allowed for this possibility. However, about midway through my time here so far – and I have been at BPL for seven years now – I felt that if this role for me is more about the service aspect of what we are about, and the library profession itself ... and less about a technologist who just happens to work in a library... I came to the personal decision that I should pursue a graduate degree in Library Science. So that's where I am now, and then of course at the time, I certainly didn't expect that I would be chosen as the head of the organization on this timeframe – it was an unexpected turn of events to say the least.

Can you describe your current roles and responsibilities as the President of the Boston Public Library?

There is a vision component and a strategic direction component, as well as operational oversight. The Boston Public Library is one of the largest libraries in the United States. The size of our collection and the custodianship responsibilities have to be a major focus of our work. We are in the very early stages – I was just appointed in June – of rearticulating a vision for the next five to ten years that I think should build upon what has come before. The daily duties of the job can span from fundraising activities, liaising with our city colleagues, because the library is a department of the city of Boston, to many traditional areas of operational management. So really, it is a combination of external relationships, library services oversight, and then administrative or operational oversight. And, we have a strong leadership team that has discipline expertise in their own areas.

Since you did not go to library school and were not trained as a librarian by profession, do you see your non-library background as an advantage? How do your previous experiences contribute to your current work as the President of the Boston Public Library?

I think those non-traditional librarian skills and experiences are actually a huge asset, and I think that is what the Board of Trustees and the Mayor saw in me as a candidate for this position. Technology is a huge part of libraries, whether it is e-books and digital content or technology services to the public, or things we haven't even invented yet. Then, equally, someone who has the strategic business understanding of how to implement and use technology is incredibly useful. Oddly enough, the sales and marketing and consulting experience I have, I think, is particularly helpful in the partnerships and development work that we are doing more of now. I happen to believe that fundraising is a form of sales or a form of consultative selling, in the best sense of those words.

Do you find measuring the successes of libraries to be challenging?

I think that my business experience is an advantage here as well. As a government and non-profit organization, using some of the good aspects of having clear quarterly goals and holding people accountable is something that is very beneficial in this world that might not traditionally be used to set expectations. I also think that traditionally, libraries have not been good at measuring their impact – sometimes not good at even measuring their output. However, we want to be cautious about how far we take that, because there are enough examples of overly measuring factors in say, the education sphere and forgetting the human element of things ... I think that with the right approach to both quantitative and qualitative measures, then we can understand the role we're playing in society, the impact we are having. Everyone would say we do great work, and they have great experiences, but are we making a difference where it really matters and how we can demonstrate that more successfully.

Can you give a brief introduction of the Boston Public Library including the highlights of the collections and services?

The Boston Public Library is an almost 170-year institution and we claim several firsts – the first large free municipal library in the U.S. We were also the first library to lend books – before BPL, most libraries were more like reading rooms rather than places where you could borrow books and take them home with you. We were also the first to have a branch library and also the first to have a designated children's library. So, that is a strong and rich history by U.S. standards.

Today, we have a central library here in downtown Boston, and the complex is almost one million square feet. We have just recently completed a $78 million renovation of the public space in our 1970s building, which really moves our public spaces into the 21st century. There are 24 branches today across the city of Boston, which for us is a pretty high density given the size of the population and the geography of Boston. But, each of these branch libraries is really linked to its local community and the local communities are very passionate about their local libraries, and that is a great platform for this organization to build on going forward.

In terms of going forward, we are really starting to talk about our mission as formed around four principles or pillars:[2] reading and literacy is still at the core,

---

[2] I have based this on work by Wayne Wiegund on the history of US public libraries.

whether it's printed materials or digital materials. The role of the physical space and the programs that we use to animate the spaces is the second core pillar of our service. The third is the rapidly-evolving 'access to information' principle, which traditionally might have been reference. Today, that is more about teaching people skills in many cases – except for the specialized collections, where specialized traditional reference still plays a key role. Fourthly is the responsibility of preserving our cultural heritage. Of the approximately 23 million items in our collection, probably about six million are treated as special collections which span everything from the history of the anti-slavery movement in Boston at a very important time in our history to the Shakespeare exhibition – that will open this evening – that contains the first folios of Shakespeare's works dating back to the 1600s. Some of these works will be on display for the very first time, and our goal in putting this exhibition together is to really drive towards greater accessibility. While it is great to see the works and appreciate them as rare items, understanding the narrative journey tells us about the evolution of language and the role that his works and his forgers and copiers had from 1600 to 1800 to today. We are also, then, building upon this exhibition by having readings of the plays and performances by local theatre companies inside a variety of library locations. It becomes not just an explicitly educational, but also a broad cultural and fun experience.

Could you describe the staffing structure inside the Boston Public Library?

Today, we have about 475 full-time employees across all of the locations and about another 100–150 part-time and contract staff. Those are organized into a number of divisions, which are either operationally-focused such as finance, operations, and technology or public service focused that are organized around programming and strategic initiatives, etc.

Can you describe your typical day at work?

Maybe a typical hour at work would be easier to describe these days! I used to say that I didn't know what I would be doing one day to the next, but it really is coming down to one hour to the next. For example, today, we were just finalising our press release for the Shakespeare exhibition tonight. Sometimes, I have to get the work I am getting my own done before the day starts because once the day starts, it's largely back-to-back meetings from about 8:00 a.m. to 5:00 p.m. Then, there are evening and weekend events, whether it's introducing an author or the opening of an exhibition or one of our partners' programs. It is a very full day and a full week.

Why did you make the decision to undertake a Ph.D. program? It is not a part of the job requirement, isn't it?

It is not, but I think it will lend further credibility to being head of this institution. While I think that the library staff here respect me because I have been here for seven years already, both the symbolic value and the substantive value of having a degree in the area is important. But, to be honest, for me personally, it is also a bit about returning to my academic roots and being able to look on this as the opportunity to blend research interests and the academic world with public service. BPL is one of two public libraries in the U.S. that is also designated as a research library. Most all of the other official research libraries are at universities (or are private). We almost have a split identity, if you will, but we walk this fine line between your typical public library but also have a lot in common with the university libraries because of the depth and breadth of our collections.

Can you describe your leadership and management style?

To me, collaborative leadership is the essence of good leadership, because it allows you to take the strengths of every individual, but also to have each individual on the team learn from each other and problem-solve in a way that is much more effective. You cannot however always do that when you are dealing with a crisis or triaging a problem – that has to be a little more authoritative and directed. I think that from a management point of view, it is more about knowing what is the right style or approach for the right situation.

I can give you one particular example, there was a big issue for us here a year and a half ago, related to the discovery that two very valuable prints – pieces of art – were missing from the collection. They were ultimately found here, and they were still in a secure area, but they weren't where they were supposed to be. That is not a situation where you sit around in a room and throw around ideas. That is a situation where you have had either a collections management failure or a security failure, and you want to basically take the triage model from emergency services or a healthcare setting to deal with that problem. It includes assessing what the cause was, addressing the immediate problem, and then putting procedures in process and in place so that it doesn't happen again – which part of the problem must you solve first and quickly and which do you regroup on later.

What part about your job as President of the Boston Public Library do you find to be the most rewarding and most frustrating?

About a year and a half ago, we opened a new children's library here, and we put a lot of thought into the design of the space – both from an interior decoration point of view but also a point of view of best practices around early literacy and the children's librarianship field. Whenever you are having a bad day, you can just pop into that space for about five minutes, and you see these young toddlers, 4–8 year olds, 8–12 year olds just making the space their own. It is really uplifting, because it reminds you of why we do what we do and that when we put the right amount of planning and thought into a project and it pays off the way we intend it, it is incredibly gratifying. At the other end of the spectrum, we have this Shakespeare exhibition that I was talking about earlier, and that will put on display some of our rarest objects in a way that should animate the whole experience. That, too, is very uplifting and an inspiring aspect of the role. What is the point of having these 23 million objects if people don't have the opportunities to appreciate them, understand them, be inspired by them, and take something away? Those are two very clear examples about why I enjoy the job.

The frustrating aspects tend to be more operational. When you are dealing with a 150-year old or older organization and you want to bring in new procedures that will make things a little bit more efficient or customer-facing – that can be an uphill struggle. But, it is a necessary one, and one that will ultimately pay off.

Boston is one of the oldest cities in the U.S. and continues to be one of the most important centers for education and culture. In addition, many high-ranked universities can be found in Boston. In this context, what roles does BPL play in the community?

From the academic community, first of all, we have very strong relationships with Harvard University[3] and MIT[4] – both on the depth of their special collections but also in some of the work around open data. Northeastern University[5] is a strong partner around digitization. Recently, there was another exhibition that we contributed to, which is a partnership between Boston College[6], the Houghton

---

3 Harvard University – Homepage. Available at: http://www.harvard.edu/
4 MIT (Massachusetts Institute of Technology) – Homepage. Available at: http://web.mit.edu/
5 Northeastern University – Homepage. Available at: https://www.northeastern.edu/
6 Boston College – Homepage. Available at: http://www.bc.edu/

Library[7] at Harvard, and also the Isabella Stewart Gardner Museum.[8] We are also trying to be a bridge between some of the academic world and the cultural institutions in Boston. We see ourselves as playing both on the education side as well as on the arts and culture side of our civic goals. That is before you get to the core of public library service, which is really about serving people of all ages in their communities, and online and a variety of needs. We know from some of the studies done in the last five to ten years that libraries are probably the last remaining trusted entity in government – there is almost a level of distrust in every single other aspect of government. We have a responsibility to continue to live up to what it means to deal with civic engagement. We are people's first and sometimes only positive interaction with government.

How do you want BPL to make a positive difference in the lives of everyone in the community?

I think that if we were to jump ahead five years from now, if you were interviewing people on the street, I would want them to say two things: (1) "The Boston Public Library makes a positive impact on my life" – it could be access to reading material for entertainment purposes, it could be that we helped them get a job, it could be that they came to find an inspiring author here at the library, it could be their third space. In today's world, we need alternatives to home and work that are not the online experience, but can mesh with that in a way that allows people to be physically present to each other. I think that libraries can play that role. (2) When they list the top five institutions that are special to them in Boston, that BPL should be one of those.

Boston versus New York City and places like Seattle – how are the attitudes and expectations of the local communities toward these libraries different from each other?

I think there are many similarities between the large, urban libraries – Seattle, San Francisco, Chicago, Los Angeles, New York, Boston. But, I think there are two things that are special about Boston and New York in particular. It is the depth of the research collection because we hold the cultural treasures that go back, in our case, over a millennium. Also, it is how passionate people are about their branch library in their local community. I think we see that uniquely in Boston and

---

7 Houghton Library – Homepage. Available at: http://hcl.harvard.edu/libraries/houghton/
8 Isabella Stewart Gardner Museum – Homepage. Available at: http://www.gardnermuseum.org/home

New York; Chicago as well possibly others. It's the uniqueness of the cities that gives the libraries their own individual uniqueness.

If a young person is inspired to become a public librarian, what sort of advice would you give to him or her?

I would say that if someone is inspired, it is probably because they have a personal connection with a librarian or library staffer that has been good to them or has helped them in some way. My advice would be to talk to that person about why they became a librarian, and then how do you evaluate the choices. The library field has many specialties within it. We see, obviously, such traditional disciplines as the children's and youth librarian, the archival specialist, the cataloging or collections specialist. But, over the last five to ten years, there is this interesting convergence between Information Science or Information Technology and Computer Science and Library Information Science. I think there are huge opportunities that go beyond working in the public library but are useful to the public library and society generally. They are simply critical to society. I would try and have a dialogue with this person that would say, "Don't think of the library as a profession that only prepares you to be in the library. Think about it as a profession or a degree that prepares you to deal with the important role of information in society as a whole."

In your opinion, why do we still need libraries?

I think if you look at recent visitor numbers and foot traffic and also the e-book borrowing and physical books circulation numbers, we are seeing a very healthy pattern now. While I think that the use and borrowing of e-books and digital materials will continue to increase, we are reaching a point where we know people still want to touch the real thing. In fact, where we have digitized, for example, some manuscripts from the medieval period, when we have that high-quality digital material available online, it actually drives people to come and want to see the real thing as well. My answer to your question is, it is not the electronic or digital version instead of the printed material, but it is *in addition to*. The foot traffic and visitor numbers that we are seeing seem to bear that out. Will some people go out and buy their own book or visit a bookstore rather than borrow it? Sure. But, do you want the high fidelity and quality e-book that you can borrow from the library, or do you want and, what is largely a poor-quality and not necessarily well-OCRed limited version that is available from other online sources? That is a choice that you will have to make. In some cases, good is good enough. In other cases, you want the fully-accessible materials. Not to mention those that can't afford to purchase their own copies.

How do you think the library will evolve in the next five to ten years?

I think we will see, and we are seeing already, the importance of spaces that you can go visit and that are warm, welcoming, and inviting as opposed to years ago, when they would have been rows and rows of books and whether or not they were inviting was immaterial. I think that the importance of civic gathering spaces is critical. I think that the role of technology will grow. But, when we are designing spaces today, we try to build in flexibility to these spaces, because we don't really know with certainty what's coming next. The important thing is to be ready for what is coming next and to be able to evolve with it. We have to continue to look at the research and the consumer trends and technology trends; continue to look at new small businesses and what new innovations are being done not just with technology, but with the nature of work itself and how people are living and working together. In some ways, the perfect library futurist is an entrepreneur, a technologist, a sociologist, a social media guru – that's the kind of skillset they need to have.

Would you like to say anything to conclude this interview?

I would like to wish you luck on your project. I am interested to read the book at some point and see how my experiences match with others. I just want to end by saying that public libraries are here to stay and are a more and more important part of, (at least, U.S.) society – I don't have the authority to speak beyond that – as long as they continue to evolve. That is the key. We must continue to evolve, but our future is bright.

17 Felton Thomas, Jr.

Director of Cleveland Public Library

Introduction

Established in 1869, the Cleveland Public Library (CPL) is the third-largest research public library in the United States. The system operates with the Main Library in downtown Cleveland and 27 branches throughout the city. In fact, the library was the first one in the U.S. to offer its users direct access to open stacks of books to browse at their convenience – in other words, library users were allowed to directly choose their desired reading materials instead of having to ask library staff to retrieve books, which was the prior standard practice. Since January 2009, Felton Thomas, Jr. has been serving as the Executive Director of CPL. Since beginning his tenure there, Thomas has furthered the mission of CPL to be "The People's University" by launching initiatives aimed at addressing community needs in the areas of access to technology, education, economic development, etc.

Thomas is also a recipient of many professional awards, including a "Mover and Shaker" by the Library Journal and acting as a fellow in the Urban Library Council's Executive Leadership Institute. Nationally, in 2015, Thomas was elected as President of the Public Library Association, and began service in 2016. In the following interview, he tells us how a 13-year-old boy of a humble background became the youngest employee at the Las Vegas Clark County Library in history, and, 30 years later, became the Executive Director of a major library system in the U.S. In addition, he discusses the ideology behind his "Drum Major for Change" management.

Fig. 17.1: Felton Thomas, Jr., Director of Cleveland Public Library (Photo: Cleveland Public Library).

DOI 10.1515/9783110533347-018

Fig. 17.2: Main Library (Photo: Cleveland Public Library).

Fig. 17.3: Main Library (Photo: Cleveland Public Library).

Fig. 17.4: Main Library, Indoor Garden (Photo: Cleveland Public Library).

Could we begin this interview by introducing yourself – for example, your professional training and educational background, what did you study at your university, do you come from a family of librarians?

My name is Felton Thomas, and I am the Director of the Cleveland Public Library and current President of the Public Library Association (PLA).[1] I received my Bachelor's degree from the University of Nevada, Las Vegas[2], a Master's of Library and Information Science from the University of Hawaii, and I am currently working on my Ph.D. at Simmons College[3] in Boston – I am a dissertation away from receiving it!

I started the whole reading and library thing in my family. My sister is a librarian and my brother works in system technology in libraries. But, everybody else is off in other things.

---

1 Public Library Association (PLA) – Homepage. Available at: http://www.ala.org/pla/
2 University of Nevada, Las Vegas – Homepage. Available at: https://www.unlv.edu/
3 Simmons College – Homepage. Available at: http://www.simmons.edu/

I read somewhere on your online biography that at age 13, you became the youngest employee at the Las Vegas Clark County Library District in history. Could you shed more light on that story?

I lived in a very poor neighborhood in Las Vegas, as my friends started getting into gangs on my way home, instead of going out and being with them, I would just go into the library. I ended up going to the library every day. When I was 13 to the degree that the librarian there told me that I should work here. I had just finished eighth grade, and the idea was that you could work when you were a high schooler. They also didn't realize that the other rule was that you had to be 14. But, I was a little bit ahead of myself in school, and so, I was actually 13. So, I was the only person to be able to be hired at 13 in the library system.

You started going to the library when you were a small child. What did the library mean to you at that time when you were still a little boy?

I was the oldest of seven, so my home was always filled with kids, and it was always loud. The idea of going to the library was that it was the only place that I could focus, it was quiet, and it was safe. It was the only place in my area and community that wasn't burned down except for the churches, so that was my choice. I was able to go there and find a safe place. I was always a reader, but this allowed me to focus and start reading all the time on things that I really wanted to read. It was a very good space for me. To get a job there was just icing on the cake.

What kind of work would you be doing at the library?

I was shelving books. I think the reason that I was successful was that I came in, and I did my work. There were always books that needed to be shelved, there was always areas that needed to be cleaned up, there was always things that needed to be done. I became known as somebody who really concentrated on and focused on their work.

When you were a teenager, did you ever imagine yourself becoming the director of a major city library?

No. Actually, it was surprising because I didn't really start thinking about being a director or even a librarian until I was probably in my mid-20s. When I was 15, people started talking to the director of the library system about me, and they said, "You should talk to Felton because he has the things, he has the smarts, he can be a director one day." Out of the blue, I was just shelving books one day, and the director came out and talked to me about being a director. I was shocked that he would take the time out of his day and schedule to talk to me. It was interesting, but even then, I had never really thought about being a librarian. I was going to do something in sports or a psychologist or something of that nature. But, that's kind of how it went.

Can you tell me about your current responsibilities and specialties at the Cleveland Public Library[4]?

My responsibilities as the Executive Director of the Cleveland Public Library are to make sure that the library is responsive to its mission, which is to be the center of learning for the whole city of Cleveland. We do it through our specialties, which we are the third-largest public research library in the country. We have some of the largest research collections in the world, and we have 27 public library branches. We do a lot in the community, and then we do a lot around research. It is very much like the Hong Kong public library system – there is a main Central Library with a lot of neighborhood branches that are very much situated around the communities.

Could you describe the economy of Cleveland? What is the city's economy based on?

It used to be situated around the steel industry and manufacturing. But, that has changed, which has caused Cleveland's economy to really decline in the 1980s and 1990s. We are trying to get ourselves back out of it now, because we have one of the best hospitals in the world, the Cleveland Clinic, and a lot of different hospitals are in the community. So, we are moving toward being biomedical.

Have you always worked in libraries? Did you have other careers before your career in librarianship?

Since I was 13, I have pretty much been in libraries all my life. When I graduated from undergrad with a degree in Psychology, I was thinking that I was ready to leave the library, and everybody was like, "We're your family. We don't want you to leave. You can go to library school." I was looking at the list, and I said that I would like to go to the University of Hawaii for graduate school.

Could you describe your career path to becoming the Director of the Cleveland Public Library? For example, where did you previously work before coming to the Cleveland Public Library?

---

4 Cleveland Public Library – Homepage. Available at: http://cpl.org/

I was born and raised in Las Vegas and worked in the library system as a page. I then moved up into the circulation department, and I moved up into the research department, then to an assistant branch manager, then a branch manager. Then, I became a regional manager, and that is where I ended in Las Vegas before the director position opened up in Cleveland. I was recruited for the job here, and that is how I became the Director of the Cleveland Public Library.

Can you give a brief introduction of the Cleveland Public Library – including the history of the library?

The Cleveland Public Library is one of the historic libraries in the country. It was founded in 1869 – almost 150 years old. The library has been situated in and based off of the New York Public Library (NYPL)[5] and the Boston Public Library (BPL).[6] We are the third-largest public research library. We have one of the largest collections of materials on chess in the world. We have some great collections in which people from all over the world come and view here in Cleveland. In this sense, one of my responsibilities is to balance the commitment to research for those folks who want to come to a research library, and do research for a variety of things they are going to do with also being a popular library for the 400,000 people who live in the city of Cleveland, and our 27 branch libraries based in the neighborhoods, and making sure that those neighborhoods have what they need to be successful.

Can you give some highlights of your Library's collections and services?

I talked a little bit about our chess collection – we have one of the largest collections of materials on chess in the world. It is ever-growing. We have one of our original board members who left an endowment to buy pretty much everything we could buy on chess. We continue to bring in chess sets and things of that nature, so it is a wonderful collection.

We also have a variety of science collections and a variety of architecture collections for the city of Cleveland that we continue to use endowments to support. I think that one of the collections that we're growing is a sports collection around Cleveland sports. Since the 1880s, we have had Cleveland sports teams.

I think that public libraries in general are starting to move their programs to being services. I can tell you a number of services that we provide in the Library. One would be that we provided 150,000 meals to school-age children last year

---

5 New York Public Library (NYPL) – Homepage. Available at: https://www.nypl.org/
6 Boston Public Library (BPL) – Homepage. Available at: http://www.bpl.org/

in the Cleveland Public Library. But then, we also provide services, for example, partnering with the Legal Aid Society[7] to have lawyers come in and help the community members, who have different legal needs at our libraries per month. We also have people who come in to provide financial aid services.

When you were talking about your library providing free legal aid services for the users, what kinds of people would come to use that service?

It could be someone who is having issues with their Social Security, maybe someone whose family member has died and there is no will, probate assistance. It would be something that is a civil case – not criminal cases – or civil law where you can sit down with them and provide them with assistance, or longer ways with talking with them through their case so they can get there. It is really amazing. We do it at one of our libraries per month, and people come in lined up at 7:30 a.m. – we open at 10 a.m. I will drive by and people will be lining up at 7:30 a.m. to be prepared to come in for legal services at those libraries.

Who designed and initiated this legal aid program at your Library?

We have a head of programming, and this person's job is to look for programs that we can provide that are going to be helpful to the community. We just started a new one. A lot of our community members have outstanding student loans. So we are working with a group that will come in and sit with people who have outstanding student loans, and talk with them about ways they can consolidate them, ways they can work with the government to clear up their outstanding loans, that they can get back on track, and how they should pay them back so that they can better situate their financial situation.

The Cleveland Public Library is the third-largest public research library in the United States after the New York Public Library and the Boston Public Library. Comparing the Cleveland Public Library with these other libraries, what are the users' needs and expectations towards the services? How are they different from other libraries?

I think that New York is off in its own place. The New York Public Library has a series of research libraries across the city of New York, and they are so big. They have huge endowments to go along with those research collections. Whereas we have all of our collections in one library, they have theirs spread over maybe a dozen libraries throughout the city. We in no way that can compare to them. One of

---

[7] Legal Aid Society – Homepage. Available at: http://www.legal-aid.org/en/home.aspx

our jobs, though, is to look at what are the collections that are the most important to the city of Cleveland. So, they may be looking nationwide for their collections, but we are looking at the collections that might be of most interest to the city of Cleveland. We have a two million-item collection of photographs about the city of Cleveland. Those kinds of things are important for us, and for any kind of researcher or individuals who either come from Cleveland, or are looking for information about institutions in Cleveland.

Could you describe your staffing structure at the Cleveland Public Library?

From top-down, we have myself as the Director, and I have a Deputy Director, and then we have two chiefs who serve as my executive team. Under that is our leadership team. Then we have managers of our main library and then managers of the branch libraries, and then, our staff.

How many professional librarians do you have in your team?

For the library itself, I think the number is that we have over 120 folks that have M.L.S. degrees. We have a total number of 700 staff.

Can you describe your typical day at work, or is there a typical day?

So, a typical day at work would probably look like this: I get in probably around 8:30 a.m., and I will start the process – I have a variety of meetings and schedules that go on through the day. I am also involved in a lot of organizations, so I will go out and do presentations before organizations. Typically, I will have some kind of lunch that I will have to do with some stakeholders in the organization or in some group. Then, I will start my series of meetings again after that with staff, with organizations, or whatever. Then, I have a dinner at night, and, hopefully, that is the only thing I have. Sometimes, I will have two dinners I have to run between – the record is three! I just run there back and forth until I get home.

What time of the day do you usually write your assignments or your dissertation for your Ph.D. studies?

I find my best writing time to be early morning. I will go to sleep around 12 midnight, and wake up at 5:00 a.m., and write for a little while before everybody wakes up. That is the time when I am able to focus and concentrate.

You are already in a top position. Why do you choose to undertake the Ph.D. program?

One of the things is that I got into a program called the Managerial, Leadership and Information Doctoral Program. The idea was that they wanted to get folks who were already practicing librarians to learn the research side, so that we could go out and become directors, and then add that research component into our directorship. I use a great deal of databases in my work as a director, which comes from understanding research and all that. A lot of folks don't do that, and that was the basis by which people go through this program. It was more about how to take that research aspect for my doctorate and then take it and do it in the real world.

Can you describe your management and leadership style?

I have been fortunate to have been in libraries for a very, very long time. So, I have done pretty much everyone's job. My inspiration is around trying to inspire folks to recognize how important their job is to the overall goal. I can sit with a page, who might be 16 and doesn't understand why it is important to have books in a certain order, and I can say, "You are the foundation of this library. If someone goes to look for a book, and you've misplaced it, they will never find that book. All the people who ordered the book, the people who have talked with the patron about the book, and have gone to look for that book is based on your important job in making sure that book is in the right space." My job is to do that same thing with everybody throughout the system. They can see how important it is for everybody to work together as a team.

In one of your online lectures, you talked about being a "Drum Major for Change." Can you elaborate more on that?

I am actually a drummer, so I looked at it from the standpoint that a Drum major is someone who leads folks – someone who goes and walks through the parade and is taking in everybody as the leader. My job is to be that role. I am not playing any other instruments, but my job is to be out in front of everybody, and have everybody walk in time. If we do that as an organization, we will be successful at what we are trying to do.

I understand that you are a very accomplished musician. Could you tell us what kind of style of music do you specialize in?

I am a drummer, so I have been in lots of different types of bands. I was in a heavy metal band when I was younger. I don't really play as much anymore, but I think that one of the things that I learned from being in a band, and learned from being in music was trying to get everyone to harmonize around what we are trying to do. You have all these different musical instruments, and they are all trying to sound good, but everybody has to do a different thing for it to all sound good for the community.

In your opinion, what traits or attributes do most successful library directors have in common?

I think the first one is that they need to be good listeners. One of the traits that I see in folks who are not as successful is that they don't listen to anyone. To me, having respect for everyone in the organization is important. Some of the most important things I find out about our organization I can find out through some of our lower-ranking staff members. I want to make sure that people are recognized, and they should be treated with the same level of respect.

Another thing I talk to our staff about is being selfless or sacrifice. As a director, I think that I have to lead by example. I have to show folks that I am willing to work extra time. You will see me working and I will be out here in the community. I will be out until 9 o'clock and I'll be at breakfasts at 7:30 a.m. so that they recognize that I am working as hard as they are and am sacrificing my comfort just as they have to. Lastly, I think that integrity is huge. I think that integrity means, to me, to do what you say you are going to do. Staff and people in the community look at you and say, "Is this a person of integrity?" I think that most successful library directors have those three traits I just talked about – they are selfless, they have integrity, and they have respect for everybody who they walk into contact with.

Which part of your job do you find most rewarding and which part do you find most frustrating?

I think I will start with what I find the most frustrating – libraries are still seen and perceived like libraries of the past. I will talk to folks, and people will say, "Do we really need libraries? I can find all of the information online, you guys are just a warehouse of books, and you guys must be doing horribly now because nobody reads books – they can just read e-books." Then, I will ask, "Have you been to a library in the past 20 years?" – because that is in no way what we are.

For the thing that gives me the most joy: this weekend, we did a big *Mini Maker Faire* inside our main building. We had folks from all over demonstrating technology – showing off drones in one of our libraries, and many other really neat innovations in technology. We had over 5,000 parents and kids coming through our library. Just seeing the kids' faces as they went from place to place doing all of this and recognizing that they had that ability to be creative. It was people from all communities here – people from all levels of class, race. It was just some really good things.

Can you describe the overall social and economic landscape of Cleveland? You had said that your library had a free lunch program for underprivileged children during the summertime. Why do you think there is a need for such a program? How is it related to the current economy of the city?

Cleveland, right now, has the second-highest level of poverty of children in the United States. While it is certainly a city that is on the rebound, that is finding its economic legs, there are folks doing really, really well here, but there is still a significant number of community members who are struggling – especially children.

What we have found was that children, during the summer, were not having lunches because at school, they would always get lunches. But, during the summer, schools were no longer providing lunch, so these kids were struggling to find nutritious food during the summer. So, a number of places – including our library – started to say, "How can we be helpful?" We pretty much started there, and we have provided around 20,000 meals per summer. But then, we started having conversations with them about their kids coming after school into the libraries, and they would be hungry. We started working with the food bank to provide meals for them, and then we would tutor them as they are getting those meals. So, they are doing after-school tutoring and giving meals and really being able to focus on getting their schoolwork done.

When you are talking about these children, would their parents be unemployed or would they be doing blue-collar jobs?

Both. We have had kids whose parents are unemployed and looking for work and then we have a number of children whose parents are underemployed, and so they are working, but they are barely making enough money to get by, so there may not be enough food at home for them. Many of them can't come home until their parents can pick them up after they get off of work. We are more than willing to help the children have a productive period of time after school. It is not just if you don't have any place to send your kids, just send them to the library. We want them to know that their children can come to the library, work on their schoolwork, get a meal or a snack during that period of time so that when they are picked up at around 5:30 or 6:00 p.m., their children have already gotten their homework done, they are not hungry, and they can be ready to go home and continue on whatever they need to do.

Where does the funding for this lunch program come from?

The food bank funds those meals, and everything goes through that. They do fundraising to make sure that they can get the funding to provide the meals. We just provide the space.

In what ways do you want the Cleveland Public Library to make a difference in people's lives in the community?

I mentioned when I came on that Cleveland had a number of deficits in the community that we need to talk about and start examine about how we can help solve them. So, we started examining what they were: one was food for our kids, one is crime, and one is education. We just started listing what kinds of programs we were doing and how we could better situate those programs, so that they could really just start solving the deficits in the community. That is what we have been focusing on for the past seven years since I have been here: what are the community deficits, how can we help solve them, and what other partner institutions can we bring into it? That is where we see all of these partners coming in. There are folks who started and went to college, they racked up a lot of debt, and they can't go back to school, they can't do anything, and they're struggling. So, let's bring folks in who can help. They can talk with them about their student debt, and give them a plan to cut the debt down while they go ahead and continue working. Those are the types of programs that we are bringing into the community to help people be more successful.

During your tenure, your library has maintained a five-star status and was named one of the top innovators by the Urban Libraries Council for its use of technology and data to inform decision making. Can you shed more light on this?

We have been very fortunate with the library system that we have been in. This year, we were named a Five Star Library again, so we are proud of the fact that while we are a public research library, the Five Star Library is based on a number of statistics. Libraries like us (public research libraries) generally aren't at the top of the list, because you have to circulate a number of books, and you have to have people come in for a variety of different things. We have been able to balance that between our research side and our popular side. To be Number 4 in the country as far as our numbers, it is just fabulous for our library system.

    We are also proud of our innovations around here. One of the big deficits we have found is that people would talk to us about their children in underprivileged communities didn't have access to the technology that folks in other communities did. We opened up our TechCentral[8] [Cleveland Public Library]

---

8 TechCentral, Cleveland Public Library – Homepage. Available at: http://cpl.org/thelibrary/subjectscollections/techcentral/

downtown, which is a technology lab, a kind of fabrication lab. We opened up four – two on one side of the city, and two on the other side of the city – different branches of similar types of smaller services so that community members in our libraries would be able to have access to 3-D printing, see laser engraving, see what they can do, and start working and creating these things.

Could you tell us about your Library's "MyTune" project? What is the driving force behind its success and how does it increase the popularity of your library in the community?

So, we are fortunate that in our library community and in our city, we have the Rock n' Roll Hall of Fame[9], which is obviously an icon as far as music and all of those things. We also have a company that also provides downloads – we pay for the downloads, and the community members are able to download music to their phones, computers, and things of that nature. It is the same as many libraries across the country, but because of our connection to the Rock n' Roll Hall of Fame, we are able to partner with, talk about, and do programming around individuals who have their music through these companies. But, we can feature some of the big rock n' roll folks because of their connection to the Rock n' Roll Hall of Fame.

MyTune, in my sense, is really important. I talked about those folks who don't believe that the library can be important to them – they have their computers at home and can have access to information there. But, we try to say, "Did you know that you can download music from your phone? That you can see a biography about Jimi Hendrix or some of your favorite artists, and connect with and download music by them just by having a library card?" That's why it is important about getting people throughout the city who might not use us to see that the library does a lot more things than just be a repository for books.

Public libraries across the country have access to different databases and database companies that sell music. Our difference is that we tie it into the Rock n' Roll Hall of Fame, which is in the city of Cleveland.

If a young person is inspired to become a librarian, what would you say to him or her if this person asks you for advice?

I would say to them that the library has allowed me to change people's lives. I speak to a group of children, and I will ask them, "How many of you want to be

---

9 Rock and Roll Hall of Fame – Homepage. Available at: https://www.rockhall.com/

a librarian?" and nobody raises their hand. Then, I will say, "How many of you want to do something that's going to make people better?" Everybody raises their hand. So, I will talk to them about the importance of what libraries do and how many people have told me how I have affected their lives and make their lives better. Then, I ask them again about how many people want to be librarians, and I still only get two or three hands, but I was able to get two or three people to raise their hands. It is at that point that people realize when I talk to folks about being a librarian, I say when you want to affect and change people's lives, then the library is a great place to do that. If you go into it with that focus, you will have a very successful career.

Before we conclude this interview, would you like to say something inspiring for the readers?

I think that I will share a quick story with you. I was fortunate to have a seat next to the Surgeon-General of the United States, and this position is the highest medical doctor in the US. She said that she is not a general, but rather a colonel and a commissioned officer. She was talking to me, and she found out I was a librarian. She said, "I'm going to tell a story, and after I tell the story, I want you to come to me because I want to tell you why that is so important."

She started to tell a story about the other commanders she would meet – it was a funny story. One of the aircraft carriers was going through the seas, and to the right, they see this light in the distance, and they are going to go right to where they think that boat is. They send a message to the boat, and they say, "We're coming through right where you are, please move 15 degrees to your left." It gets a response, "Well, we're not going to move. You move 15 degrees to the south." They're super upset, and the captain finally screams at them, "We're a US aircraft carrier. We will run you over! Will you please move 15 degrees to the north?" It finally comes back with a response of, "Do what you have to do. We're a lighthouse."

The idea was that they would run through and kill a lot of people because of running into a lighthouse. Afterwards, I stopped and talked to her, and she said, "Felton, the reason I wanted to say that story for you guys is, because I think that libraries are lighthouses. Many people in their life are in boats going through rocky waters and on the rocks. Think of it as you guys are the light that helps people make their direction during those difficult times." I tell that story a lot when I go and talk to staff members in other libraries because they need to recognize that the libraries are the lighthouses for difficult communities. They need to realize that their job is to keep the light on.

Further Readings

Cleveland Public Library History [YouTube]. Available at: https://www.youtube.com/watch?v=YHxg2iPH5zU

Cleveland Public Library - The Drum Major for Change: Felton Thomas at TEDxCLE 2013 [YouTube]. Available at: https://www.youtube.com/watch?v=YtsrHrvmPK0

Felton Thomas 10.16.13 [YouTube]. Available at: https://www.youtube.com/watch?v=IL46cwPGyfs&t=6s

Felton Thomas, Jr. - Cleveland Public Library. Available at: http://csreports.aspeninstitute.org/Task-Force-on-Learning-and-the-Internet/2014/participants/details/122/Felton-Thomas

Felton Thomas Jr. continues a legacy at the Cleveland Public Library. Available at: http://www.hawaii.edu/news/2015/09/30/uh-alumni-profile-felton-thomas-jr-continues-a-legacy-at-cleveland-public-library/

Gaining and Educating Public Library Stakeholders – Felton Thomas [YouTube]. Available at: https://www.youtube.com/watch?v=7dg71J9RufE

Library Director Felton Thomas Elected as 2016-2017 Public Library Association President. Available at: http://cpl.org/library-director-felton-thomas-elected-as-2016-2017-public-library-association-president/

Message from the Director - Felton Thomas, Jr. [YouTube]. Available at: https://www.youtube.com/watch?v=zwhIK8Bn5jw

Oder, Norman. (December, 2008). *Felton Thomas named Cleveland Public Library Director. Library Journal Archive Content.* Available at: http://lj.libraryjournal.com/2008/12/managing-libraries/felton-thomas-named-cleveland-public-library-director/

Our Advertisers: Cleveland Public Library [YouTube]. Available at: https://www.youtube.com/watch?v=JhIACqHeZKU

The People's University: A Look Inside the Cleveland Public Library [YouTube]. Available at: https://www.youtube.com/watch?v=pKGUDiCorBA&t=569s

PLA President Felton Thomas Jr. releases statement on public libraries and inclusiveness. Available at: http://www.ala.org/news/press-releases/2016/11/pla-president-felton-thomas-jr-releases-statement-public-libraries-and

VIDEO: Cleveland Public Library Shows Off Renovations [YouTube]. Available at: https://www.youtube.com/watch?v=scZcfw7xCc0

VIDEO: TechCentral at Cleveland Public Library [YouTube]. Available at: https://www.youtube.com/watch?v=6jlfx2N6mzw

18 Mary Anne Hodel

Director/CEO, Orange County Library System

Introduction

The Orange County Library System (OCLS) is a major public library system located in Orlando, Florida. The whole system is made up of a total of 16 different locations – that is, one main library (the Orlando Public Library, the headquarters located in downtown Orlando), and 15 other branch libraries spread throughout the whole Orange County. Highlights of the OCLS services include a great variety of gaming, lifelong learning programs, computer classes taught in both English and Spanish and Haitian Creole, and professional studios like the Melrose Center, etc.

A Political Science major and MLIS graduate from the Catholic University in Washington, D.C., Mary Anne Hodel has spent a number of years working for different libraries – once at a consulting firm, a US Air Force base library, and academic libraries – before finally landing a career in public librarianship. Hodel became the CEO of the OCLS in 2002. In the following interview, Hodel discusses the challenges and joys as well as the rewards for being the leader of a library system with staff that truly believe in the phrase "No Boundaries. Only Possibilities!"

Fig. 18.1: Mary Anne Hodel, Director/CEO, Orange County Library System (Photo: Orange County Library System).

Fig. 18.2: Eatonville Branch (Photo: Orange County Library System).

Fig. 18.3: Melrose Center (Photo: Orange County Library System).

Fig. 18.4: Orange County Library System's Learning Central (Photo: Orange County Library System).

Could we begin this interview by first introducing yourself, for example, your professional training and education background? For example, what did you study at university?

I earned a Bachelor's degree in Political Science with minor in Economics and History from the University of Wisconsin (Madison)[1] and a Master's degree in Library Science from Catholic University in Washington, D.C. I also did further study in an Executive Education program at the University of Michigan[2] in Ann Arbor.

Have you always worked in libraries? Could you tell us more about your path to becoming the Director/CEO of the Orange County Library System (OCLS)[3]? Could you also describe your current role and areas of responsibility as the Director/CEO of the Orange County Library System?

I have always been attracted to learning in all forms, and I have worked in libraries my entire career. After finishing my master's degree, I worked for a library-consulting

---

1 University of Wisconsin - Madison – Homepage. Available at: http://www.wisc.edu/
2 University of Michigan – Homepage. Available at: http://umich.edu/
3 Orange County Library System – Homepage. Available at: https://www.ocls.info/

firm doing a serials inventory contract. I then worked for the U.S. Department of the Interior[4] as its project manager for the automation of its very extensive serials collection on natural resources. I worked in Germany at a U.S. Air Force[5] base library (Ramstein Air Base[6]) that served the reading needs of U.S. troops, and their families stationed in the western part of Germany, near Saarbrücken. Later I worked at Edward Bennett Williams Law Library of Georgetown University[7] in Washington D.C., supervising a team to update the collection's holdings and automate the library's bibliographic and holdings records. From there, I went on to manage the central library of the Enoch Pratt Library[8] in Baltimore, Maryland.

Subsequently, I was selected to be the Director of the public library in Ann Arbor, Michigan when it split from the Ann Arbor Public School System[9] to become the Ann Arbor District Library. This meant establishing the library as its own independent entity, including setting up brand new library accounting system, banking and investment accounts, state and local reporting systems, budget, purchasing agreements, vendor contracts, as well as the library's own policies, business practices, internal rules and procedures, customer and service standards, legal advisors, property leases, union contracts, pay scales, position descriptions, human resources, financial and customer software systems and investments, millage, elected board, board meeting reporting formats and eventually, new services and branches, etc. The library won the Library Journal's Library of the Year Award in 1997.

In 2002, I became the Director/CEO of the Orange County Library System (OCLS) in Orlando, Florida, an independent unit of local government with its own governing board and an operating budget that is approved but not decided upon by the county. One of the Director's responsibilities is being the fiduciary for the library's employee multiple pension plans and health self-insurance fund. When staff have issues dealing with the public, they bring those issues to the Director for resolution, so I am the arbiter for the Trespass Review Committee and have the final word on customer Rules of Conduct infractions. Strategic planning, setting the vision and direction for the system for future services, facilities and training are critical functions of the Director's job.

---

4 U.S. Department of the Interior – Homepage. Available at: https://www.doi.gov/
5 U.S. Air Force – Homepage. Available at: https://www.airforce.com/
6 Ramstein Air Base – Homepage. Available at: http://www.ramstein.af.mil/
7 Georgetown Law Library, Georgetown University – Homepage. Available at: https://www.law.georgetown.edu/library/about/
8 Enoch Pratt Library – Homepage. Available at: http://www.prattlibrary.org/
9 Ann Arbor Public Schools – Homepage. Available at: http://www.a2schools.org/

In legal terms, the following information is summarized from the Orange County Library System's By-Laws. Per these By-Laws, the Library Director shall:
- "Have responsibility to employ, supervise, and terminate employees of the Library.
- Have supervisory charge, control and management responsibility of library facilities, as well as all employees in and about the same; shall draw up rules and regulations for work of library employees, assigning duties to each.
- Be held directly responsible for the care and preservation of the property in charge of the Board; the quality and efficiency of the library services; the accuracy of records; the reliability of the Library's accounts and resources; enforcement of rules; the cleanliness and good condition of the facilities, grounds, and sidewalks, the proper heating, lighting, and ventilation of the facilities; and proper performance of any duty the Board may require.
- Make regular reports of the operations of the Library.
- Have the payrolls properly prepared based on accurate reports of time of the employees and shall be responsible for the prompt payment of employer and employee taxes.
- Provide for orderly and prudent investment of such Library monies as are available beyond current needs."

Could you please provide a brief introduction of the Orange County Library System?

OCLS is established under Florida state law as a unit of local government, specifically an Independent Special Taxing District. This means that the library district is funded by its own line item on county property tax bills. An operating board of five citizens appointed by the city and county approves policies, contracts and purchases over $100,000. It also has the authority to hire and fire the director. The director reports directly to this Board. The library's staff currently numbers approximately over 400, 60% of whom are full-time staff with typical benefits, while 40% are part-time staff. The library operates 16 branch locations and provides free home delivery of materials to over 1,000+ squares miles in Central Florida. The OCLS service area is home to more than 1.2 million people.

In addition to the traditional printed books and magazines for adults and children, the library also supplies DVDs, audio books, MP3s, and a host of digital materials: books, music, databases, videos, movies, sound recordings all in digital format. Digital materials are available for free to download from home or office, and the library system offers training in a wide range of basic, advanced, and professional software packages. We have hands on classes in technology and software from Microsoft Office to Adobe Creative Suite to Python and Maya programming.

A regular set of children's programs, including pre-K and kindergarten readiness, bubble playtimes, language learning for pre-schoolers, toddlers' programs and story times, are offered at all locations throughout the year. There are also programs for special needs children as well.

All of our branches offer a wide array of events and programs for adults, too. We host cooking demonstrations, parenting programs, book clubs, technology meetups, English as a Second Language courses, financial-literacy events and databases, and so much more.

What is the current collection size of the Orange County Library System? Could you also describe what you deem are the highlights of the library collection or services of the whole Orange County Library System?

The physical collection contains approximately 1,600,000 items. Thousands more are available digitally. In addition to offering traditional library services (checking out materials, providing meeting rooms, and providing children's programming, etc.), we have a heavy focus on lifelong learning, specifically technology classes ranging from computer basics to sophisticated software, such as electronic engineering and digital publishing. Adult programming is another example of lifelong learning.

A vibrant and very successful children's summer learning program is conducted in the spring and summer. It features story times, singers, magicians, live animal demonstrations and more. It also offers hands-on Science Technology, Engineering and Math (STEM) programs, featuring introductory circuitry, electronics, coding and programming. Last year, more than 102,930 participated in our summer programs. Besides theses services, the Library conducts family fun programs, featuring local presenters who teach as well as entertain the whole family with music, live animals, actors, engineering lab programs, and science and animal discovery events, etc.

OCLS also offers events for teens and tweens throughout the year, including Battle of the Bands events, dance competitions, clothing swaps and costume events, a comic and graphic-novel club, as well as a teen library corps to help plan teen programs and gaming events.

For adults, the library offers programs in everything from cooking demonstrations with local chefs through our Cuisine Corner program[10] to writers programs that help local authors develop their writing/editing skills and connect with published authors who can coach them through the publishing process. Last year over 355,250 attended our programs system-wide.

---

[10] Cuisine Corner – Orange County Library System – Homepage. Available at: https://www.ocls.info/cuisine-corner.

We also host Book A Pro reservations with librarians to help with specific research questions, as well as Job Finding, Resume and Interview preparation classes for the job seeker. Mind Your Business programs that are geared to the entrepreneur are offered throughout the system.

Right Service Right Time is an OCLS created database that covers the entire state of Florida designed to help fill the emergency needs of residents who have hit hard economic times, like job loss, home eviction, or emergency health or family needs. This automated interactive system supplies up-to-date information from social service providers for available overnight beds, food, diapers, clothing for individuals and families, all geared to any postal zip code in the state. Besides creating the system, OCLS maintains the system and keeps the providers listing current. www.rightservicefl.org/orange/servicetypes.

OCLS is home to a significant genealogy collection, and we host regular events to teach people how to trace their family roots. We also have programs for seniors, and classes for immigrants who wish to prepare for the U.S. Naturalization test / interview and people who need English as a Second Language instruction and support in pronunciation, conversation and writing. OCLS even offers some of its classes – technology classes, in particular – in Spanish and Haitian-Creole. More recently, we've begun to offer sewing and knitting classes, which have proven to be extremely very popular with patrons, young and old alike.

OCLS is also home to the Melrose Center, located in the Orlando Public Library in downtown Orlando, which features professional audio, video, photography, and recording studios, a Maker Space, as well as a simulation lab that offers people instruction and intensive practice in flying aircraft, driving vehicles, operating excavation equipment and forklift machinery. The Melrose Center, which opened in 2014 thanks to a generous donation from the Kendrick B. Melrose Family Foundation, is a very high-tech addition to the library, and it offers training in all of the equipment and software it houses, including the Adobe Creative Suite, VIVE virtual reality software, podcasting and sound booths, and more. This past year, more than 18,982 people used the Melrose Center to learn professional digital skills. These activities in the Melrose Center demonstrate the future direction and role, which all libraries will eventually fulfil for their communities. We are in the process of "Melrosing our branches" to equip them to offer similar programs to local neighborhoods throughout our service area.

The library is also a champion of preserving local history. We operate Orlando Memory[11], a digital compilation of Orlando history created by residents of their favorite memories and stories. Some of the stories, photos and videos were created

---

11 Orlando Memory – Homepage. Available at: http://dc.ocls.info/

by local citizens. Others consist of oral history recordings and photographs done by library staff to supplement the historical record. All are stored digitally at the library and available on the web at http://dc.ocls.info/. We also operate EPOCH (Electronically Preserving Obituaries as Cultural Heritage), a project created by OCLS for the community to save local personal histories, photos, videos, documents and recorded memories of loved ones. By engaging community members to memorialize those they have lost, the fullness of the legacies of the deceased can be preserved for family, researchers and future generations. These can be found at www.epochlegacies.org

Another significant program we operate is ePulp, the library's own e-book platform, designed to host self-published e-books. The e-books in this collection have been reviewed by local community and are available for check out to community card-holders. Learn more about it at www.ocls.info/epulp-submit-ebook.

Please describe the staffing structure at the Orange County Library System?

The Director/CEO reports to the Library Board and in turn has six direct reports who head up the Division of Business Operations (Human Resources, Finance and Facilities), Division of Technical Support (Acquisitions, Computer Operations, Web Administration, Circulation, Special Services (home delivery), Technology and Education Center, and the Melrose Center), Administrator for Life Long Learning (Youth and Adult Services and Learning Central), two administrators for the Division of Public Services (operations for all 15 branches), and Community Relations (Graphics, Promotions and Outreach, Social Media and the Friends of the Library). Fully 75% of our staff are directly involved with delivering services directly to the public and about 25% of staff are responsible for behind the scenes support, both physical, technical and digital infrastructure support. Typical staffing is 11 to 15 staff at large branches. Most large departments/branches include of a mix of both full- and part-time staff.

Could you describe your typical day at work? Is there ever a typical day at work?

A typical day for me varies quite a bit, but each day includes meetings with staff. Frequently, during meetings with administrators we discuss (and hopefully resolve) problems. We are a large organization, so there is no shortage of challenges to be addressed. Meetings with managers also include consideration of ideas for future services as well as the logistics of implementing them. A focus on new services is always a high priority. Meeting and communicating with rank-and-file staff at large is critically important, but a bit of a challenge given our size and the widespread location of our facilities. It is imperative that I meet with staff on a regular basis. Talking to customers, and our partners and other organizations is also a regular responsibility. As complaints bubble up through the layers of

Director/CEO, Orange County Library System — 243

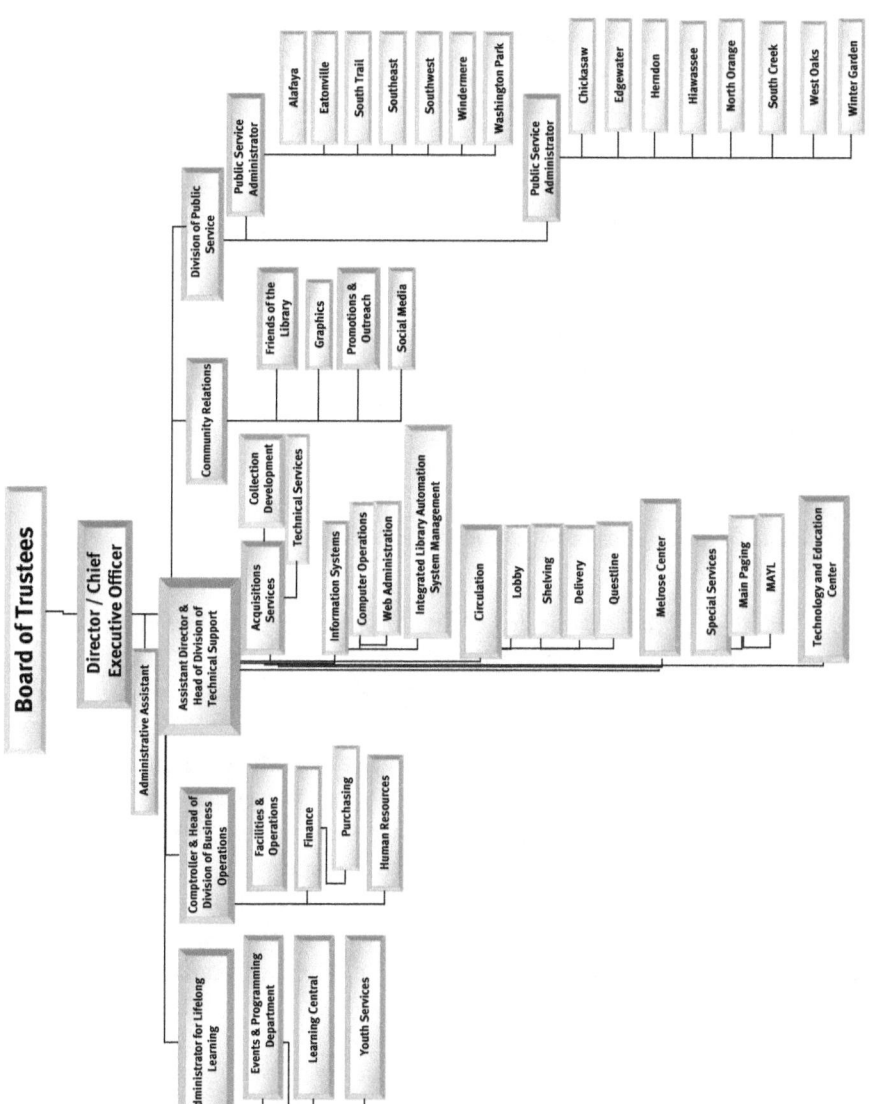

Fig 18.5: Organizational Structure (Diagram: Orange County Library System).

management, the customer who still is not satisfied has the opportunity to address his/her concern with the Director. Depending on the issue, meetings with elected officials, such as members of the Board of County Commissioners also comes with the territory. Lastly, preparing the monthly Board agenda and informational packet and participating in the Board meetings are critical to move solutions forward.

Is fundraising a major part of your job as the Director/CEO of the Orange County Library System?

I feel it is a political necessity for the taxpayers and the political leaders in our community to see that the library actively seeks out donations and aggressively applies for competitive grants to supplement tax revenue. This demonstrates that the library is not just counting on the tax revenue but is using it to leverage local donations to provide goods and services not funded by the local millage. Fundraising is critical both to supplement our current services and provide for new services. If not for significant donations from the Melrose Family, for instance, we would not have the Melrose Center[12], with all its innovative and fantastic digital services we provide to the community.

What scholarly and professional associations are you a part of, and how do they inform you in your work?

I am a member of the American Library Association (ALA)[13] and three of its divisions, Library Information and Technology Association (LITA)[14], Library Leadership and Management Association (LLAMA)[15] and Public Library Association.[16] With regard to LLAMA, I serve on the Management Practices Committee of LLAMA-SASS, where I have been extremely active as the Program Manager for the last few years. I put together informative programs on timely subjects that involve using and promoting various management initiatives and techniques, like the use of mystery shoppers to improve customer service, integrating the use of highly skilled technical professionals into the ranks of the current librarian workforce, and using annual employee surveys. I read the respective journals of these organizations on a regular basis, both to follow the trends as well as to get

---

[12] Melrose Center – Orange County Library System – Homepage. Available at: https://www.ocls.info/classes-events/library/Melrose%20Center.
[13] American Library Association (ALA) – Homepage. Available at: http://www.ala.org/
[14] Library Information and Technology Association (LITA) – Homepage. Available at: http://www.ala.org/lita/
[15] Library Leadership and Management Association (LLAMA) – Homepage. Available at: http://www.ala.org/llama/
[16] Public Library Association – Homepage. Available at: http://www.ala.org/pla/

new ideas. I have been elected a member of ALA Council, the legislative body of ALA, so this requires that I follow the group's varied discussions on its listserv on a daily basis. I strongly support the Public Library Association and have been asked in the past to stand as a candidate for PLA presidency. On a local level, I am a member of the Florida Library Association (FLA)[17], a former member of its Executive Council and a former FLA Treasurer and a current member of the Advocacy Committee that recommends advocacy efforts on the local and state levels.

Could you describe your management and leadership style? Mentorship is such an important theme in leadership – both mentoring and being mentored. Could you please tell us about your experiences about both?

I believe in risk taking, strong encouragement, and giving staff the green light to try new experiments and ideas. I feel it is best not to micromanage people about every small detail, but I do want to be kept informed. I prefer to give staff the learning experience and let them take the lead in implementing a new service, while still making sure that the library is in compliance with all applicable local, state and federal statutes. That is a good way to grow future leaders. I like for our staff to be learning new things, new approaches and new techniques. I want them to be good communicators and good bridge builders between staff and our community. Staff are in front of the public every day and they are the face of our library. I want that face to be smiling, cheerful, welcoming and knowledgeable, willing to take the time to listen to the customer's needs and trying to provide the best service the library can possibly offer. I believe in investing in staff and strongly encouraging them to improve their skills. I want this library to be fair to our vendors and community partners, offering them new opportunities that might not be possible if we did not work together in a harmonious and constructive way.

Our community is changing, along with the worlds of publishing, reading and learning. New trends are constantly emerging and the library has to be ready to adapt and be a participant or provider to those trends that fit within our service umbrella of learning. By investing in staff development, the library stands ready to be a part of and participate in these new emerging trends. This library is very innovative and forward thinking, and it must continue pursuing the future.

Hiring the very best employees the library can find and investing in their success, pays off in employee tenure and employee satisfaction. When staff know that they are valued, it leads to better productivity and greater confidence and increased ability to adapt to new challenges and emerging trends. It is always more expensive to hire someone new to replace someone who did not work out: lost time,

---

[17] Florida Library Association – Homepage. Available at: http://www.flalib.org/

lost wages, lost opportunities. Allowing staff skills to grow stale or be out-dated will cost the organization dearly. That is not consistent with our goal to be innovative and responsive.

I never had the great experience of being mentored, but certainly wish that had been the case. I think I missed out on learning some things that I eventually had to learn the hard way, through painful experiences. At OCLS, we have offered mentorship opportunities, but it has been more of an informal process. For example, I have mentored several front-line mangers and the Library's administrators have done the same. There is no formal structure, but rather it is left up to each mentor how to interact with his/her mentee. Through Executive Edge, administrators coach a select group of managers to work together to explore solutions to problems and give them executive coaching experiences that will prepare them for higher responsibilities in the organization.

Which part(s) of your job as the Director/CEO of the Orange County Library System do you find most rewarding? What is the most frustrating?

The library gives service awards to employees who have been here 5, 10 15, 20, 25, and yes, even 30 years. This is a very rewarding part of my job: to be able to thank the individual who has devoted so much time to the success of our organization in the community. I love meeting with staff at all locations, as I do on a regular basis in their work areas, hearing their ideas, listening to their concerns and dialoguing with them about whatever it is that is bothering them or their ideas and new proposals. Some of our best services have come from staff thinking about how the library could do "x" better or thinking it would be really super if the library could do "y" or what if we did "z?" They know what our customers are asking for and they know our capabilities. If they are willing to stretch to try and meet new emerging demands, why should the library not try to step it up and implement these new ideas? This approach keeps us fresh and our employees engaged and feeling appreciated.

Thankfully, frustrations are few. Inflexibility and petty office politics do not play a role in our organization. Fortunately, we have a good and excellent team of staff and thus, many of these frustrations are minimized. A big frustration is having many more ideas for new services than money to fund them.

Orange County – in what ways would you want the Orange County Library system to make a positive difference in the lives of everyone in the community?

I would want more in the community to experience our services. Many in our community have come here from other places and they assume the Orange County Library System is just like the library in their former community. I hear all the time, "I did not know the Library had a class on Photoshop Unity or Maya!" for example, or "I did not know that I could learn to do 3-D printing at my library!"

We have a high level of satisfaction with our services, with high "net promoter" scores. I wish that we could reach more residents in the community and break down those old stereotypes of what a library is. We are a very vibrant organization and our services are very surprising to many in the community. I wish that all in the community knew and use our services as well as recommend us to their new neighborhoods who just moved in across the street.

The local communities in Orange County (the local media, both regular and non-regular users of the Orange County Library System) – how do they usually describe the Orange County Library System?

Occasionally, the press will run a story on a specific topic (a contract dispute with a vendor is the most recent example) that is not complimentary, but largely we receive very favorable press. The public at large, even those who may not be regular users, do value the library as part of the fabric of a healthy community. Residents in new housing developments in the county contact us about the need for a branch library in their community. Any attempt to close a branch location or relocate it brings an outcry from that community. When meeting with elected officials about the Library's budget, compliments are common and complaints infrequent. The perception is the Library is well run and provides good service and excellent value to the taxpayers. That perception is accurate. Many recognize that the Library is innovative, offers services that are surprising for a library, provides value for the tax money invested, is a good organization with which to partner, and is cautious in the use of taxpayer dollars.

Orange County versus Los Angeles County versus San Francisco County – the attitudes and expectations of the local community towards their respective city libraries – how are they different from each other?

We are much smaller than Los Angeles County, population wise and territory wise. We are not nearly as wealthy and not nearly as spread out geographically. Los Angeles County has a population over 10 million spread out over a large area of 3,531,905 square miles. It is a very liberal and progressive community of voters who support strong public services and are willing to tax themselves to get better services. That library is part of a very large county administration, so I would think that makes it hard to move quickly on a new idea that has not been already proven.

San Francisco has a smaller population than Orange County, 845,600 people compared to our 1,182,511 population. San Francisco has about $135.90 income per capita versus our $29.26 per capita (2015 figures). So San Francisco has greater financial ability to start new services without risking curtailing current services. It is a community of very tech savvy, high-income earners with a very liberal leaning, progressive tax base willing to raise the taxes for public services. Since the **median** cost of housing there is $765,700 while ours is $161,900, a small increase in the property rate there yields a lot of revenue. Orange County Library System is not part of the local county government. We are an independent taxing district. We have a predominantly blue-collar work force, a large part of which works in the entertainment and hospitality industries. So, our home values are much lower than the other two areas. Orange County's **average** home price is $250,000, which yields about $75 in Library tax revenue. Although we have lower taxes than the other two jurisdictions, we are not part of a larger governmental unit, which allows us more flexibility in our undertakings. As a result, this library is more nimble, since we are not held back by the constraints of coordinating with county or city administration. We can take an idea, try it out and see how it works on a small scale before implementing it system wide.

If a young person is inspired to become a librarian as a career, and comes to you for advice, what would you say to him/her?

Pay attention to trends, especially in technology. Look down the road to see what is coming, not just in the next months or so but way down the road well into the future. Learn and know computer coding, study information and computer systems, work to sharpen one's management skills, budgeting skills, negotiation skills, presentation skills. Solid communication skills are surely needed for use within the library workforce and the community as well. Today's library leader needs all of these skills and more. A commitment to lifelong learning and a willingness to be flexible are keys to success.

Further readings

Becoming an American Citizen at the Orlando Public Library. [YouTube]. Available at: https://www.youtube.com/watch?v=eD5KXjVD0w4&t=44s

Chickasaw Branch Library Banner Ceremony. [YouTube]. Available at: https://www.youtube.com/watch?v=WTXvTtDIwnY

The Genealogy Collection at the Orange County Library System. [YouTube]. Available at: https://www.youtube.com/watch?v=RbnAWH32rUg

Mary Anne Hodel | Orlando Science Center Testimonial Series. [YouTube]. Available at: https://www.youtube.com/watch?v=eD5KXjVD0w4

Melrose Technology Center (Orange County Library). [YouTube]. Available at: https://www.youtube.com/watch?v=9X1xT7EAPvY

Orange County Library System. [YouTube]. Available at: https://www.youtube.com/watch?v=NoiqOXKayD0

Orange County Library System- Brainfuse Recorded Training. [Youtube]. Available at: https://www.youtube.com/watch?v=hWeGzVYqgXw

Supporting The Community After The Pulse Tragedy. [YouTube]. Available at: https://www.youtube.com/watch?v=Lw8YcgQ0uKU

19 Misty Jones

Director, San Diego Public Library

Introduction

Established in 1882, the San Diego Public Library (SDPL) system currently consists of the Central Library, 35 branch libraries, and an adult literacy program office, READ San Diego. The new building for the SDPL, designed by architect Rob Quigley, opened in 2013, and it is considered one of the most attractive landmarks of the city of San Diego.

An MLIS graduate of the University of South Carolina, Misty Jones is the current Director of the SDPL. Prior to that, she served as the Department's Deputy Director – overseeing Support Services, which includes Building Services, Budget Development and Administration, Information Technology, and so on. Jones started her career in librarianship at the Greenville County Library in South Carolina. She then worked for nine years at the Charleston County Library, working her way up through several positions of progressive responsibility from a Librarian in Children's Services, Business Librarian, Assistant Head of Reference, and Regional Branch Manager for the Main Library. In the following interview, Jones discusses her "lead by example" attitude as well as what kinds of unique experiences she wishes to bring her patrons with the unique architectural design (both interior and exterior) of the SDPL.

Fig. 19.1: Misty Jones, San Diego Public Library Director (Photo: San Diego Public Library).

Fig. 19.2: San Diego Central Library (Photo: Joan Λ Irwin Jacobs Common).

Fig. 19.3: San Diego Central Library Reading Room (Photo: San Diego Public Library).

Could we begin this interview by first introducing yourself, for example, your professional training and education background? What did you study at university? Do you come from a family of librarians?

I came to librarianship as a second career. I previously worked in the Social Services and Mental Health fields. I have a BA in Psychology. I decided to go back to graduate school and change directions because I was burned out. To be honest, I just sort of fell into this profession, because it seemed like an interesting field. So an effortless decision to change fields turned into the perfect career for me.

Do you come from a family of librarians?

No. In fact, I never understood the true importance of libraries until I started working in them. This is why I am so passionate about advocacy. I know there are so many people out there that were like me and just never thought about libraries. I want to change that.

You previously worked in the Social Services and Mental Health fields – how have your previous professional experiences in social services and mental health field contribute to your current work as a librarian?

I would say they have helped a tremendous amount. Working in a public library means you see and help all members of the public regardless of race, religion, status, etc. This also means you often interact with many vulnerable members of society. My background has given me the advantage of being able to listen and talk to people, to understand and try to help them find their own solutions and to just empathise.

When you were undertaking your MLIS program at university – were there many classmates like you, undertaking the MLIS program, with the hope of undertaking a career change?

I did encounter many fellow students that were changing careers. Many teachers were leaving the classroom and moving into libraries in schools and other institutions.

Have you always worked in libraries? Could you tell us more about your path to becoming the Director of the San Diego Public Library?

I have worked exclusively in libraries since starting library school. I have held nearly every possible library position including Children's Librarian, Business Librarian, Assistant Head of Reference, Branch Manager and Central Library Supervisor. I came to San Diego Public Library[1] from Charleston County Public Library[2] for the position of Deputy Director of the Central Library and oversaw the completion of the Central Library building project. Shortly after moving into the new building the Director retired and I was appointed Director.

---

1 San Diego Public Library – Homepage. Available at: https://www.sandiego.gov/public-library
2 Charleston County Public Library – Homepage. Available at: http://www.ccpl.org/

Could you also describe your current role and areas of responsibility as the Director of the San Diego Public Library?

I oversee 36 library locations throughout the City of San Diego.

Could you please provide a brief introduction of the San Diego Public Library?

The City of San Diego Public Library serves the informational, educational and recreational interests of San Diego through 35 branches, Central Library, the READ/San Diego[3] literacy program and an online presence. The mission of SDPL is "to inspire lifelong learning through connections to knowledge and each other."

What is the current collection size of the San Diego Public Library? Could you also describe what you deem are the highlights of the library collection or services of the whole San Diego Public Library?

a. more than 5.3 million books, including e-books and audio-visual materials
b. 3,138 periodical subscriptions
c. 1.6 million government documents; and
d. more than 265,295 books in 25 languages other than English

In September 2013, the City opened the state-of-the-art and award-winning San Diego Central Library @ Joan Λ Irwin Jacobs Common[4] that better serves our entire region, and has put us on the map internationally.

The IDEA Lab exposes students and adults to cutting edge technology that will make them more competitive in a digital economy. The Lab features 10 high-end computers that offer software for graphic design, photo editing, architectural design, music production, video editing and technology such as 3-D printers, multi touch collaboration platforms and design tablets, etc.

The La Jolla/Riford branch of SDPL[5] has created what is probably the first instructional Bio-Safety Level 1 laboratory biology lab of its nature inside a public library anywhere in the world.

The Information, Innovation, & Incubation Lab (I^3 Lab or "I Cubed" Lab) has popular rapid prototyping tools used in professional incubator spaces, such as a

---

[3] READ/San Diego - Adult and Family Literacy Services – Homepage. Available at: https://www.sandiego.gov/public-library/services/adulteducation/read
[4] San Diego Central Library @ Joan Λ Irwin Jacobs Common – Homepage. Available at: https://www.sandiego.gov/public-library/locations/central
[5] La Jolla/Riford branch of SDPL – Homepage. Available at: http://lajollalibrary.org/

laser cutter, vinyl cutters, CNC (Computer Numerical Control) mills, 3D printers and other electronics with the goal to provide entrepreneurs with the tools, space and support they need to make, build or invent. The I³ Lab leverages resources from the adjacent Patent & Trademark Resource Center[6], part of an officially-designated nationwide library network maintained by the U.S. Patent and Trademark Office (USPTO)[7], to provide a one-stop-shop for entrepreneurs and inventors.

Please describe the staffing structure at the San Diego Public Library?

We have full-time, half-time and hourly employees making up approximately 800 total employees. These employees range from Library Aide to Supervising Librarian.

Could you describe your typical day at work? Is there ever a typical day at work?

I have forgotten what a typical workday looks like. Usually, it starts with answering emails and returning phone calls. I spend a lot of time in meetings ranging from programming, strategic, budget or personnel related. I always have to think big picture but still handle all of the little details. It is never dull.

What scholarly and professional associations are you a part of, and how do they inform you in your work?

I am a member of the American Library Association (ALA)[8], Public Library Association[9] and the National Management Association. I am also heavily involved in the California Library Association[10] and served this past year as President.

Could you describe your management and leadership style? Mentorship is such an important theme in leadership – both mentoring and being mentored. Could you please tell us about your experiences about both?

I can't say I had one specific mentor, but I really tried to learn from everyone that I worked with. I admire people that are ambitious and challenge themselves but still remain grounded. This is what I try to do. There is so much truth to the statement "lead by example" and this is always what I keep in mind. I am a big thinker

---

6 Patent & Trademark Resource Center – Homepage. Available at: https://www.uspto.gov/learning-and-resources/support-centers/patent-and-trademark-resource-centers-ptrcs
7 U.S. Patent and Trademark Office (USPTO) – Homepage. Available at: https://www.uspto.gov/
8 American Library Association (ALA) – Homepage. Available at: http://www.ala.org/
9 Public Library Association – Homepage. Available at: http://www.ala.org/pla/
10 California Library Association – Homepage. Available at: http://www.cla-net.org/?

and like to get things done. I'm not afraid to make the tough decisions or have the tough conversations. I like change, I like challenges and I love libraries. I have high expectations of my staff because I have even higher expectations of myself. But I am fair and open.

Which part(s) of your job as the Director of the San Diego Public Library do you find most rewarding?

We are in the unique position to constantly redefine ourselves and provide new opportunities for the public. Being able to empower people with knowledge is incredible. What is the most frustrating? There is never enough time or budget to be able to get all the things accomplished.

San Diego Public Library – in what ways would you want the San Diego Public Library to make a positive difference in the lives of everyone in the community?

Our new vision statement is "The place for Opportunity, Discovery and Inspiration" and this is what I want to achieve for every person in San Diego. I want SDPL to be the place that can help them achieve their wildest dreams, discover their passion and then inspire those around them to be better. Ultimately, the knowledge is the great equalizer and libraries are the place that everyone came come for knowledge.

The San Diego Public Library, designed by architect Rob Quigley, opened in 2013 – is considered one of the landmarks of the city of San Diego. As the Library Director, can you describe the overall architectural design (both interior & exterior) of the San Diego Public Library? How are the library staff making the best out of the interior design and the layout of the physical library – in order to bring a unique experience for the users?

The nine story Central Library has a total square footage of 497,652 sq ft with 366,673 sq ft of library space. Floors 6 and & are home to e3 Civic High, an innovative charter school. The 366,673 square-foot, nine-story, downtown Central Library includes an outdoor garden courtyard/café, three-story grand lobby entrance, 320-seat auditorium, three-story domed reading room, 22 study rooms, dedicated teen center, Dr. Seuss themed children's library, homework center, technology center, special event space with two terraces overlooking the city, Special Collections room and an art gallery and sculpture garden.

The public and the staff are extremely proud of this building. We get over 3,000 visitors per day which is 4 times that number of visitors to the old Central Library.

San Diego versus Los Angeles versus San Francisco – the attitudes and expectations of the local community towards their respective city libraries – how are they different from each other?

I can't really speak for LA and SF but San Diego is a big city full of small communities and neighborhoods and each of these communities in unique. Each of these communities also really love their individual library no matter how small.

If a young person is inspired to become a librarian as a career, and comes to you for advice, what would you say to him/her?

In my opinion, this is the best time to get into libraries. There are so many opportunities on the horizon for us to do some incredible things and really push the boundaries. But you have to like change and be ready to change quickly in order to stay relevant.

Further readings

Bill Moyers on the Difference the San Diego Public Library Makes [YouTube]. Available at: https://www.youtube.com/watch?v=zye_m5yhNYA

Misty Jones, San Diego Public Library Director. Available at: https://www.sandiego.gov/public-library/about-the-library/admin/directorbio

New Vision for San Diego Public Libraries [YouTube]. Available at: https://www.youtube.com/watch?v=DLAiR-Gstic

San Diego's New Central Library - a center for learning, literacy and education [YouTube]. Available at: https://www.youtube.com/watch?v=-1us-dfkINs

San Diego Central Library opens to the public [YouTube]. Available at: https://www.youtube.com/watch?v=4XHFo8L5HDE

San Diego Public Library Deputy Director Misty Jones discussed Central Library [YouTube]. Available at: https://www.youtube.com/watch?v=-krExQ3FNHU

San Diego's New Central Library Tour [YouTube]. Available at: https://www.youtube.com/watch?v=SWDf8YUs_W0

20 Marcellus Turner

City Librarian, The Seattle Public Library System

Introduction

The city of Seattle, Washington, is well known for many things – especially Starbucks, rainy weather, and for being "sleepless," a cliche that is, of course, inspired by Tom Hanks' popular romantic film made in the early 1990s. Seattle is also the home to many famous landmarks and architectural sites. The Seattle Public Library's Central Library is the flagship library of the Settle Public Library (SPL) system, and it is also one of the most notable landmarks of the city. The Central Library is most celebrated for its beautiful architectural design, user involvement initiatives, and particularly noted for its bold steel and glass design, its grand public spaces, cityscape views, all-red meeting floor and 30 miles of books arranged in the only Books Spiral in the world.

In 2016, the SPL celebrated 125 years of service to the city of Seattle. The whole system operation has nearly 700 staff members. Overseeing SPL, which includes the world-renowned Central Library and 26 new or renovated branches is Marcellus Turner. Prior to joining SPL, Turner served as the Executive Director of the Jefferson County Public Library in Lakewood, Colorado, and Assistant Executive Director of the Rockford Public Library in Rockford, Illinois. In the following interview, Turner describes his unique management and leadership style as well as his valuable advice for any young person who aspires to choose public librarianship as a career.

Fig. 20.1: Marcellus Turner, City Librarian for The Seattle Public Library (Photo: Seattle Public Library).

DOI 10.1515/9783110533347-021

Fig. 20.2: Exterior of Central Library (Photo: Seattle Public Library).

Fig. 20.3: Interior of Central Library, Assembly (Photo: Seattle Public Library).

Fig. 20.4: Interior of Central Library, Reading Room (Photo: Seattle Public Library).

Could we begin this interview by first introducing yourself, for example, your professional training and education background? For example, what did you study at university?

I'm Marcellus Turner, City Librarian for The Seattle Public Library.[1] I have a master's degree in Library Science from The University of Tennessee[2], and a bachelor's degree in Speech Pathology and Audiology from Mississippi University for Women.[3]

In an online Interview, it says you started out in 4th grade shelving books in your school library in Mississippi – as a young boy who grew up in the south – was it a 'cool' thing to do among your peer at school? What were the reactions among your peers towards your love for using the school library?

I don't know if it was a cool thing to work in the school library, but it certainly was fun. Many students in my elementary school had to work in a school office or department starting in 4th grade. In 5th grade, I was assigned to the nurse's

---

[1] The Seattle Public Library – Homepage. Available at: https://www.spl.org/
[2] University of Tennessee – Homepage. Available at: http://www.utk.edu/
[3] Mississippi University for Women – Homepage. Available at: http://www.muw.edu/

office. In sixth grade, I started out in the principal's office. I did that for one month, and then finished out the remainder of the year back in the school library, which I enjoyed. I'm not sure what the reaction was among my peers, but I guess I thought it was cool to have been allowed to complete a second stint in the library.

Have you always worked in libraries? Could you tell us more about your path to becoming the General Director of the Seattle Public Library System? Could you also describe your current role and areas of responsibility as the General Director of the Seattle Public Library System?

Short of my work study assignments in college, all of my paid professional work has been in libraries. Although I have a degree in library science, my course concentration during school was in records management. I thought I might someday like to work in a records center for a national company. That did not happen, however, and my first couple of jobs post-graduation were in academic universities as a reference or instruction librarian. I did that for about six years and then moved to public libraries, where I led a variety of departments, including the circulation and reference departments. After a couple of years in these positions, I took an assistant director post at Rockford Public Library[4] in Illinois, and then joined the Jefferson County Public Library[5] in Colorado, where I served as head of public services and then deputy director of the system. I was eventually selected and served as executive director of Jefferson County Public Library for three years prior to joining to The Seattle Public Library.

My job as city librarian is to set the direction for the Library, and to ensure the provision of Library services to our community. In doing so, I help build the budget to support our work, speak on behalf of the Library and represent the library at the state, national and international levels.

Could you please provide a brief introduction of the Seattle Public Library and its associate system?

The Seattle Public Library is celebrating our 125th anniversary in 2016. Our system is made up of the world-renowned Central Library in downtown Seattle and 26 neighborhood libraries. Our mission is to bring people, information,

---

[4] Rockford Public Library – Homepage. Available at: http://www.rockfordpubliclibrary.org/
[5] Jefferson County Public Library – Homepage. Available at: http://www.jeffcolibrary.org/

and ideas together to enrich lives and build community. We use five strategic service priorities to chart the future of the Library system. Those priorities are: Youth and Family Learning; Community Engagement; Technology and Access; Seattle Culture and History; and Re-Imagined Spaces. The Library's 2016 operating budget is $67.2 million, which includes $13.7 million in funding from a voter-approved 2012 Library levy that will run through 2019. Library Journal has awarded us the top rating of five stars among large public libraries for six consecutive years, and an international survey of public libraries ranked us first in circulation per capita among systems of similar size.

What is the current collection size of the Seattle Public Library and its associated library system? Could you also describe what you deem are the highlights of the library collection or services of the whole library system?

The Library's collection of about 2.3 million items for children, teens and adults includes:
- Books, audiobooks and large print books;
- Music (CDs) and movies (DVDs);
- Magazines and newspapers;
- One of the largest digital collections among public libraries in the U.S., with nearly 300,000 files. We also have one of the highest digital circulations, which in 2015 was 2.2 million.

We also have free online resources – books, movies, music, audiobooks, newspapers and magazines. We have excellent collections on genealogy and Seattle culture and history, including the histories of the 1962 Seattle World's Fair and the Pike Place Market. We have one of the largest collections of African-American literature and history on the West Coast.

We provide access to more than 800 Internet-enabled computers across our 27 locations; each location also offers free Wi-Fi. In 2015, we began lending Wi-Fi hotspots for patrons to use on the go or at home. We offer more than 10,000 educational classes and events each year to patrons of all ages, including story times for children, English-as-a-second-language classes for immigrants, in-person homework help for students, health seminars, self-publishing workshops, author programs, and more.

We also serve people in the community through our innovative Books on Bikes program, our mobile services to patrons who are unable to use their local libraries because of age, disability or illness and our mini-libraries that pop up at community events such as farmers markets, concerts and summer festivals. Our Museum Pass program allows patrons to use their Library card to reserve, and print out an admission pass to participating Seattle museums for free.

Please describe the staffing structure at the Seattle Public Library and its associated library system?

The Library is governed by a five-member citizens' board of trustees, appointed by the mayor of the city of Seattle and confirmed by the City Council. The Library Board hires the City Librarian, who oversees the Library system. Several directors report to me and are responsible for areas such as Library Programs and Services, Administrative Services, Human Resources, Communications and Marketing and Online Services. We have divided our service area into seven regions, each of which has a regional manager who is responsible for oversight of the libraries in that geographic area, or in the case of the downtown region, oversees all the public service departments at the Central Library. We have nearly 700 employees.

Could you describe your typical day at work? Is there ever a typical day at work?

Surprisingly, there is a sort of rhythm or pattern that suggests a typical work day. First, my schedule / routine is pretty much the same every day. I'm in the office at my desk each morning by 7:30 a.m. and I try to leave between 5:00 p.m. and 5:30 p.m. each evening. And somewhere in the course of the day between 11:30 a.m. and 2:00 p.m., I usually have a scheduled hour for lunch, which I always try to take to get out of the office more so than to eat. With luck, I also get a bite to eat.

The content of the day's work is pretty much the same – meetings. Each day has on average, 5 scheduled meetings, though they may be weekly meetings with direct reports (Communications, Marketing, Human Resources, Finance and Administration, or Library Programs and Services), attending a department meeting to talk to staff and answer questions, a meeting with a board member or someone from another city division or a meeting for a special project or work. On top of that, I usually have a few "pop-in" meetings, where I or someone needs at least five minutes to talk about something. Over the course of a week, I have maybe one or two lunch, breakfast or dinner meetings with someone interested in the work of the Library and possibly one speaking engagement. These meetings generally start at 9 a.m. and I use the time between 7:30 a.m. and 9:00 a.m. to handle emails or review reports and briefings for later use, and make phone calls.

What scholarly and professional associations are you a part of, and how do they inform you in your work?

I'm a member of the American Library Association[6], the Public Library Association[7] and the Black Caucus of the American Library Association. I serve on the boards of United for Libraries (Trustees, Foundations and Friends groups), The University of Tennessee College of Communications Board of Visitors, and The University of Washington[8] MLIS Advisory Board.

Each of these affiliations provides an opportunity to connect with leaders in the profession, thereby increasing awareness, and understanding of the work and future of our profession, and a chance to share ideas and thoughts for resolution and consideration.

My work on the university boards keeps me connected to both the instruction, and content that our library schools are teaching and how our students are prepared to work in our libraries.

Could you describe your management and leadership style? Mentorship is such an important theme in leadership – both mentoring and being mentored. Could you please tell us about your experiences about both?

As the City Librarian and Chief Executive Officer (CEO) of the organization, my job is to determine the direction and work that we will take as a system. I do that by focusing on how society is responding to technology, convenience, access to information and the needs of our city. I pair all of that with what we do best, and where we can make a difference and let our staff go from there.

My management and leadership style is one that is collaborative, open, supportive and relaxed. I lead from the middle by hiring great talent to deliver on the direction, and work that we will do as a system. I share with them what we should do and let them determine how we will do it.

Mentoring is a concept that I respect both for myself and for others. In serving as a mentor or as the mentee, I steer away from the traditional approach to mentoring and look at it as an opportunity to share, and exchange thoughts and ideas that strengthen both of us in our thinking. I approach them as conversations, unhampered by formal sessions or roles, but enhanced by just talking and asking questions, and offering insight and referrals to others who have found themselves

---

6 American Library Association – Homepage. Available at: http://www.ala.org/
7 Public Library Association – Homepage. Available at: http://www.ala.org/pla/
8 University of Washington – Homepage. Available at: http://www.washington.edu/

with similar concerns. It has no set boundaries of time other than recognizing when it is no longer needed.

Your Library has been constantly voted as one of the most beautiful public libraries in the world in mass media (particularly the Internet) – as the Library Director – what do you have to say to respond to that? Do you think the attractiveness of the physical library building plays an important role in drawing in the general public to use the library's facilities and resources?

We are immensely proud that the Central Library is so well regarded internationally. When the building opened on May 23, 2004, people lined up by the thousands to be the first inside. By the end of opening day, more than 25,000 people had toured the building to see our soaring atrium, the all red meeting room floor and the 30 miles of books organized in a four-level spiral. *The New York Times*' late architectural critic Herbert Muschamp wrote: "Seattle's new Central Library is a blazing chandelier to swing your dreams upon"... and described it as "the most exciting new building it has been my honor to review" in more than 30 years of writing about architecture.

Ten year later, tourists, librarians, architects and media representatives from around the world continue to visit the iconic building. The Central Library is more than an architectural marvel – it is a functional library that combines spaces for core functions, such as areas for children and teens, with flexible spaces such as the open and airy street-level "Living Room," which invites patrons to gather and read.

Likewise, though the building is striking, and may initially inspire a member of the general public to visit, it is the expertise of our staff and the depth of our program of services, and resources that keep patrons coming back to use our facilities and resources. Our staff members help patrons have personal and meaningful Library experiences.

Which part(s) of your job as the Librarian do you find most rewarding? What is the most frustrating?

There are many parts of my job that I find rewarding. However, knowing that we are meeting the needs of our users is most rewarding. When a patron sees me and says how much they like what we are doing, I can't help but smile and be proud of the work of my staff in making that happen. What I find frustrating is something that affects most industry, and that is our inability to be as nimble as we need to be. The pace at which our world is changing requires every industry to be more nimble, and we haven't mastered that just yet. But we are trying and I'm encouraged.

I understand you have always been a keen reader, and truly believe in the idea of reading for the pure pleasure of it. If you were to find yourself castaway on a desert island, and told that you could only take one book with you, which book would you take with you?

Ahhhh. That is a really hard question. I could answer it by saying that I would take one series (Harry Potter), one author (David Baldacci) or one genre (Elizabethan historical fiction), but for it to be one book. Aargh. I'll go with *The Book of Questions* by Gregory Stock. The book asks a lot of soul-searching questions and I would hope my time alone would give me an opportunity to know my true self.

In what ways would you want the Seattle City Library to make a positive difference in the lives of everyone in the community?

It's funny that you ask this question because I've always said that as city librarian, I have one job and that is to increase the ways that The Seattle Public Library makes a difference in the lives of our residents and users. I've said that ever since I started this job. And to do that, we have to bring people together. If we can bring people together through books, our programs or services, we are making a positive difference. I believe that through and through.

If a young man is inspired to become a librarian as a career, and comes to you for advice, what would you say to him?

This one is easy. I say it every time I speak to a class of library school students or someone new to the profession asks. Take the time to work in circulation. It is one of the hardest jobs in the library and it brings you in contact with everyone who uses the library. You will gain a whole new respect for what we do and the impact that we make.

Further readings

City Librarian - The Seattle Public Library. Available at: http://www.spl.org/about-the-library/leaders-and-organizations/city-librarian

Election Candidate: Marcellus Turner - United for Libraries. Available at: http://www.ala.org/united/about/board/election/turner

Getting to Know Your City Librarian - The Seattle Public Library. Available at: http://www.spl.org/about-the-library/leaders-and-organizations/city-librarian/getting-to-know-your-city-librarian

Marcellus Turner City Librarian Visiting at the Magnolia Library [YouTube]. Available at: https://www.youtube.com/watch?v=I8ri-zKxx2U

Nordstrom Gifts with Personality: Meet the Modernist [YouTube]. Available at: https://www.youtube.com/watch?v=pwisz6oRXjU

The Seattle Public Library: Central Library 10th Anniversary [YouTube]. Available at: https://www.youtube.com/watch?v=ueSDb5R7M4k

The Seattle Public Library Foundation: Global Reading Challenge [YouTube]. Available at: https://www.youtube.com/watch?v=-gROaXneqxs

The Seattle Public Library: online special collections [YouTube]. Available at: https://www.youtube.com/watch?v=l4DXWqtMsgo

21 Kate P. Horan

MLS, Library Director, McAllen Public Library (Texas)

Introduction

From its humble beginnings in 1932 when the McAllen Study Club opened a one-room library at the McAllen Chamber of Commerce, to being the largest single floor public library in North America, the McAllen Public Library has come a long way.

After 60 years in downtown McAllen, Texas, the old Main Library closed its doors and the Public Library relocated to its current location at a repurposed Walmart retail big box store, a bold vision conceptualized by local government officials and community residents.

Director Kate P. Horan discusses how the space was overhauled into its 123,000 square foot home in central McAllen, tripling its former size and doubling its services. Since becoming director, the library thrives under Horan. It immediately became a globally recognized public library, winning first place in the American Library Association and the International Interior Design Association's 2012 Library Interior Design Competition. With its new home, new look and new direction, McAllen Public Library welcomes record numbers of visitors daily and offers a variety of services to support lifelong learning, cultural opportunities and civic engagement to the region.

Fig. 21.1: Kate P. Horan, Library Director in the adult stacks with a beehive inspired service desk just behind (Photo: City of McAllen).

Fig. 21.2: A view of the outdoor mall leading to the facility. The far end of the mall area includes two limestone bubbler fountains and a small water feature (Photo: McAllen Library).

Fig. 21.3: OPACs on custom endcaps are scattered throughout the stacks and provide point-of-need patron convenience (Photo: City of McAllen).

Could we begin this interview by first introducing yourself, for example, your professional training and education background? What did you study at university? Do you come from a family of librarian?

I received my Bachelor's Degree in English, Summa Cum Laude, from SUNY (State University of New York)[1] at Stony Brook University[2], Stony Brook, NY, and my Master's Degree in Library Science from St. John's University[3], Flushing, NY. I do not come from a family of librarians, but my mother always took me to the library when I was growing up in Jackson Heights, Queens. My eldest daughter is a Montessori K-8 School Media Specialist. She is now a Librarian III with Prince George's County Library System.

When you were at South Country Library, you served as the Adult Reference Service Librarian, could you tell the readers about the work you did for musical programming and special programming?

I took over musical programming by providing an eclectic mix of styles. South Country Library[4] is located on the South Shore of Long Island, and is often referred to as "the quiet Hamptons." Performances ranged from a Frank Sinatra sound-alike, to a jazz quartet, a classical guitarist, a solo artist performing songs from the American songbook, and a small opera troupe performing well-loved arias. I organized all the performances at the start of the season so I could promote it the way a performing arts center does. The program resulted in high quality musical entertainment, free to the public, and each performance was well attended.

At one point, I wrote a grant and received funding to launch a poetry series. The idea was to pair an established, published poet of regional renown with a lesser-known poet who might just be starting out. The program helped the younger poets to hone their performance skills while observing the more experienced poets, and taking the opportunity to ask questions about improving their own writing.

Could you tell us more about your path to becoming the General Director of the McAllen's Public Library System (MPLS)? How did you become the General Director of such a major public library system at such a young age?

I have been working in libraries since 1991. I worked as Circulation Supervisor for a mid-sized public library, then as Assistant Circulation Supervisor and

---

1 State University of New York (SUNY) – Homepage. Available at: https://www.suny.edu/
2 Stony Brook University – Homepage. Available at: http://www.stonybrook.edu/
3 St. John's University – Homepage. Available at: https://app.applysju.org
4 South Country Library – Homepage. Available at: http://wordpress.sctylib.org/

Stacks Manager for SUNY Stony Brook, where I scheduled and supervised student pages. I finished my MLS in 2003, and took my first professional position at South Country Library in Bellport, NY. In 2005, I moved to Texas and became the Branch Manager of McAllen Public Library's[5] south branch. In 2009, I was hired as Assistant Director of Public Services, in part to assist the Library Director with relocating to our current location and to expand programming. The Director retired in 2012 and the City of McAllen hired me as Library Director. It was a huge change for me to move from NY to South Texas, but I am living my dream job. I am the Director of an award-winning, 123,000 square foot facility that was repurposed from a Walmart.[6] I have the best staff of dedicated, enthusiastic and talented professionals and paraprofessionals, and, through our many partnerships, we are able to offer a vast array of educational and literary programming to our citizens.

Could you please provide a brief introduction of the McAllen Public Library and its system of branch libraries and the city that they serve? For example, could you describe the economy and the demographics (cultural and literary scenes in particular) of the city of McAllen, Texas?

Nestled in the heart of the Rio Grande Valley of South Texas, a four-county region at the southernmost tip of Texas, McAllen Public Library serves residents and visitors of McAllen and the lower Rio Grande Valley, offering a dynamic civic resource that promotes the open exchange of ideas through free access to information, and connecting a culturally diverse population with the global community. The resources of McAllen Public Library system include the Main Library, and two, 11,000 square foot branches, Lark Branch to the north and Palm View Branch to the south. MPL offers its patrons a wide gamut of free resources, services, and programs to meet the demand of the city's active residents and visitors.

The original McAllen Public Library opened its doors in November of 1932, located first in a room at the McAllen Chamber of Commerce, then to a local church room, and the basement of a park bandstand. It remained there until May 1950, when the next facility opened on Main Street. There it grew from a one-story building to a 40,000 square foot, three-story structure. Eventually, the collection outgrew the space and, after a thorough community assessment, the need for expanded parking and public meeting space was determined.

---

5 McAllen Public Library – Homepage. Available at: http://www.mcallenlibrary.net/
6 Walmart – Homepage. Available at: https://www.walmart.com/

The new facility opened for business on December 10, 2011, with more than 10,000 people attending Opening Day activities, undeterred by the day's heavy rainstorms. The new library has 123,000 square feet of public and staff areas and was once a Walmart store. The new location tripled the size of the library, making it what is considered to the largest single-story public library in North America. In just one year after opening, the library has welcomed almost 600,000 visitors through its doors, doubling its services to children and tripling its services to teens. Today, the library has over 85,000 registered cardholders. Additionally, 276,000 users access MPL's website, generating more than 822,000 page views per year.

In 2012, McAllen Public Library received an ALA/IIDA (American Library Association/International Interior Design Award) for a Public Library over 30,000 Square Feet. MPL and the design firm of Meyer, Scherer & Rockcastle, Ltd. were honored for modern and forward-thinking design, which takes as inspiration motifs of growth and movement and the Fibonacci sequence. News of the big-box-store-cum-modern-library went viral on major new networks and continues to garner attention and praise in print and online.

What is the current collection size of the MPL? Could you also describe what you deem are the highlights of the Library's collections and services?

The collection size of physical materials is just under 324,000 and digital holdings are about 10,000. In 2008, we gave the Spanish language physical collection a cash infusion and since then, we have grown a sizable collection of high quality Spanish language materials in a variety of formats. Our Children's collection takes up the square footage of our former location's first floor, with over 21,000 board books and picture books in child-friendly, browseable bins; easy readers, chapter books, non-fiction, a large bilingual section and Spanish language section, and an ever-growing parenting collection, as well as music CDs, audiobooks, and DVDs/Blu-Rays. Our YA collection features books in English and Spanish. We also have a growing collection of high quality graphic novels for children, teens, and adults.

Please describe the staffing structure at the MPL?

The Main Library is comprised of an Administration, department Supervisors (Children's; Teens; Circulation; Reference); a Marketing team of three FTEs; 31 para-professional FTEs; and 32 part-time positions. The two branches have a Branch Manager (MLS) plus one MLS Librarian; a Circulation Supervisor; 6 para-professional FTEs; and two part-time positions.

Could you describe your typical day at work? Is there ever a typical day at work?

Each day is different with its own set of challenges and successes. However, I like to begin each day around 5:30 by looking over my schedule and mentally establishing goals for the day. Sometimes I send a reminder list email to myself so I can get right to work when I arrive at the office around 7:45. I love Peter Bregman's book, 18 Minutes, and I try my best to put my work into a context of "why" before starting to read emails. Everything we do, every resource and service and program, has to align with our mission and goals. To ensure that requires thoughtful leadership, so I like to think along those lines before plunging into emails.

Many days have back-to-back meetings to discuss grant operations or compliance, track the progress of new project launches, or talk with department Supervisors or my two Branch Managers about personnel and operational topics. I meet weekly with my two Assistant Directors to review operations in more detail and budget expenditures.

In a facility this large, it's essential to walk around the library to greet patrons and get a general sense of what's going well and what needs to be improved. I believe that it is good leadership practice to speak with staff, not only in meetings, but also at points of service. Staff can ask to meet with me at any time by phone or in person, and I also make myself available to every patron who requests a meeting with me.

Could you describe your management and leadership style? Mentorship is such an important theme in leadership – both mentoring and being mentored. Could you please tell us about your experiences about both?

I believe in situational management because staff and situations are different and require a variety of management methods. When possible, I favor consensus and participation in making decisions which will impact operations. A recent example involved inviting Adult Services MLS Staff to participate in revising the Reference Librarian job description. We met a couple of times and went through several iterations before reaching consensus. This was necessary, not only because the job description needed revision, but also because I wanted to place less emphasis on desk duty and more on each MLS Staff having a narrow but deep focus, for example, outreach, community events, adult education, and digital management, etc. My staff know I like to get things in writing: proposals, guidelines, instructions, expectations, and procedures. The potential to be misunderstood is ever-present, but it's a good leader's responsibility to minimize or eliminate misunderstanding to the best of our ability. My preference is to hire highly motivated staff with whom I can share general expectations (and specifics, where necessary), and then let them go do their best work. Supervisory staff submit weekly reports of their accomplishments and other items on their radar, and those reports are a tremendous help to me as Director. They act in part as conversation starters and in part as confirmation that what I expect is getting done.

It says on your biography that you are under the supervision of the Deputy City Manager of McAllen, Texas – could you describe the working relationship between you and the Deputy City Manager? What issues do you both usually discuss at the work meetings?

I have a standing, weekly appointment with my Assistant City Manager (there are three in our city). I keep him apprised of anything I feel the City should know about; major facility maintenance or personnel issues; grant progress and compliance; staff continuing education; any changes to programming, technology, or capital projects. I also share flyers and information about upcoming events (SRP, Teen Read Week, our annual McAllen Book Festival, author events, etc.) and any successes or accolades the library has received. We have an excellent working relationship based on trust and communication, and I know I can count on his support and counsel. This year, we had an amnesty campaign whereby I would dye my hair pink if we reached our goal of returned items. At the campaign's success press conference, my ACM showed up wearing a pink blazer! It's that kind of personalized support that makes me feel grateful for a great working relationship.

Your library has been voted as one of the most beautiful public libraries on the Internet. As the General Director of the MPL, what would you say to respond to that?

Of course, we're very proud to have been named the most beautiful library in Texas, as well as having received an ALA/IIDA award for our interior design. You will not find any traditional library furniture or somber colors here, and I frequently receive questions about where we bought our furniture. In fact, our furniture comes from designer manufacturers like Knoll, Vitra, Emeco, Coalesse, Nienkamper, and Herman Miller. Our entire facility is based on a motif of growth and movement.

The interior design is a nod to the Fibonacci sequence (a mathematical pattern found throughout nature) and local plant and animal life. The themes of movement and growth can also be found in the fractal designs on the children's tables and chairs and throughout the library.

The new Main Library is home to Area 3918 (the Teen Dept.), an acoustically separated lounge for teens ("3918" refers to the teen area's square footage).

When people talk about the MPL, what unique features (architectural design, services, facilities) would first come into their mind?

McAllen is one of the fastest growing cities in the nation and this library was designed with the current and future community in mind. The library is filled with great places for the community to gather. McAllen Public Library boasts a 180-person auditorium, 16 rentable high-tech meeting spaces, 14 free group study rooms that can be reserved online, 3 computer labs (adult, teen, and children), a café, and a quiet reading room. Tables with electrical outlets are located throughout the library. These provide users with ample places to plug in laptops and devices while they take advantage of free Wi-Fi access. The Library also has self-checkout stations and an automated drive-through drop box to return borrowed items. The drive-through conveys returned items on a belt that runs invisibly across the library and drops the automatically checked-in items into sorting bins, reducing the time from check-in to shelf.

The library itself is a green alternative, having used the existing structure instead of tearing it down to build another. Other green features are a state-of-the-art chiller system that utilizes condensation, and the "111 Chair," which is made from 111 recycled soft-drink bottles and scattered throughout the facility.

Boldly colored mega-pendants are large way-finding signs in English and Spanish make the high ceilings feel a bit lower. Under them are reading nooks, referred to as respites, with comfortable couches and handy tables.

A laser-cut wood panel begins in the lobby and extends along the length of the building, which provides visual interest and serves to divide public stacks from the computer lab and the Lobby Art Gallery and Meeting Center rooms.

Summer Reading Program – could you talk about the Summer Reading Program launched by the MPL under your direction – could you tell me why marketing, and outreach for children and teens in their local community are so important, when most schools in the US already have their own school libraries staffed by trained professionals (school librarians). In addition, reading materials are so easily available on the Internet?

I feel that the public library is uniquely poised to step into the role of providing literacy initiatives to support children's and teens' education. We are now providing SRP for babies through high school. It's very important for parents to begin interacting with their children, even when they're babies, because their child's future largely depends on the sheer number of vocabulary words acquired by age four. MPL provides the bridge from birth to school for our youngest citizens. I like to say that we're changing lives, one baby at a time! We also support parents who are conscientious about maintaining their children's reading over the summer. We do so with fun, periodic incentives through the summer and wide variety of programming to keep children and teens interested in reading and using the library. This is especially important in the Rio Grande Valley, where the poverty rate is 26 percent of the population and a literacy rate of only 50 percent. In that regard, the library plays a critical role in providing free access to physical and digital materials, keeping in mind that many of our youngest citizens may not have access to their own books, Internet, or computers.

Could you tell the readers about the grant awarded for creating and launching McAllen Public Library smartphone app – how has this app service helped the MPL outreach to its users, as well as enabling the users to access MPL's resources more easily?

MPL received a $10,000 Texas State Library and Archives Impact Grant to develop and launch an MPL app. We launched the app in early 2017 and expect that the ease of use will drive more users to use our catalog and digital services, such as language acquisition, e-books and e-audiobooks, medical databases, and much more. We have a well collected e-branch component to our website, and I believe the app will help to point users to well-curated resources that will delight and inform. The app had 1,117 unique downloads in the first month. Based on the downloads to date, I expect more than 5,000 will have downloaded it by the end of the calendar year.

MPL – what are the general attitudes and expectations of the local community towards MPL, and in what ways would you want the MPL to make a positive difference in the lives of everyone in the community?

Our tagline is "Where people and ideas meet and connect." We make a difference every day in the lives of people who use MPL. They can look for jobs or learn to write resumes, take classes for the GED or ESL exams, transact business or study in our free study rooms, or rent space in our Meeting Center for a performance, meeting, or presentation. They can attend storytimes, homework help, or relax with other teens in the teen department. And, of course, they can browse the stacks and read whatever is important to them. Our building was designed to bring all these services to the public and the public expects and appreciates all that we do. Our many partners assist us in providing necessary services, such as free tax returns through AARP, teaching coding to children and teens, free computer instruction, and providing critical information to veterans. During the summer months, we partner with the USDA and our local school district to provide free lunches and snacks to children and teens. Every year, we provide the only book festival exclusively for children and teens in the Rio Grande Valley, offering children and teens the opportunity to meet and talk with established authors and illustrators. I believe this is why we have more than 60,000 per month entering our library.

Which part(s) of your job as the Librarian do you find most rewarding? What is the most frustrating?

The most rewarding part of my job as Library Director is knowing that our resources, services and staff change lives in ways big and small. Nothing makes me happier than knowing I am part of enacting positive change in my community.

The most frustrating part? That's easy: There aren't enough hours in the day to do everything I want to do in service to our citizens. But I'm honored each day to do my utmost for a better future.

Throughout your career as a librarian, do you have any regrets or second thoughts? Was there anything that you would have done different if you were given a second chance?

I honestly can't think of anything I regret. Certainly, there are no second thoughts. If I hadn't been in library school at the same time that I was a single mother raising three children, during a time when my mother was ill, I would have been more involved in pursuing an academic career. But I don't regret the choices I made to be with my family during that period of my life. I have spent most of my adult life in the library in some capacity and each year feels like the best year ever.

When you said, you would have been more involved in academic activities, does it mean that you could have become an academic or scholar?

I had considered becoming an academic, but the timing wasn't right for me. I still hold it as an option for the future.

If a young person is inspired to become a librarian and asks you for advice – what would you say to him or her?

I would say the following to this person:
1. If you aren't currently working in a library, try to volunteer to get a sense of what a library actually does.
2. Find the most rigorous MLS or MLIS program you can afford, and be sure to explore your selected university's array of scholarships before taking on a student loan. Take courses in digital management and overall management. These two areas will help you no matter what you will ultimately specialize in.

3. Once you are hired, don't hesitate to take on projects that put leadership into practice. Look for a mentor in your department, even if it's an unofficial mentorship. You will learn leadership best by observing others' successes and putting leadership into practice. Be sure to follow through with every project, not matter how small. Great program ideas and passion are plentiful, but the ability to follow-through is the most valuable asset. Library Directors prize staff they can count on.
4. Last, but not least, be courageous! You will find your place if you work hard and persevere.

Could you give me a list of major achievements accomplished by your Library in 2016?

This year (2016) was our third annual McAllen Book Festival, a day of literacy and fun expressly for children and teens in the Lower Rio Grande Valley. The MBF has its own website (http://mcallenbookfestival.com/), social media, and mission: *The McAllen Book Festival is a celebration of culture and imagination by linking readers of all ages with authors, performers, and publishers, and fulfilling the mission of McAllen Public Library as a place where people and ideas meet and connect.*

The McAllen Book Festival has a committee that begins planning in January of each year for the November festival. Our sponsors have included local restaurants, food vendors, local and regional booksellers, local media, and City of McAllen Departments.

This year, based on feedback from the public and from staff, we expanded from a small, but successful, festival of children's and teen authors, to a festival atmosphere that included outdoor rides, popcorn, cotton candy, raspas (a local favorite of shaved ice and syrup), a rescue animal show, and an improved location for families to purchase participating authors' books and engage in one-to-one conversations with authors and illustrators. We tracked attendance through the distribution of wristbands with great results. The first year attendance was around 2000; year two inched up to just over 2500. This year, attendance was more than 4500!

This year's authors were a definite draw. Newbery Award Winner Matt de la Pena read from *Last Stop of Market Street*, a book with a sweet but powerful message to Latino/a children. Carolyn Dee Flores held a Sketch-Off Storytelling whereby children could see story ideas come alive on paper. Kid Chef Eliana, author of *Cool Kids Cook*, treated families to a healthy cooking demonstration and catchy songs. Storyteller Dianne De Las Casas read from her delightfully silly book, *Cinderellaphant*.

Further readings

Bigger in Texas: Town Turns Abandoned WalMart into Biggest Library in America [YouTube]. Available at: https://www.youtube.com/watch?v=vtVxg4phTio

Bong Lap Demo at McAllen Public Library [YouTube]. Available at: https://www.youtube.com/watch?v=zcWxB5x-dr4

Enjoy McAllen Public Library [YouTube]. Available at: https://www.youtube.com/watch?v=rml2WWg6DVU

The Fooducator™ Interviews the McAllen Public Library Director - Fooducation™ Movie Series [YouTube]. Available at: https://www.youtube.com/watch?v=Eksj5tyON24

Happy Holidays McAllen Public Library [YouTube]. Available at: https://www.youtube.com/watch?v=-el7yw09IrA

Hilda Salinas - New McAllen Library - Teen Area [YouTube]. Available at: https://www.youtube.com/watch?v=hoBRAugYzT4&t=24s

Manga Madness at the McAllen Public Library [YouTube]. Available at: https://www.youtube.com/watch?v=07xHf706iH8

McAllen Public Library Director Receives Worldwide Recognition. (2016). Available at: http://www.rgvproud.com/news/local-news/mcallen-public-library-director-receives-worldwide-recognition/633239766

McAllen Public Library Grand Opening [YouTube]. Available at: https://www.youtube.com/watch?v=h1-e089mh-0

McAllen Public Library Named Most Beautiful Library in Texas [YouTube]. Available at: https://www.youtube.com/watch?v=EAWmbJXcWWA

McAllen Public Library: National Library Week [YouTube]. Available at: https://www.youtube.com/watch?v=dHIrV2WpDS0

McAllen Public Library Wins AIA Honor Award [YouTube]. Available at: https://www.youtube.com/watch?v=HkOiTTgsJME

Siu Lim Tao Demo at McAllen Public Library (Kung Fu Demonstration) - Sept 17, 2011 [YouTube]. Available at: https://www.youtube.com/watch?v=Jn81YyVvogo

Smith, Sonia. (September, 2012). Making something out of nothing. *Texas Monthly*. Available at: http://www.texasmonthly.com/articles/making-something-out-of-nothing/

Take a Tour of McAllen Public Library [YouTube]. Available at: https://www.youtube.com/watch?v=VOFn-Rgckac

Team Tiger Demo McAllen Library [YouTube]. Available at: https://www.youtube.com/watch?v=JVcRxuFgY5Y

Tour of New McAllen Library Building [YouTube]. Available at: https://www.youtube.com/watch?v=5k69X9qQ1wg

The Wing Chun Punch - from a Demo at the McAllen Public Library Sept 17, 2011 [YouTube]. Available at: https://www.youtube.com/watch?v=SFxUodEot4k

22 Dr. Hannelore Vogt

Director, Cologne Public Library

Introduction

The Cologne Public Library (CPL) is one of the largest and most important public library systems in Germany. It is made up of the Central Library (as a part of the *Kulturquartier*, a 'cultural hub,' near the Neumarkt), 11 other branch libraries, and a mobile library. The CPL provides local residents (about one million inhabitants in total) with information resources for education, training, as well as a wide range of other recreational and social networking activities. Furthermore, a large number of people from nearby regions and other neighboring countries (e.g., Belgium, the Netherlands, Luxembourg) are also known to be frequent users of CPL.

In addition to its vast and significant printed and digital collections, CPL is also internationally renowned for being a multicultural meeting place, as well as its long list of innovative digital initiatives. Overseeing this major public library system is Dr. Hannelore Vogt, who became the Director in 2008. Before coming to CPL, she was the Head of the Wurzburg City Library, which was the winner of the national library rankings (BIX) four times in a row and was elected "Library of the Year." In 2015, Cologne City Library was also elected to the same position – making it the best library in Germany.

On top of her long list of achievements, Dr. Vogt is also a member of the IFLA Metropolitan Libraries Standing Committee, a longtime chair of the Advisory Board "Information and Library" of the Goethe Institute and worked as a Strategic Advisor and Reviewer for the Bill and Melinda Gates Foundation (Global Libraries, Global Development). She was elected "Cultural Manager of the Year" 2016 in Cologne. Apart from having a degree in librarianship, she also has a Ph.D. in Cultural Management in the field of library marketing. In the following interview, Dr. Vogt shares with us the secrets behind her leadership qualities and the overwhelming success of CPL.

Fig. 22.1: Dr. Hannelore Vogt, the library director (Photo: Cologne Public Library).

Fig. 22.2: Kamishibai for kids taking part in a Lesestart event (Photo: Cologne Public Library).

Fig. 22.3: Sprachraum a place of learning for refugees/immigrants and their tutors (Photo: Cologne Public Library).

Could we begin the interview by introducing yourself, your professional training, and educational background?

I am the Director of the Cologne Public Library[1] since 2008. The Cologne Public Library is one of the biggest public library systems in all of Germany. I was also the Director of the Würzburg City Library, which is a library in Bavaria in a medium-sized university city. Both of these libraries became Library of the Year in Germany. I got this award two times.

By the "biggest public library system," I mean that it is a combination of the number of staff, collection size, branches, etc. While the size of the collection is important, the actuality of the collection is more important. We try to have relevant and up-to-date materials.

For my educational background, I first started studying Library Science. At that time, there were Diplomas in that subject. Then I got a Master's degree in Cultural Management, and this is the same subject I did my Ph.D. I specialized in marketing and especially customer orientation. I always liked being in contact with and together with people. I love reading, but that is not what you are doing as a professional librarian all the time. I worked in libraries all of my life, and this is my passion. I have worked in them since 1982! I started in a small, one-person library, and as I moved, the libraries got bigger and bigger. As a result, I know all of librarian work from scratch. When I started, I worked as a librarian for ten years, and then I stopped and got my Master's degree. I also wrote my doctoral dissertation at night while I was working. I picked a topic that was really close to my practical life. I did all of the research on customer orientation at night, and I could practice in the daytime! This was a very good combination.

What role does the public library play in people's lives in Cologne?

I think that the core topic for this is not reading, but rather knowledge and education, participation, and community engagement. Our role is to bring people together and to give them the infrastructure to explore and to learn. Cologne was the first public library in Germany to have a 3-D printer. We are looking at technology trends and at what could be interesting for people. We are providing them with not only information in books, but also with technology that they can try out – they can see it, they can learn things they didn't know that they wanted to learn. When we started with the 3-D printer, people came with files, and they wanted them printed. We asked them, "Could you go out and tell other

---

[1] Cologne Public Library – Homepage. Available at: http://www.stadt-koeln.de/leben-in-koeln/stadtbibliothek/

citizens how to make such a file?" Some of them agreed, and we started a system of volunteers – also with pupils from a nearby school. They are doing training for adults. We started a whole system of workshops and learning units – only short introductions.

We are also reacting quickly on social needs. When all of the refugees came into Germany last year, we offered an extra space that we called the Language Room. We opened this room to volunteers. They are giving training to the refugees, and we are providing them with space and materials, and we are bringing them together and providing them with a network. So, we are working with a lot of partners in our city and also unusual ones. We have a program called "Kids at Cologne," so it is for youth and we also have science labs. We have all of these things that people don't really expect at the library. But, it's all learning and knowledge – that is our goal.

How did you end up becoming the director of the Cologne Public Library?

I was headhunted, but I had to apply through the regular procedures. In Germany, you have to apply and give a presentation and persuade people that you are the right person. I got a call, and they said, "Wouldn't you be interested in working in Cologne?" They contacted me in advance, but there were other people as well, so I had to do a good job when I had to present myself.

Why do you think they chose you over the others?

I think it was because I look forward. I had a vision for this library. When I was presenting, I was not only talking about what I did before and how great I did it, but I was actively thinking about this library. When I talk about libraries, you feel that I love what I do, and I think that people feel this and feel the passion. On the other hand I am a very strategic person.

Can you briefly explain the cultural landscape of Cologne? How has all of this shaped your policies at the library?

There is a lot of creative industry, so this was one thing we looked at. Then, we looked at our customers, and 70% were under 40 years old. We are part of the municipality, and we are paid by them. In many other cultural institutions, they have many older audiences. So, I looked at what makes us special, and what makes us special to our audience and politicians. Our audience are digital natives, so we have to adapt. Staff members understood that Internet, e-books and social media transform the society and that we have to transform, too, because our audience is expecting that.

Another point that I could say is that the library has more visitors. Cologne has many museums and is very proud of them. But, I could tell them that the Library has more visitors than all of the museums together. This is another thing that makes us special, and it was more important for financial support.

With the users being so young and being digital natives, why do you still need a physical library?

We learned that people want to come to a space – a kind of co-working space. They come to learn as a group, and we are providing spaces where they can talk with each other and learn together. It's not only a quiet place. That is very attractive for them. It is kind of like in Hong Kong, where people do not have much space at home where they can learn together, so they come to the library. Then they need a space to have a coffee, so you have to offer them an attractive space to rest.

Is continuous learning important for people who are already working in Germany?

For the people who are working, they use the library on weekends with their families. We just started, for example, workshops for fathers reading to kids. They come with their whole families, they find things they don't expect like 3-D printing, and they say, "Oh great! I can do this in the library," and then you offer them online lessons and resources on how to learn all kinds of things. It is important to bring them into the building so that they can see that the library offers more than just reading novels. We will be getting a renovation of the library for 40 million euros because our politicians understood that they need the library as a consume-free public space.

The Cologne Public Library was selected as the best public library in Germany. Could you describe the criteria for selecting the best libraries in Germany?

I can tell you the criteria that the German Library Association[2] applied: it is quality and innovation, future orientation – again, it's not looking backward, it's looking forward, sustainability, attractive services, and also PR, international engagement, partnerships and networking. We are doing all of this.

---

[2] German Library Association – Homepage. Available at: http://librariesforall.eu/en/best-practices/dbv-deutscher-bibliotheksverband-german-library-association

Why is international engagement so important for a public library that is devoted to serving the local public?

The local public in Cologne is made up of people from 180 nations. 35% of our community don't have German origins. We also have 25 sister cities all over the world. So, our local community is also international. And we are learning by exchanging ideas with the colleagues abroad.

Can you describe the staffing structure of your library?

We changed all of our counters into self-service, so we don't need so many unskilled people. I only hire skilled people who have librarian or professional training, or you can become a trainee and get a three-year training in the library to become a library assistant. We are also looking for people with other educational backgrounds like social workers and so on. We want skilled people, and they all get special training when they start working in our library. We have a four-week training, and it's modular. They have to learn about customer orientation or how to deal with difficult customers. They learn what we expect from them, and we are focusing on knowledge management. They are working with wikis, and all information is put on a wiki – new staff members have to go through this and learn all of our expectations.

Why would you choose someone who has experience as a social worker?

As I said before, we are working with those who are refugees, so it's good if you have somebody who has special training, and they will get the basic librarian skills in the library. For instance, the social worker has skills like teaching, working with traumatized people. We are collaborating with adult training centers – aside from the training they can get there, they can get experience working in the library. For these reasons, we need educators and also social workers.

Can you describe your typical day at work?

I think that there isn't a "typical" day, but there's a lot of management, strategy, talks – not long meetings. When we start a meeting, we have an agenda and have a limited time. For me, the interaction with my staff members is very important. Once a day, I do management by walking around. I walk through the building so that my staff members can see me, and they can easily ask me something. All of the things that need concentration I put together in about three hours – no phone, no visits, just working. So, I am a very structured person. Every morning, I plan what I am going to do today, and in the evening, I make a plan for the next day and for the week.

Who are the majority of users at your library?

It's different between the Central Library and the branches. If you look at the branches, there are a lot of children, teenagers, and older people. We need these branches because these children won't come to a big central library. For reading promotion and grassroot education, you will need branch libraries.

In the Central Library, it is different. But it also depends on the day. Like on Saturdays, you have all of the families coming in, and during the week, it's younger people. People who are visiting the library are more educated and well-trained. They are reading e-books, but they are also reading paper books. To get the children of the lower-income groups, you have to get contracts with schools and get all of them to the library.

What is "grassroots education" like in Germany?

Along with the regular education system, we support reading programs, working with the illiterate, refugees, schools. We collaborate with schools when children start. We have a program called "A Library Card for Every Schoolchild," where they get a library card and can get this grassroots education.

Can you describe your management and leadership style?

I think that I am a very open-minded person, and I like my staff. I think that as a leader, you have to have a vision, you have to have a goal, and you have to make decisions. But, before you make your decisions, you should listen to people, and you should inform them. Participation and information are very important. For example, I learned that if you don't inform people in the early stage, they hear something and it's like "mouth propaganda." The content changes and people get afraid, because they hear that something is coming up and they don't know what. So, it's better to inform and to talk. In the end, you have to decide what to do because you are responsible. That's my leadership style. When I first started here, I began inviting my staff members in for their birthdays. Every month, I invite the staff members who had birthdays that month into my office where they have a cup of coffee and a piece of cake. We talk about work and their daily lives as well.

What part of your job do you find the most rewarding?

The most rewarding part is working with and meeting so many people – you meet so many different people. You meet with authors, but you are also meeting children, refugees, staff members, so you learn about a lot of different people.

You have worked in libraries for many years, but is there something that you wish you had learned before becoming a director?

Well, I had found out that I had missed some things because they were not a part of the training when I was becoming a librarian. I think that all kinds of management skills are very important, and therefore, I studied again.

What are the main elements for survival of public libraries for the next five to ten years?

I think that we should adapt to changing needs and we should not complain. Many people are complaining of lacking resources – it is boring. If you take the customer's point of view, if the librarians say that they are underfunded and in a bad situation, why should they go there as visitors if this is such a miserable place? You should be creative in thinking, and you should not be afraid to make mistakes. If you are an early adopter of new things, you can make mistakes because you are so far ahead. I also think that we should make the library as an attractive place to be, and to have a comfortable surrounding. The library should have zones where you can do quiet work and meditate as well as noisy zones, where you can collaborate or you can meet your companion and have coffee. We should focus on lifelong learning, and we should be where our customers are both physically and online.

Anything you would like to say to conclude this interview or any advice you would give to a young person who wants to be a librarian or director of a public library?

I would like to say that library work is never boring because we have to work with people, and we have to cover so many fields from education to new technology to management. There are so many opportunities for someone who wants to work in the library if you are innovative and not afraid of adapting to the changing world.

Further readings

Hannelore Vogt - Future Library 2015. Available at: http://2015.futurelibrary.gr/index.php/speaker/hannelore-vogt/

Interview with Dr. Hannelore Vogt: Always One Step Ahead: On the New Library Concepts. Available at: https://www.goethe.de/ins/cn/en/kul/mag/20731015.html

23 Christine Brunner

Director, Stuttgart City Library

Introduction

Designed by Korean architect Eun Young Yi, the Stuttgart City Library has been praised internationally by experts, visitors, and on social media as being one of the most beautiful libraries in the world since its grand opening in October 2011. With its exterior shaped like a perfect cube, the library building has a futuristic look to it. The building is entirely white, with the idea being that the environment leads patrons to put all the focus on the colorful books lining the shelves. In fact, the heart and core of the library follows the design of the ancient Pantheon in a form of a square and surrounded by shelves of books. In addition to books, the library also contains a number of meeting rooms, a café, and a rooftop terrace, etc. Equally intriguing is the library's "Insomniacs" feature, as there is a small collection of books available 24 hours a day for late-night patrons.

Managing this ultra-modern, space station-like library is Christine Brunner, who took up the position of Director of the Stuttgart City Library in 2013. In the following interview, Brunner describes the unique architectural and interior design of the library, in how such distinctive features are supportive to the new ways we learn and enjoy books in the digital age.

Fig. 23.1: Christine Brunner, Director, Stuttgart City Library (Photo: Stuttgart City Library).

Fig. 23.2: Stuttgart City Library (Photo: Meike Jung).

Fig. 23.3: Gallery, Stuttgart City Library (Photo: Martin Lorenz).

Fig. 23.4: Thematic area, Stuttgart City Library (Photo: Günther Marsch).

Could we begin this interview by first introducing yourself, for example, your training and background? Could you also describe your role as the Director of the Stuttgart City Library?

My professional background is as follows:
- Since April, 2013   Managing Director City Library Stuttgart
- Until March, 2013   Head of the new central library in Stuttgart
- Until September, 2010 Head of 17 city district libraries and the 2 mobile libraries

I am also an expert in the following:
- Planning and building public libraries
- Last project was the city library of Stuttgart
- In-house Change Management
- Innovative solutions: state of the art library technology based on RFID
- Presentations and publications on a great range of different library issues
- Managing cultural events in the library and the European Quarter
- Library Management

Could you tell me which universities did you attend, and what subjects did you study at university?

I studied Library and Media Management at the Stuttgart Media University.[1]

How many different languages have you mastered?

German, English and French.

Could you please provide a brief introduction about the Stuttgart City Library? In addition, what is the current size of the Stuttgart City Library's overall collection, including its special collections? Could you also describe what you deem are the highlights of the collection?

We have a total offer of almost 1.3 million media items with about 500,000 media items in the central library. The branch libraries stock about 67,000 media in bigger branches and about 13,000 media in the smallest one. As a public library we don't have special collections, but our 40-year-old Graphothek has 2,800 artworks of famous international artists. We had a permanent exhibition of the authors of Stuttgart and the region. Their books are in the special area "Literaturscene" and we present these authors in films when they read their texts in our "gallery b." We also have a cooperation with the *International Trickfilm Festival*. All the festival films can be seen in our Online Animation Library.

The presentation of digital art on the 16 screens of our "gallery b" is fascinating for big and small visitors. The literature and music scene of the city and area of Stuttgart, and now also the Stuttgart movie scene have been presented in the library for many years and emphasize our function as a showcase of the cultural life in the city and the region.

The citizens of Stuttgart love our "library for sleepless people" which is small but open 7 days a week, 24 hours a day.

Does your Library work closely with other libraries across Germany? What about the rest of the world? If so, could you tell us about such cross-national or global collaborative projects? What are some highlights?

Yes we do. We work together with libraries in Stuttgart – in February 2016, we organized the *Inet-Bib Congress* together with the library of the University of Stuttgart. We help to develop a project for a new central library in Berlin and there are

---

[1] Stuttgart Media University – Homepage. Available at: https://www.hdm-stuttgart.de/english

good connections to the city library of Munich and Frankfurt. We developed an international standard for RFID-Chips in libraries together and created a common e-learning platform. We also talked about our library in Helsinki, Milan, Novosibirsk, Rio de Janeiro, Sao Paulo, Straßburg and Bratislava. In September 2016, one of our colleagues is "Librarian in Residence" in New York.

What is the role of technology and innovation at the Stuttgart City Library?

Our favorite guideline is: "Welcoming the future" and we define our library as a mediator of key competency. Our approach in Stuttgart is to strengthen the competency in handling the world of media not only in the classical way of reading support for children and young people, but also by initiating a critical discourse on digital development.

We support the reflection on media development and have created digital laboratories (also in several branch libraries), where our visitors can follow up on current topics at up-scaled high-end-computers. Testing new information technology, the security in the Internet and serious games as an alternative to violent games are only a few of the offers for our visitors.

Meetings with selected specialists in the field of digital art, the cooperation with the *Chaos Computer Club* in Stuttgart, the participation in pedagogical media projects like "Safer Internet Day" or "I can computer" makes the current developments in the digital world transparent and tangible for all.

At the moment, this task field is definitely the most challenging part of our profile and most focused on the future. With its special offers it constantly marks our strong position in the network of educational and cultural facilities of the city.

We experimented with technical solutions which can be helpful for our users. We were the first RFID-Big City-Library and have created an easy-to-handle self-service. Wi-Fi is in every one of our libraries and we created "intelligent media boxes", were you can lend a laptop for one day in the library. Adults and children love our sorting machine, where media are transported behind glass walls to one of the eight platforms.

Please describe the staffing structure at the Stuttgart City Library?

The Stuttgart City Library is managed by teams. I have a team of six colleagues. They are responsible for managing the central library, the branch library and mobile library, the offers for children and young people, central coordination services and the expanded library.

In the central library one team on every floor is responsible for media, information and events. The same is the case in the branch-libraries. Nearly 30 teams are working here, 180 full-time workplaces, 340 staff members.

Could you describe your typical day at work? Is there ever a typical day at work?

No, I have no typical days. But there are many meetings, visitors and guided tours. Developing new ideas and projects, fighting for money, planning the 18th branch library and opening ears for problems of the staff are just some examples of the things I have to deal with. There are too many emails, long days and short nights.

What scholarly and professional associations are you a part of, and how do they assist you or supplement your work?

Our library is connected with all educational and cultural institutions of the city. We create common learning and information projects and have several long-lasting series of events with the University of Stuttgart, with cultural institutions, with the *Schriftstellerhaus* (House of Authors) and the *Literaturhaus* (literature house), with intercultural institutions and the *Volkshochschule* (adult education center).

Schools and kindergartens are important cooperation partners for us. The *Verein Leseohren* is closely connected to the children's library and helps us to mediate (digital-) reading competency programs.

Who are the majority users of the Stuttgart City Library? That is, who comes to see you about your collections, programs, and services?

We have no "major"-users, but our media-collection has some priorities: International media in all European and the most important world-languages, art, music and literature. The presentation of digital art is fascinating for big and small visitors. The literature and music scene of the city and area of Stuttgart and now also the Stuttgart movie scene have been presented in the library for many years and emphasize our function as a showcase of the cultural life in the city and the region.

Another field of attention that is of great importance for us is the integration of citizens from more than 170 nations. All our facilities are intercultural libraries with offers to learn and to train numerous languages, this is particularly valuable for refugees.

Last but not least, our long opening hours are attractive for families and working citizens.

It has been said that the Stuttgart City Library was planned since 1997. Why did it take so long for it to be built? How much time did it take for the building to be physically constructed?

We opened the new central library building after 14 years of building and planning in the center of a new city district of Stuttgart, the so-called Europe Quarter. There were many discussions in the city about how to build this new quarter and especially the new railway station nearby. The library was the first building in this new area and a sign that "Stuttgart 21" would now be realized.

The physical construction took only three years from the ground-breaking ceremony to the opening ceremony 21st October 2011.

Could you describe your management and leadership style? Mentorship is such an important theme in leadership – both mentoring and being mentored. Could you please tell us about your experiences about both? Do you still have mentors that you go to?

I love to work with my team – it is important and inspiring for me. Unreserved discussions, asking for advice, creating unconventional ideas and opening the doors to new cooperation – all this works better for me within a team. At the end I decide and carry the responsibility – even if something goes wrong.

Fortunately, I regularly meet my predecessor and long-time boss. It is good for both of us to discuss my decisions – I think she is one of the most important persons in my professional life and so – if you want – more than a mentor.

When people talk about the Stuttgart City Library, what image or library service first come to their mind? What kind of words or adjectives would they use for describing the Stuttgart City Library?

Many visitors are pleased with the service and praise us and our media offers. But my favorite quote is the answer of the literature editor of the *Stuttgarter Zeitung* to the question: "Why do we still need a public library in the beautiful digital world? A building full of dead trees in form of paper, cardboard and shelves?" And she answered herself: "We need it exactly for this future because the public libraries open the doors to knowledge, they are realms of knowledge and realms of freedom, sites of participation and education for all."

Could you describe the unique characteristics behind the architectural and interior design behind the physical building of the Stuttgart City Library?

By day the library is a white cube, by night it is a blue cube. Our architect created this shiny and bright building and determined that media and visitors will bring the color.

The central rooms HEART and Gallery Hall are symbols for fertile places where knowledge can grow.

Your Library has been constantly voted as one of the most beautiful libraries in the world on different online social media. As the Library's General Director, what would you like to say to respond to that?

It is an honor and of great importance for the city. We are proud to work in this ambitious building. The great number of visitors (yearly 1.43 million persons) underline the great success of the library and its service concept. We were twice voted to be one of the most significant institutions in the city of Stuttgart.

Which part(s) of your job as the Librarian do you find most rewarding? What is the most frustrating?

It is rewarding for me to meet interesting people from around the world and to create services for the citizens of my city that supports them in their professional, scholarly and daily life.

The security requirements are so high and strict in Germany that we sometimes can't realize our interesting ideas – this is really frustrating.

Further readings

The New Stuttgart City Library [YouTube]. Available at: https://www.youtube.com/watch?v=8gk0ERMb_I0

Prizeman, Poriel. (February, 2012). Stuttgart City Library by Yi Architects. *Architectural Review.* Available at: https://www.architectural-review.com/today/stuttgart-city-library-by-yi-architects/8627149.article

Stuttgart City Library: The Book Cube - Goethe-Institut. Available at: https://www.goethe.de/en/kul/bib/20365687.html

Stuttgart's Municipal Library – LibraryBuildings.Info. Available at: http://www.librarybuildings.info/germany/stuttgarts-municipal-library

24 Sandra Singh

Chief Librarian, Vancouver Public Library

Introduction

Vancouver, British Columbia, is a city that is internationally known for its diverse communities, multiculturalism, and social inclusion. Serving the needs and reading interests of such diverse user groups in this beautiful West Coast Canadian city is the Vancouver Public Library (VPL) – consisting of a Central Branch, located in downtown Vancouver, and 20 neighbor branches situated throughout the city.

Managing the operations and strategic planning of this major library system is Sandra Singh, who took up the role as the Chief Librarian in late 2010. Prior to joining VPL, Singh worked as a library professional for a number of public libraries, an academic library, and an Internet company. Under her direction, VPL has undertaken unprecedented changes – re-imagining its services, finding new and innovative ways to expand the system and enhance access in all respects. According to her, public libraries matter more than ever as places for exploration, understanding, and community connections. "Libraries represent the best in people and society – the willingness to share and contribute to the greater good." Given its inherent merits, multiculturalism has undoubtedly led to a complex range of issues and challenges posed to the traditional library service provision. In the following interview, Singh shares with the readers how she got to be the head of such a major public library system within such a short career span, as well as the joys and challenges of serving as the Chief Librarian of VPL.

Fig. 24.1: Chief Librarian Sandra Singh (Photo: Vancouver City Library).

Fig. 24.2: Exterior of Central Library (Photo: Vancouver City Library).

Fig. 24.3: Atrium at the Central Library (Photo: Vancouver City Library).

Could we begin this interview by first introducing yourself? Namely, your major duties and roles as the Chief Librarian at the Vancouver Public Library?

I am Sandra Singh, and I am the Chief Librarian at the Vancouver Public Library.[1] I completed my BA at the University of British Columbia (UBC)[2], English Literature. I did my Master of Science in Library and Information Science (MLIS) at the UBC School of Library, Archival, and Information Studies.

As the Chief Librarian, I serve as the Chief Executive Officer of the library. The library itself, as a public library in British Columbia, is governed by a thirteen-member board appointed by City Council. We have 10 community member appointees and three elected officials – one city council member, one elected park board commissioner, and one elected school board trustee. These

---

1 Vancouver Public Library – Homepage. Available at: http://www.vpl.ca/
2 The University of British Columbia – Homepage. Available at: https://www.ubc.ca

13 board members provide governance, oversight, and strategic direction for the library. My role as the Chief Librarian is to support them in their work in this capacity and provide strategic leadership to the operations of the library. We have an annual (2017) budget of approximately $50 million dollars and we have just over 700 staff. We operate just under 500,000 square feet of space in the city of Vancouver. We are an extraordinarily busy public library by any standard, and so it is my job to make sure that we deliver relevant, innovative, high-quality library services to the city of Vancouver.

You've had a number of positions in libraries: special, public, and academic libraries. How have these experiences shaped your career and thinking about the library?

I have worked across sectors and in different types of libraries. I have also worked in different roles in libraries. When I started my career, I started as a cataloger, then moved to reference services and website design at a public library. I then moved to an Internet company and worked as a metadata specialist as well as working with the team on information architecture. I then moved into public library management and then senior management at a large urban library, and then to UBC (University of British Columbia) Library. What I have found, is that working across a diversity of sectors, different library types, and different types of jobs attached to the library has provided me with a really useful cross-sectional view of library operations as well as allowed my practice and my thinking to be enhanced by the expertise and experience of my colleagues. The non-siloed career has been very helpful and has enabled me to think outside the box and think differently and more expansively about the role and opportunities – in this particular context now – of public libraries.

What best prepared you for your work as the Chief Librarian?

I kind of happened into the role – it wasn't something that I had seen on my career trajectory. I think that there were a few things: the first is good, solid management training and practice. I think that sometimes in our field, and in the academy as well, despite the fact that we have schools of management, it is often viewed as a pejorative. I actually think that a good management approach and a respect for management technique and the discipline of management is critical as a foundation for leadership. That has been very important. I think that some of the most important skills development as well has been around interest-based negotiation, which provides a very different way of working with the community and with staff to achieve good outcomes despite differing opinions and approaches. The financial mentorship by good financial managers has been essential, as well as access to and participation in strategy setting and development for the broader organization.

As soon as I had the opportunity to be involved in broader discussions, either at the city or at the university, it was extraordinarily helpful to my practice rather than just working and thinking only within the context of the library. So, thinking about the broader ecosystem and stakeholders that you are serving.

Let's move on to the Vancouver Public Library more closely. Could you describe the highlights of the collection?

I think that as a large, urban public library, we sit in an interesting position between what a community would expect of a public library in terms of recreational reading and support of mid-level research and expectations of a large research library. We consider ourselves a resource library. Our collections are really strong – I have a very strong commitment to maintaining collections as a core library service. I think that regardless of everything that is stored on the Internet for free collections remain a fundamental purpose and role for the public library. I know within the discourse of libraries right now, there is this idea that great libraries don't build collections, they build communities. I would argue that that is a simplistic polarization, and that one of the many ways that we build great communities is by supporting lifelong learning and knowledge creation and sharing. One of the key ways we do this is by building great collections. We have a very strong commitment to our collections at VPL.

In terms of the special areas of our collections that are maybe unique compared to other libraries, We have a strong commitment to recreational reading, nonfiction, and digital collections. I would say that some of our unique collections that are emerging and are important to us as we head into the future are some of our local history and our hyper-local collections. Some of these items are digitized version of existing historical artifact, but some of these are heritage and cultural collections that we are working with the community to create and provide access to. So it's no longer the library being a source of secondary sources and information – we're actually working with the community to create primary sources at a very local level. For example, oral history collections with our immigrant communities, and other types of collections working with local communities here in Vancouver.

Do you work closely with other public libraries across Canada, and are there some examples?

Absolutely. We do work actively with other public libraries across Canada. The most useful network for that work is the Canadian Urban Libraries Council, in which we are a very active member. That is a society of large, urban libraries here in Canada – libraries that serve over 100,000 people. We work with them on a number of different initiatives. For example, we worked with the Canadian Urban Libraries Council[3] to develop a national approach to providing better access to alternative formats for Canadians with print disabilities through our libraries in partnership with the Canadian National Institute for the Blind. We have worked on projects collectively with Canadian independent publishers to develop a better understanding of our reading ecosystem, as well as to improve access to Canadian independent publisher materials in public libraries. We've worked with this group on advocacy around copyright and policy issues, and projects such as benchmarking library services.

Reference service is slowly fading away. Some schools don't even teach it anymore. What are your thoughts on reference services and how has it changed at VPL since your time there?

Reference services at VPL have changed significantly since I started. We undertook a very extensive review of our information services and then significantly altered it based on the findings. We had seen a dramatic decrease in the use of our reference services since 2007. As a result, we dramatically changed our reference services model. We are trying to have library technicians and paraprofessionals deal with the first line of reference rather than putting our reference librarians in the triage spot. No other institutions put their highest-paid professional staff on the front desk: they triage things, so we worked to implement that principle. Our hope is that over the next few years, our information services librarians can go out into the community to work with community organizations and businesses to really hone in and support their information needs. I think that, absolutely, we have seen a lot of dialogue on the demise of reference, and we've implemented significant changes here.

That said, I have worried that we have been swinging the pendulum too far, and that there is an important role for research and reference specialists in libraries to support community research – especially as information proliferates. It's becoming harder and harder for people to find the information they need, and they are settling for "good enough" or what they perceive to be good enough in the interest of convenience. I think that our complacency as a field around this contributes to a general decline in thoughtful decision-making, opinion-forming, and engagement by the broader community. I think that we can see this all over the place in social media and digital engagement, where we are becoming more and more inclined as people to develop opinions on very

---

3 Canadian Urban Libraries Council – Homepage. Available at: http://www.culc.ca/

little information and expecting those opinions to be valued as fact in research. I think that libraries have a role to play in encouraging research and rational, thoughtful approaches as essential to democracy, social exchange, and healthy communities. I don't think we've nailed it yet, but I think that the platitude regarding the demise of reference over recent years maybe has taken us down a less strategic path.

Could you describe the staffing structure at VPL? What are the working relationships with the various branches and central VPL departments in such a vast and large system?

We have 20 different branches and a large central library. At the senior level, we have a Director who oversees neighborhood and youth services. We also have a Director who oversees collections and technology. The Director of Library Experience has responsibility for the service experience in the central library as well as the strategy and coherence around common services – primarily, information services, programming and learning, and circulation services across the whole system. This person works closely with the Neighborhood Services Director and at the management level, the portfolio managers for reference services, circulation, information services and programming, and learning work closely with the Neighborhood Services managers that manage the day-to-day operations of the branch network. So, we have a bit of a hybrid model or a matrix model in terms of responsibility. In terms of children's and teen services, we have moved to an evidence-based allocation of child and teen services effort throughout the library, and our staff now work in specialty cohorts within Neighborhoods. When I say "specialty cohorts," I mean early year specialists, middle year specialists, and teen specialists. They then work as a team within an area of about four or five branches, providing services within that area. We also have a Director of Human Resources, a Director of Planning and Projects, and a Director of Corporate Services.

Could you describe a typical day at work, or is there a typical day?

For me, there is no typical day at work. Well, I would say that a typical day involves a lot of meetings. I know that it seems that a lot of meetings are unproductive, but I actually think that meetings are critical to an organization that is committed to collaboration. When you are committed to collaborating with a lot of people to get your work done, you have to meet with them – whether it be teleconference or in person. So I would say that in a typical week, I spend anywhere from half a day in meetings with the City of Vancouver, and I spend quite a bit of time in meetings with staff working on various issues or in charge of portfolios and spend time on community, whether it be Vancouver communities or library communities-initiatives. And, of course, there are meetings every month with the Board of VPL and conversations with various Trustees throughout the month. It is a bit of a mix, but lots of conversations and meetings.

You're currently the president of the Canadian Library Association. What has it been like and how has it complemented your position as Chief Librarian?

Taking on the presidency of the Canadian Library Association, I had anticipated one thing and it turned into something else. When I put my name forward and was elected as vice-president, I thought that I would spend a year as president and represent the CLA making presentations at the federal level and working with my executive council to respond to various policy issues that arose and organizing the annual conference, which is pretty much "business as usual" for the CLA. Instead, what I found was that the association was no longer sustainable and we were in a position in which we needed to enact significant change to preserve a national voice for Canadian libraries. My year as the vice-president and then this year as president has been much more intense as we worked with association partners across the country to try to find a new way forward for a national voice for Canadian libraries, and eventually, with the membership to determine that dissolution would be the best approach forward. Right now, we are working on the dissolution of the Association. It has not been a typical presidential year by any means.

In terms of how it complements my work, I think that certainly the types of skills and approaches that you need to lead a large organization like VPL such as collaboration and facilitation skills came to be very handy. I think that what was most important in my work with the CLA. Also, VPL had been a longstanding member of the CLA since it formed – it has never dropped its membership – and I have been a CLA member for many, many years. That commitment to national engagement was critical to being both passionate and dispassionate in terms of the work of the last year and a half or so.

Are there any other scholarly or professional associations that you're a part of and how do they assist you in your work?

I am a part of a few other associations: there's CLA, there's the Association for BC Public Library Directors, the InterLINK Federation, and the British Columbia Library Association.[4] At this point, that rounds out my memberships. I also serve on a number of different types of committees and boards outside of professional engagement. What I think I would say is that the types of professional

---

4 British Columbia Library Association – Homepage. Available at: https://bclaconnect.ca/

engagement that I find most helpful for me in my role is the interaction with the Canadian Urban Libraries Council because these are people working in similar situations with me professionally. It has been really helpful having them there as a source of information, inspiration, and mentorship. The areas where I most look now for professional development are areas that are outside of the profession. So areas around public policy development, strategic planning, and city urban planning – fields like that where I see it's important to bring some understanding and knowledge of that field, even if it is just one-centermeter-deep, into my work so that I know what types of questions to ask and how to better interact with these professionals who have such a profound impact on the role and future of libraries and the community.

Who are the users of VPL?

We have a really diverse range of users here, and I don't mean that we are unique when compared with other large, urban libraries. We have a very high use by children and families. Vulnerable populations that face various types of marginalization or exclusion, and by newcomers who are seeking support for their settlement and integration into Canada. We have a high use by seniors. We tend to lose people in their 20s and 30s – often, they will come back with children. What we're trying to understand better is how to support those communities with what they need from the library. We also tend to have higher use with those with medium to low income, but what we find is that many people who don't even use the library still support it because they see the socioeconomic imperative of having the library in the community. In the last year, almost 300,000 people used their library card – either for access to our physical collections or access to our digital services. That's very high in terms of usage.

Could you give us some examples on the types of new programs and services at VPL that you have found to have been successful or innovative?

Last year, we launched the Inspiration Lab, which is a creative digital media lab that includes sound booths for video and sound recording, digitization software, and different types of creation software for the community that does not have access to this type of technology or that might have it but does not know how to maximize it. That has been enormously last year, we also implemented a number of public realm interventions. In an attempt to highlight the literary heritage of Vancouver, we launched Literary Landmarks; plaques that highlight local writers are dispersed throughout the community, and we are adding to that collection every year. We also launched another collection of landmarks – we called them Reading Lights – that are intended to celebrate children's writers and illustrators in British Columbia and inspire kids to read by placing little literary interventions in spaces where kids and families hang out. For example, at playgrounds and parks around the city. We have implemented our digital repository this year and we have seeded it with a number of oral history collections – so, histories of growing up in the West End, stories of growing up in Chinatown. Our intent is to grow this resource in order to both capture our history, stories, and memories before they disappear and also to showcase them for the community and provide a good sense of continuity and build understanding of the rich diversity of Vancouver. I think that those three are good highlights.

Recently, there has been an announcement to expand the VPL Central Branch to have a new tenant and new outdoor spaces for users. Could you elaborate on those plans, and what is the direction of the library in the next few years?

What we are able to do is to move the library to take over the top two floors of the Central Library. So altogether, we will be adding about 35,000 or so square feet of public space to the public through this expansion. There will be a whole suite of new community meeting spaces and programming rooms for use by the library to offer community programs and for use by the community for their own programming and organizing. There will be a 60-seat theatre for use by the library and the community, an exhibition space, and an area we are calling "Vancouver Stories." So we will have spaces for our mentors – our aboriginal storyteller in residence, our writer in residence, and any other creative residencies that we might create in the future. There will be creative space and workshop space in there as well. We will also be opening two outdoor terraces for public use and an 8,000 square foot learning garden – it is going to be designed intentionally to support individual contemplation and use, as well as learning events and community event programs. It will be quite a flexible space.

As a part of the second phase of this expansion, we will be bringing the City of Vancouver Archives onto the seventh floor of the Central Library, and that will happen after we move into levels eight and nine. So we hope by 2021, we should have all of that wrapped up, and we should have a different experience on the top floors of the library. We also plan to revitalize a few other areas of the library, including the Children's Library, which is on the lower levels. We need to expand and refresh that space. When this library was built in 1995, the Children's Library was seen more as a resource library to support children's services throughout the branches, because there was not such a large residential community in the downtown core. Now, 20 years later, there's a huge residential community, and it's growing. Those families use the Central Library as their neighborhood branch.

On the second floor, you get quite a traditional library experience – you see a lot of books on shelves, computers, and a circulation area. What we really want to do is to transform this space, where as soon as you walk in, you see a whole range of learning activities happening beyond what you would traditionally expect from a library, which is people accessing collections and people using the Internet. We want to have transparent programming rooms, community meet-up spaces, reading spaces, and of course digital technology. We really want to celebrate the diverse platforms that people use to learn and engage in lifelong learning. We need to work on the third floor as well.

Mentorship is such an important theme in leadership – both mentoring and being mentored. Could you please tell us about your own experiences with both, and do you still have mentors that you go to?

I have found that mentorship in my career has been quite informal and unstructured, but extraordinarily important. There have been a number of people whom I have sought advice from over the years or have had the opportunity to have worked closely with and learn from. That has been very important. In my view, almost everyone I encounter in my work is someone I can learn something from. Whether that person reports to me, works side-by-side with me, or I report to the person, I think that I can learn something from everyone. There are some people in my organization that are working here as branch heads or supervisors, and I still learn from them. Certainly, there are a number of people over the years in leadership positions whom I have counted on as people to go to and call for advice, and it is incredibly important to have them in my life.

In terms of mentoring other people, what I have mostly done to date is to make myself available to those who want my thoughts or my opinions on something. I have served as a mentor at a leadership institute and will do so again this.

What part of your job as the Chief Librarian do you find the most rewarding? What would you say is the most frustrating?

I think that I find the most rewarding piece to be when we are able to implement a service that can clearly be tied to an important social outcome or impact in the community and hearing the feedback and the stories about the service. I find it really rewarding to see the staff come together and implement these types of services, and I'm always amazed by the passion, diligence, and conscientiousness that they bring to these projects. It is really rewarding to see our work make a real difference in people's lives.

I think that the most frustrating thing that I face in my work is the public sector move to quantifying everything. The positive part is that it challenges our organization to really be able to articulate our outcomes and impacts – we've only ever articulated our output. However, the enormous amount of work that goes into measuring things like impacts and outcomes can, at times, detract from over ability to deliver services that can make a difference. I am hoping the pendulum swings back to what feels like a more reasonable level so we can better balance measuring and doing.

25 Shih-chang Horng

Director, Taipei Public Library

Abstract

As a cosmopolitan Central Library, the Taipei Municipal Library, in line with the principles of "comfortable, convenient, advising enriched, serious, kind, and reader satisfaction," strives to provide a variety of activities for public services. It has become one of the public facilities Taipei people most willing to enjoy. Here, we interviewed the library director Shih-Chang Horng (洪世昌)[1]. In the following interview, Taipei Public Library Director, Shih-Chang Horng explains the significance of the library to the entire city of Taipei, from which the library staff stand united to meet the needs of the local community, and strive to promote Taipei to become a dynamic metropolis Imbued with happy reading and enthusiastic in learning.

Fig. 25.1: Shih-chang Horng, General Director of Taipei Public Library (Photo: Taipei Public Library).

---

1 http://www.tpml.edu.tw/ct.asp?xItem=1101938&ctNode=62450&mp=104021

DOI 10.1515/9783110533347-026

Fig. 25.2: Main Library of Taipei Public Library (Photo: Taipei Public Library).

Fig. 25.3: East Metro Mall Intelligent Library of Taipei Public Library (Photo: Taipei Public Library).

Fig. 25.4: Beitou Branch of Taipei Public Library, the first diamond-level green building in Taiwan (Photo: Taipei Public Library).

Director Horng, could you please introduce yourself. What did you study at college? Before working at Taipei Municipal Library, where did you work?

I majored (undergraduate and postgraduate) in Social Education, with a focus on Library and Information Science. After graduation, my first job was already in the Taipei Municipal Library. During my career as a librarian, I had worked for eight years at a university library, and then returned to performing public library services in Taipei. So far, I have been working in the library field for over 20 years.

Since books and other reading materials are so easily available on the Internet and local bookstores nowadays, why do people still choose to come to use the Taipei City Library?

Every year we conduct a survey on reader satisfaction and usage behavior. We found that most readers come to the library for the following three main purposes: first, to borrow and return books; second, to read newspapers and magazines; third, to self-study and prepare for exams.

Who are the majority of users at the Taipei City Library?

Different readers come to our library for different purposes. In general, more elderly people come to read newspapers and magazines. Youths and young students come to study by themselves and to prepare for exams. Students in secondary and elementary schools come to do homework and to borrow books. Especially, during weekends, a lot of parents come with their elementary-school-age children to the Taipei City Library to borrow books and do their homework.

By what means does your Library try to meet the reading interests and information needs of people from the local community?

We buy books via two different channels. First, our librarians examine new publications of the year, and choose books based on their professional judgment. Second, we accept book recommendations from the general public all year round. After receiving the book recommendations, we shall include them onto our purchase list – eventually these recommended books will go through a review mechanism.

Now there are so many free e-books freely available on Internet. There are also many mega bookstores in Taiwan, while the average book price is not expensive. Why would they still need to go the public libraries?

I think those who buy books, are those in relatively good economic conditions. They can certainly spend a lot of money to buy books and whatever they want to read from the local bookstores. But there are still many low-income families in Taipei. When their want to read, they probably need to come to our public libraries. Eventually, there will be a limit in terms of the amount of money one can spend on buying books from whatever bookstores and for whatever reasons. So, if this person has a tendency to read a lot, he/she simply cannot pay money to buy every single book he/she desires to read. In other words, providing free reading materials to the millions of individuals living in Taipei is one of the core functions of the Taipei City Library.

The majority of the Taipei City Library users, which social classes from the local community do they represent?

We did not do surveys on our library visitors, to find out more about the profile of our book borrowers. However, we found that most readers are between the age 31 to 50. But we did not further analyze their income, occupations, and so on.

Do you know whether a majority of the users come to borrow books from the Taipei City Library for recreational or for self-study purposes?

Different people borrow books for different purposes. For example, a majority of the white-collar office workers might come to borrow books for sheer leisure reading. Whereas for the local elementary school students, they are likely to borrow books that are assigned by their teachers – to read them as homework. For the elderly, many of them would come to read books for recreational purposes, or to fulfill their information needs related to their daily activities, e.g., information about health and old age. Books on tourism are particularly popular among the elderly use group.

Do you also find a large percentage of young children, youths, retirees and disabled people in your existing user group?

As I just said, most of the borrowers are in the age group between 31 and 50 years old, while the second largest user group is 7 to 12, i.e., elementary school students. We also have a very high proportion of children in our user group. Special services are provided at the Taipei City Library for these young children. Every weekend, we have library staff and volunteers reading stories to these children as part of our Library's weekend service highlights. For the elderly (over 55 years old), our Library has established a "Learning Center for Senior Citizens" – aiming at offering different recreational programs in a variety of areas, for example, computer literacy, painting, calligraphy, by making their life more colorful, less socially isolated – thereby giving them a sense of achievement, as well as allowing them to make new friends.

Does your Library also provide any special services that are tailor-made for the users who are school-aged children?

We have different plans for different student groups. For preschool children, we have reading classes for toddlers and young children. For elementary schools students, every year we have summer reading programs. We design reading materials based on different themes, thereby allowing them to complete or to facilitate their learning journey as a young child. For teenagers, we have this "Winter Reading Festival" activities during the winter break. For college students, we encourage them to come to our Library to serve as volunteers, in particular, carrying out different kinds of library duties – for fulfilling their job internship requirements.

Do many university and college students also come to serve as volunteers at your Library?

Such volunteering services are in collaboration with the local universities academic courses and internships, as part of the curriculum for the students to earn or accumulate academic credits.

Are there any ongoing collaboration between your Library and the local school libraries?

Our Library has formed close partnerships with many local primary schools. We have several approaches. First, schools or classes can apply for a group library card for borrowing up to 50 to 200 books to their school library for doing book exhibitions or other reading promotion activities. Second, we send professional librarians out to the local schools to provide guidance, say, on how school librarians and school children can use our library's information sources, thereby developing their information literacy skills.

What library activities are the most popular (such as lectures, seminars, training, guidance, etc.) amongst your existing users? When are these activities generally held?

For children, weekend storytelling activities are very popular. Book exchange is one of the most popular activities amongst the adults, which is held on the last Sunday of each month. Other popular monthly events include "Books of the Month" and "Meet the Author," via which we invite the general public to meet with their authors in person – thereby allowing the audience to hear their favorite authors to read their own work, or to autograph their books.

Each library has its own collection characteristics, they are sometimes defined by their unique collections or special services. Can you tell us what makes the Taipei City Library special?

Under the Taipei City Library system, each branch library is responsible for developing its own collections, as well as its own promotional or outreach activities, e.g., book fairs and lecture series, etc. For example, we have a branch library that specializes in developing a collection that is devoted to sports, e.g., ball games and physical education, etc. During the year of the world's important tournaments, such as the Olympic Games or the Asian Games, this branch library will hold exhibits, book displays and talks focusing on sports, and will invite some outstanding athletes or outstanding people in the field of sports to share their experience with the readers.

When is the peak season for such cultural program and activities?

The most popular time for such promotional programs and cultural activities are probably weekends, especially on Saturday afternoons; also during the summer (July and August) and winter (January or February) vacations. On average, the whole Taipei City Library system holds up to 1,300 events each year.

In order to increase visibility and enhance the public image of the Taipei City Library, what means of publicity do you employ?

Our Library homepage plays an important role in creating an institutional identity for our Library, that is retaining our users, and encouraging them to return to our Library. For Taiwan, the most popular online social media is Facebook. Our Library has also created our own Facebook fans page, using it as a platform to communicate with our users, that is to "get our message out" about our Library's events and information, etc. In addition, we have also been very active in using YouTube in self-marketing and outrearch, e.g., using YouTube to introduce our world famous Beitou (北投) Library to the general public.

To better address the learning needs of the local community, has Taipei City Library established partnerships with any arts, cultural and educational organizations other than school libraries?

We work closely with many types of organizations in Taipei. Of course, our most frequent cooperation is with the local primary and secondary schools. This is followed by a number of cultural and educational foundations. With them, have jointly organized many lectures, film shows that have drawn both record attendance and critical praise.

Could you describe the working or organizational relationship between the National Central Library and the Taipei City Library?

In Taiwan, the public library system functions like this: we have a National Library, that is under the Ministry of Education at the national level. In the city of Taipei, we are under the Taipei City Council. We do not have administrative subordinate relations with the National Library. However, the National Library provides advices to all public libraries at the local level.

Am I to understand that all the public libraries located within the city of Taipei, they are all under your leadership and management?

Yes. The main library is responsible for all the operations and administration of all public branch libraries within the city of Taipei. Each branch has its own director or branch manager, and is responsible for reporting to the General Director at the Main Library. All funds, all personnel are managed and allocated by the main library. And I am the General Director of the Main Library.

How many branch libraries are there in total that are operating under your leadership?

We have different types of service points, currently 44 branches, 11 public reading rooms (smaller ones). In addition, we have 7 unmanned intelligent libraries, and 7 "FastBook"[2] automatic borrowing booths and they are all under my management and leadership.

What kind of initiatives has the Taipei City Library undertaken to encourage people to make good and maximum use of the physical spaces inside the library, regardless they are using these spaces for sheer entertainment, recreational, formal learning or even just for social networking purposes?

In order to encourage more people to use the physical library, I believe the library first needs to create a very comfortable and inviting environment. Secondly, to provide very rich resources for learning and recreational reading in many different formats, including paper books, electronic books, journals, newspapers, magazines, etc., in order to attract people to physically come to the library to use the resources available. Third, to provide a very convenient system for borrowing books, such as "inter-branch loan services." All our books are interlinked between branches, meaning that our users are given the option to request a book to be delivered from and to another branch library. Finally, to attract people to come, we have been very active in conducting different outreach and promotional activities under an ongoing basis, such as children story-telling, meeting with writers, reading club for sharing reading experience, and so on.

What is your philosophy behind your library services?

What sets the Taipei City Library and our library services apart from other public libraries in Taiwan is that: our reader service system has passed the so-called ISO quality system certification. Under this quality management system, our standards for Quality and Success can be summarized as follows: comfortable, convenience, information rich (resourceful); serious about quality of services, user-friendly, reader satisfaction. Our mission behind the Taipei City Library is to shape Taipei into a and vibrant city that is imbued with happy reading and enthusiastic learning. We truly believe that the Taipei City Library plays a vital role in the community, and we aim to translate our visions into library services that could be enjoyed by everyone in Taipei, regardless of their social and economic backgrounds.

---

2 http://english.gov.taipei/ct.asp?xItem=94775268&ctNode=8472&mp=100002

Other libraries

26 Father Maximilian Schiefermüller O.S.B.

General Director, Admont Abbey Library

Introduction

Admont Abbey is a Benedictine monastery located on the Enns River in the town of Admont, Austria. As the oldest remaining monastery in Styria, Admont Abbey contains the largest monastic library in the world as well as a long-established scientific collection. Known for its beautiful Baroque architecture, art, and manuscripts, the Admont Abbey Library is considered the largest monastery library in the world. As General Director of the Library, Father Maximilian is responsible for all general aspects, including preserving the history of the Abbey in the form of the extensive source material (files, documents, photographs, collections, etc.) held in the archives. As the curator of the collection of antique art, vestments and paraments, Father Maximilian works closely with numerous conservators and prepares the annual exhibitions in the Abbey Museum, particularly those staged in the Museum of Fine Arts.

Fig. 26.1: General Director of Admont Library and Archive, P. Maximilian Schiefermüller O.S.B. (Photo: Admont Abbey Library).

Fig. 26.2: Benedictine Monastery of Admont (Photo: Admont Abbey Library).

Fig. 26.3: Baroque Abbey Library (Photo: Admont Abbey Library).

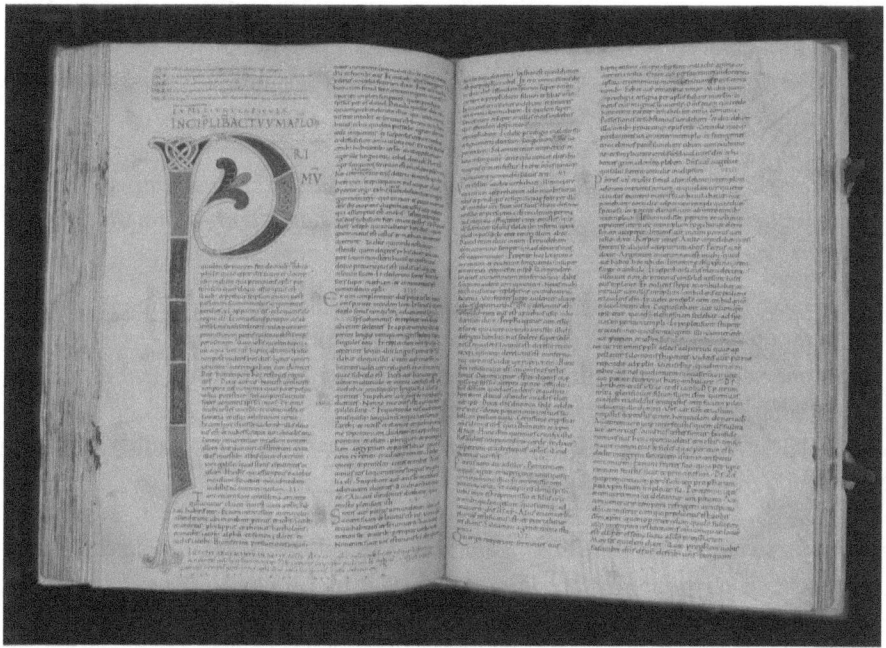

Fig. 26.4: Admont Library, Cod. D „Admonter Riesenbibel" / Giant Bible (Photo: Admont Abbey Library).

Could we begin this interview by first introducing yourself, for example, your training and background? Could you also describe your role as the General Director of the Admont Abbey Library?

My name is Father Maximilian Schiefermüller O.S.B., and I am a Benedictine monk in the Admont Abbey[1] in Austria. Admont is one of the oldest abbeys in Austria, founded in 1074, with an uninterrupted tradition. After my entrance into the monastery, I graduated in History and Catholic Theology at the University of Salzburg[2], was ordained a priest in 2009, and I have since worked in pastoral care in three parishes near the monastery.

Because of my training, I am responsible for the rich collection of ancient art and liturgical texts. In addition, I completed various courses and training in the field of Archival and Library Science. At the end of 2013, I was appointed the

---

[1] Admont Abbey (Austria) – Homepage. Available at: http://www.stiftadmont.at/en/
[2] University of Salzburg – Homepage. Available at: https://uni-salzburg.at/index.php?id=52&L=1

librarian of the largest monastery library in the world and the archivist of the richest monastery archives of Central Europe. As a librarian in Admont, I oversee the collections and supervise a number of academics and students, who work with our library and archival collections.

How many different languages have you mastered? Do you still use Latin to communicate with other members of the Roman Catholic Church both within and outside of Austria on a daily basis?

I can speak German, English and Latin, and I am also capable of reading them. In the monastery, we pray some parts of our daily prayer in Latin, church music, and some services (in Latin) are celebrated in the ancient liturgical language. For communication purposes within the Catholic Church, Latin is, however, no longer being used. If I write a letter to the Vatican archives in Rome, this is usually done in English, German or Italian.

There are so many abbeys in Europe that are equipped with their own libraries with precious collection – what are the reasons that the Admont Abbey contains the largest monastic library in the world?

Since the Middle Ages, the monks of Admont have placed a lot of emphasis on studying and training. Admont was founded in 1644, and was the first school to emphasize knowledge. In the Middle Ages, the monks in Admont were very productive in manufacturing manuscripts. In 1776, the new Admont Abbey Library[3] was completed with a space to reflect the ideal life of the Baroque and the love of science, art and culture, etc.

The Melk Abbey Library versus the Admont Abbey Library – how are their physical libraries and the collections different from each other, in terms of collection size, usage, range of services, and user groups/types?

The Melk Abbey[4] Library has a large collection of books compared to Admont; however, Admont is spatially the largest library of the two. Regarding the differences in the collections: Melk Abbey has a number of valuable medieval manuscripts, and a large inventory of Baroque literature.

---

3 Admont Abbey Library – Homepage. Available at: http://www.stiftadmont.at/en/?s=library
4 Melk Abbey – Homepage. Available at: http://www.stiftmelk.at/

In the 17th and 18th centuries, the Abbey reached a highpoint of artistic productivity – any reasons that the Admont became the highpoint of artistic productivity during that period? Was this artwork created for the purpose of teaching/spreading the Roman Catholic faith? Were they meant to be signs of the personal devotion of the artists to the Catholic Religion?

Not only in Admont, but also in all the monasteries in Austria and southern Germany, the Baroque era has clearly been reflected. There were large-scale remodeling of monasteries and churches. Admont was the exception, however, with the Catholic faith, the glory of God (in art), which plays an important role here.

What were the situation and state of operations of the Admont Abbey Library during World War I and World War II, and even the early war against the Turks?

The Turkish wars did not affect Admont, but rather, the monastery incorporated parishes in the south of the country. There was a lot of destruction and plundering.

During World War I, Admont was not part of the military clashes. World War II, however, brought the expulsion of the monastic community by the Nazi regime and brought the utter dispossession and occupation of the monastery. The Library was partially closed and valuable books were moved to Graz and Vienna. After World War II, the monastery was returned to the Benedictine, and gradually, the land.

Have you always worked in libraries? Could you tell us more about your path to becoming the General Director of Admont Abbey Library?

I have always loved books. Dealing with historical matter has always been my career choice. Through my studies and my training, I had an easy path for taking over the management of the monastery library and the archives, even if this was not sought out from the beginning. Following the retirement of my predecessor, Abbot Bruno had the confidence to entrust me to my current position.

Could you please provide a brief introduction about the Admont Abbey Library?

The Library of the Admont Abbey houses about 200,000 volumes. Of these, 70,000 books are kept in the baroque library hall, which was completed in 1776, as the "Eight Wonders," as it was called, and is still the largest monastic library room in the world. In addition, the Admont Abbey owned about 1,400 valuable manuscripts, of which half date back to the Middle Ages. The number of incunabula, the printed book until 1,500, amounts to 530 pieces; that is slightly more than 400 printing units that are available from the period 1501 to 1520. The manuscripts and more than 930 incunabula are no longer placed in the Library Hall since the early 20th century. Today, they are in air-conditioned safety vaults.

The Library Hall, built in 1776 from designs by the architect Joseph Hueber, is 70 meters long, 14 meters wide and 13 meters high, and is the largest monastery library in the world. As the General Director, what type of oversight is involved in maintaining the physical fixtures of the library?

It requires permanent conservation measures. The Library Hall was completely restored a few years ago and was recently fumigated. We are currently working on cleaning all 70,000 books in the Library since dust, pests and climate have greatly worn on the stock in recent decades. Furthermore, the Library is a tourist attraction of the region, and it is visited annually by about 60,000 people. This also has an effect on the climate of the library, however, as it is not always conducive to the safety of collections inside the Library and thus requires constant monitoring.

The abbey possesses over 1,400 manuscripts, the oldest of which, from St. Peter's Abbey in Salzburg, were the gift of the founder, Archbishop Gebhard. How does your library preserve these rare and special collections?

The valuable manuscript inventory of the monastery, which dates back to a large extent from the Middle Ages, is kept in private, air-conditioned rooms that are technically perfect conditions to meet all conservation requirements. In addition, we are working to digitize many of our valuable manuscripts, so that these works can be made available online to many people while the originals are preserved.

Could you also describe what you deem are the highlights of the collection?

Highlights in the holdings consist of the monastery archive from its foundation. In terms of the library, the highlights would be the manuscripts from the Middle Ages as well as the three-volume "Giant Bible" from around 1070 AD. Also included is a gospel book from the same period with exquisitely decorated illuminations. From the mid-12th century, the Admont Abbey had its own scriptorium, in which many books were produced either for its own use or for other monasteries. In addition, there are also books of the Baroque period, which you would not expect in a monastery library, such as literature of liberalism, the Enlightenment and of the French revolutionaries.

Usage of the Admont Abbey Library and its collections – how have usage, expectations and information needs have changes over the past centuries?

The use of the collection of the library has changed to the extent that we have arrived at the monastery in the electronic and digital age. Our collections can be found online, and we manufacture scans and digital copies of manuscripts. Information regarding archival and library requests are usually via email from around the world.

Do you also work closely with other libraries across Austria and Europe? Such as on cross-national or global collaborative projects? What are some highlights?

There are projects that we carry out with other Austrian ecclesiastical libraries, including digitizing the library of the Augustinian Canons in Klosterneuburg. European libraries do not hesitate to contact us when it comes to loans of the Admont manuscripts for exhibitions. Moreover, we are a member of various German associations of libraries with historical collections.

Please describe the staffing structure at the Admont Abbey Library. For example, what are the working relationships between the various Heads of subject/cataloging departments and the branch heads in such a vast and large system?

My close colleague, Dr. Karin Schamberger, is a librarian and expert in the field of book inventory and in the field of medieval manuscripts. Two book restorers work for our library as well as five employees in the field of conservation measures (book cleaning). We also hire students to work for us. These are valuable aids in the digitization and cataloging.

Could you describe your typical day at work? Is there ever a typical day at work?

My day is marked by the monastic rhythm of life: that is, times of prayer in the monastic community and the celebration of worship in my parishes. Otherwise, I am overseeing the use of our archive and library, answer queries that are addressed to me, as well as write articles and reviews for various magazines.

Who are the majority users of the Admont Abbey Library? That is, who comes to see you about your collections, programs, and services?

Over 60,000 tourists annually visit our monastery library. But, these are not users of collections. Most users of the archive and library holdings are scientists and students from various universities around the world – including regional historians and individual researchers, who just want to get to know their own history, or are interested in various topics.

"Most users of the archive and library holdings are scientists" – why would the scientists want to use the collections and services of the Admont Abbey Library?

Our collections are very valuable, and – just the medieval area – often consist of unique pieces. There are scientists who not only want to explore the world, but often, also the stylistic, artistic, or calligraphic components of the manuscripts.

What's the role of technology and innovation at Admont Abbey Library?

We are very open to innovative projects that facilitate researching and working with our book collections. So, we specialize just in the field of handwriting digitization, but also work with international partners of libraries and archives.

Do you work closely with numerous conservators and prepare the annual exhibitions in the Abbey Museum – particularly those staged in the Museum of Fine Arts?

Yes, it is part of my job as a curator of the Ancient Art Collection or liturgical textiles to always keep contact with various restorers. I am also responsible for annually changing the exhibitions in the Kunsthistorisches Museum of the Admont Abbey. As Benedictines from Admont, we are responsible for our heritage entrusted to us. It is in our nature or dictated by the Rule of St. Benedict that we preserve the goods entrusted to us, carefully handle it and preserve them for posterity.

Could you describe your management and leadership style? Mentorship is such an important theme in leadership – both mentoring and being mentored. Could you please tell us about your experiences about both? Do you still have mentors that you go to?

In monastic rule, it is certainly the most important thing to have a spirit of cooperation and everyone can function in a community. Personally, I feel that I am in a good working environment, an open atmosphere, somewhere we can happily and honestly work with each other. Work should be fun and everyone can use his or her applied talents. It is very important not to lose sight of the common goal. However, it also sometimes requires a corrective hand of the supervisor.

What kind of professional knowledge, skills and personality traits that are necessary to serve as the General Director of the Admont Abbey Library?

In my personal case, it is knowledge as a theologian, historian, scientist, and archivist.

Why is it the having the knowledge of a "scientist" is necessary for doing your work at Admont Abbey?

It is primarily connected to my work as a scientist at the Abbey Library and the archives. As a monk and priest, one must have undergone theological education. As a historical archivist, training in library and archival sciences is absolutely necessary.

Which part(s) of your job as the General Director do you find most rewarding? What is the most frustrating?

I am glad that when people are interested in our work, and if they can find access on the science of God, particularly when we can change negative views of the Catholic Church and its monasteries by learning about the openness of our Admont Abbey and appreciate it. Every day is different, and it is always exciting and always surprising and enlightening. I am glad that I never cease learning. As Benedctine monks, we should always be listening and learning. It is however frustrating coming across the ignorance of some people against monasteries and the Church, especially the many false prejudices that exist.

Where would these ignorance and false prejudices usually lay? How would they usually affect your work?

There are prejudices against the Catholic Church as a whole, and they are always brought up by the media and church critics from time to time – and sometimes justified, but sometimes completely unreal. As a priest, this complicates the work and pastoral care even enormously at times since the access to the people by negative publicity is often difficult.

During the Nazi occupation – the Admont Library was partially closed and valuable books were moved to Graz and Vienna – for the Nazi regime – what were their purposes for relocating the valuable collections away from the Admont Library to Graz and Vienna? What benefits would the Nazi gain by doing so?

The fellowship of the Benedictine monks had to leave the monastery. A part of the valuable collections has been taken away to ensure their safety or to use them for research. The Nazis seized the Monastery Admont, all of its valuables and its inventory. They did this to many other monasteries as well.

Your predecessor, Abbot Bruno – could you describe his working style and his work ethics? What were the most important job skills and knowledge that you have learnt from him?

In his work, Abbot Bruno focuses on a life in religious community, prayers, and also a life and work according to the Rule of Saint Benedict. As our monastery's abbot, he has to make decisions in a range of other fields as well, particularly when it comes to matters in economy, staff and construction. An advisory board assists him in these matters.

Could you tell me what are the differences between a Franciscan monk and a Benedictine monk or monks from other Roman Catholic branches?

There are big differences, especially in spirituality, tasks and rules of the Order. I am sure you can find further information in the literature.

27 Dr. Cornel Dora

Director, Abbey Library of Saint Gall

Introduction

Situated in a city in the northeastern part of Switzerland, near the Lake Constance, the Abbey Library of St. Gall Monastery is one of the earliest, and most important Carolingian monastic libraries in the world. The cathedral and the library are the main features of this remarkable abbey's architectural complex-reflecting 14 centuries of continuous activities. In fact, the entire abbey was declared a UNESCO World Heritage Site in 1983. Some of the most striking features of the Abbey Library are the Baroque frescoes and the wooden balconies shaped into decorative flowing shapes and beautifully curved moldings. The heart of the library collection consists of 2,100 manuscripts with the earliest item dating all the way back to around 400 C.E., as well as 1,000 incunabula. Managing the daily operations of the Abbey Library is Dr. Cornel Dora, a graduate of the University of Zürich, who spent 12 years serving as head of the St. Gallen State Library (Vadiana) before becoming director of the Abbey Library of St. Gall. In the following interview, Dr. Dora discusses the essential professional skills and knowledge that are required for serving as the Director for one of the oldest surviving libraries in Europe.

Fig. 27.1: Dr. Cornel Dora (Photo: Abbey Library of Saint Gall).

Fig. 27.2: The building with the Abbey Library of Saint Gall from outside (Photo: PaterMcFly).

Fig. 27.3: Baroque Hall (Photo: Abbey Library of Saint Gall).

Could we begin this interview by first introducing yourself, for example, your training and background? Could you also describe your described role as the Director of the Abbey Library of Saint Gall?

I was born in 1963 in Saint Gall and grew up in the parish of the city, and I was involved in the cathedral as a server and lecturer during masses. So, I have a close and emotionally balanced relation to the Catholic Church. I studied English, History and musical science at the University of Zürich[1], where I had a small appointment as lecturer for Old and Middle English after my studies. In my professional career, I started out as archivist of the diocese of Saint Gall and then got an appointment as librarian at the Abbey Library[2], where I became deputy director in 1996.

I finished my doctorate with a dissertation about one of the Bishops of Saint Gall, and this was followed by a diploma for scholarly librarian at the Zentralbibliothek Zürich (Zürich Central Library).[3] In 2001, I was appointed director of the Kantonsbibliothek Vadiana Saint Gall (State Library of the canton of St. Gall)[4], where I was able to launch a process of positive changes, introducing a merger with the city library and the acquisition of new premises in the central post building of Saint Gall, establishing the largest e-library for public libraries on the continent and preparing the first modern library law in Switzerland that passed parliament in 2013.

In November 2013, I returned to the Abbey Library as director. It was a good moment after having completed the projects mentioned at the Kantonsbibliothek.

As the director of the Abbey Library, I am responsible for one of the most important historical libraries in the world – a gift of history to our times. Compared to other libraries, it is small, with permanent staff of fifteen persons. We have three branches: (1) One of the most successful museums in Switzerland with 130,000 visitors per year, (2) A library still active and playing an important role in the digitization of manuscripts as founding partner of e-codices (www.e-codices.ch). (3) A scholarly institute working together with quite a number of universities in the German-speaking countries and worldwide.

Are you a Roman Catholic priest? Are there any reasons why some abbey libraries would appoint Roman Catholic priests to manage their library collections (e.g., the Admont Abbey), while others do not?

No, I am a layman, married, and have three children – one of them just 2 years of age. That is why I reduced my appointment from 100 to 90 percent this year. The

---

[1] University of Zürich – Homepage. Available at: http://www.uzh.ch/en.html
[2] Abbey Library of Saint Gall – Homepage. Available at: http://www.stibi.ch/en-us/info/exhibition.aspx
[3] Zentralbibliothek Zürich (Zürich Central Library) – Homepage. Available at: http://www.zb.uzh.ch/index.html.en
[4] Kantonsbibliothek Vadiana Saint Gall (State Library of the canton of St. Gall) – Homepage. Available at: http://www.sg.ch/home/kultur/kantonsbibliothek.html

Abbey Library has since 1981 been directed by lay people. Of course, a certain affinity or closeness to the world of the church and the monasteries is important in order to lead an institution like this credibly, with good feeling and a long-term approach, but other skills for example in communication, scholarship or management are just as important.

How many different languages have you mastered? Do you still use Latin to communicate with other members of the Roman Catholic Church both within and outside of Switzerland on a daily basis?

I am a German native speaker and learned French at school, as all Swiss do, English – I studied English literature and linguistics at the university – a little bit of Italian, and Latin. As director of the Kantonsbibliothek, Latin was not so important, but since I returned to the Abbey Library the skills in Latin are of course very useful. However, I am happy to have at least two scholars in my staff that are extremely good in Latin, who can assist when I have problems with a text. There is not so much communication with the church as you might expect, and this communication is in modern languages nowadays.

What makes the Abbey of Saint Gall and its Library so internationally famous?

I usually mention three facts to explain the importance of our library: (1) It is one of the most beautiful ones in the world with a breath-taking baroque hall built 250 years ago. (2) It is one of the oldest libraries still existing, going back to the $7^{th}/8^{th}$ century, and it is still functioning as a living scholarly library. (3) Its collection is of very high quality in three respects: It is the largest collection of a library going back before the year 1000 in Europe. In the Carolingian period the monastery was very conscious of good transmission (8th to 10th century), so the Saint Gall manuscripts often represent a very good, sometimes the best and in a few cases even the only transmission of a text basic for the cultural development of western Europe. On the whole, the Abbey Library is indeed a gift of the past to the present.

There are so many abbeys in Europe that are equipped with their own libraries with precious collections – what are the major differences in terms of the setup, collections, user groups and the daily operations of the Abbey Library of Saint Gall by comparison that sets it aside from other abbey libraries in Europe?

Since the early Middle Ages, Saint Gall has been one of the best collections of manuscripts, and with the elapse of time and the suppression of abbey libraries either in the Reformation or in the Secularization period it finally became the only one of importance, that was saved in a good state, and it survived even the suppression of the Abbey in 1805. It is important that the Abbey Archives also still exist, and they also have a unique collection going back to the early 8th century. The two collections together form a wonderful corpus. There is no other human community from the 8th to the 11th century we know so much about as the monastic community of Saint Gall. Compared with other abbey libraries, Saint Gall today is one of the most active in the three fields mentioned in the answer to the first question: a museum, a library, and a scholarly institution.

In the 17th and 18th centuries, the Admont Abbey (in Austria) reached a highpoint of artistic productivity? Did the Abbey of Saint Gall also experience similar highpoints or artistic heights around the same periods?

Yes. In Saint Gall, also, there was a new cultural climax during the Baroque period. The buildings of the Abbey church and the library are testimonials to this. However, there was a period in distress from 1712 to 1720, when the Cantons of Zürich and Berne conquered and plundered the abbey and the library. It took a few decades to recover from this. But, on the other hand, the monks that took care of the library and archives during that period were great scholars, especially Pius Kolb, Johann Nepomuk Hauntinger and Ildefons von Arx.

What were the situations and the states of operations of the Abbey Library of Saint Gall during World War I and World War II?

The first decades of the 20th century are a transition period in the history of the library, moving from a library that leaned a bit towards a public library to a scholarly library focusing on its own collection and the worldwide interest for it. Of course, the wars did not create a background that was favorable to international learned networking, but after 1945, the library developed very quickly into what it still is today: a highly reputable institution of major interest for all scholars dealing with historical libraries, monastic culture and the Carolingian and Ottonian periods.

During World War II, the manuscripts were moved to a more secure place in Switzerland.

Have you always worked in libraries? Could you tell us more about your path to becoming the General Director of Abbey Library of Saint Gall?

I started out as the archivist of the diocese of Saint Gall in 1988, and I moved to the Abbey library as simple librarian in 1993. Because of health problems of the director, I had to take over more and more managerial functions, and I launched a very successful exhibition about the *Scrolls from the Dead Sea* in 1999. In 2001, I transferred to the Kantonsbibliothek Vadiana Saint Gall, and in 2013 I was able to return "home" to the Abbey Library as director.

Could you please provide a brief introduction about the Abbey of Saint Gall?

The Abbey of Saint Gall was the largest monastery in what is today Switzerland for more than a thousand years and an important center of art and learning from the 9th to the 11th and the 16th to the 18th century. It was dissolved in 1805, leaving a wound in the history of Saint Gall, and eastern Switzerland, since the later political institutions never became as prestigious as the Abbey had been. But, that is a different story.

What is the current size of the Abbey Library of Saint Gall's collections, including its special collections? Could you also describe what you deem are the highlights of the collection?

The library holds in all 170,000 items that came together during a period of 1,400 years. This is unique. At the heart of the collections lies the manuscript section with 2,100 manuscripts from late antiquity to the present. 400 of them date back to the Golden Age of the Abbey, which lasted from around 800 to 1080, a period otherwise not well-documented. Some of the later manuscripts are famous and important also, for example the Saint Gall Nibelung manuscript (Cod. Sang. 857) or the sketchbook of Georg Franz Müller, a soldier who served in East India in the late 17th century. There is also a nice incunabula collection with around 1,000 pieces. You can look at the library from different angles, its collection is always of high quality. It is in fact a miracle that it has come down this way to the present.

Usage of the Abbey Library of Saint Gall and its collections – how have the usage, expectations and information needs of the public changed over the centuries?

From the beginning and to the end of the 18th century, the collection of manuscripts was for the needs of the ritual services of the church and for the scholarly interests of the monks. It was an in-house institution – loans to other monasteries or the courts of emperors and kings were rare. When the monks had left, the Catholics of the Kanton Saint Gall took over the property and adapted the institution quite wisely to the new post-feudal world. The last librarians of the monastery, who were excellent scholars, had prepared the grounds for this by showing the uniqueness of the collection. The beautiful library building helped to underline the importance of the institution that over the years developed into the academic library it now is. A very important leap into the present world was made when the library launched the e-codices project 12 years ago. Today, this manuscript digitization platform for Switzerland ranges among the best and most profiled enterprises of digital humanities. Our library thus figures among the leading libraries that engage in manuscript digitization worldwide. And, we have a state of the art studio for digital photography in our buildings.

E-codices have revolutionized manuscript studies worldwide in the past decade. It is like a huge, worldwide reading room with free access, and it triggered the interest in medieval manuscripts. We have entered a new sphere in manuscript studies. Lately, we have started to organize successful summer schools for manuscript specialist in Europe. We will proceed further on this path.

Do you also work closely with other libraries across Switzerland and Europe? Such as on cross-national or globally collaborative projects? What are some highlights?

With the help of e-codices our network of libraries has increased considerably. It includes the monastic libraries in Switzerland, and a number of other important manuscript collections in- and outside the country, such as Wolfenbüttel, Munich, the Bodleian Library[5] or Trinity College in Dublin.[6] Important fields of collaboration apart from digitization are the cataloging of manuscripts that needs to take on a more over-nation view, and react to the new conditions that the Internet has brought on.

Could you describe the staffing structure at the Abbey Library of Saint Gall?

Our library is a machine of output as a library, a museum and an academic institution, but our staff is not very big, only 15 people. Director and administration: 2.7 fte (3 persons), academic section: 2.1 fte (3 persons), library section: 2.6 fte (6 persons), museum and shop section: 2.1 fte (3 persons). In addition to that, our staff includes about 20 more people working as security and surveillance officers, at the shop, and as guides. All in all, we are about 35 very motivated employees.

---

5 Bodleian Libraries, University of Oxford – Homepage. Available at: http://www.bodleian.ox.ac.uk/
6 Trinity College, Dublin – Homepage. Available at: https://www.tcd.ie/

Could you describe your typical day at work? Is there ever a typical day at work?

There is no routine and no typical day of work. I deal with management, give tours and talks, plan expositions, work together with other institutions like monastery libraries, touristic institutions or universities. My professional world is full of miracles and surprises. All in all, it is a real dream job.

Could you tell me why you believe it is a dream job that is full of miracles and surprises? Can you provide some examples to illustrate your point?

I am at the center of a UNESCO World Heritage[7] site, working in a wonderful building, surrounded by treasures of unique quality, the wisdom of the past. Our library is to some extent independent of the pressure and the uniformity that is more and more determining scholarship and university life. I also love the spiritual aspects of what we do here.

What are the skills and knowledge that are necessary for work as a librarian for an abbey library?

I think that at first, a positive attitude and a good intuition in the field of monastic and historical libraries is most important for the library staff. Secondly, of course, the skills of librarians, including the cataloging of old prints and knowledge that helps understand the collections and the research that is being carried out, such as Latin, history, theology, paleography, literature, etc.

Who are the majority users of the Abbey Library of Saint Gall?

The majority of users of the library and its collection are scholars worldwide. There are a few users that visit our reading room to see the original codices, but most of the users look at the manuscripts on e-codices, our digitization platform. In the museum, we have visitors from all over the world – over 100,000 per year.

What is the role of technology and innovation at the Abbey Library of Saint Gall?

For us, technology is a means, not a purpose. But, of course, it is important today when you want to keep interest in your collection or reach your goals in communication. However, we are a small library and – apart from manuscript digitization – there is no field we have a leading function in.

---

7 UNESCO World Heritage – Homepage. Available at: http://whc.unesco.org/en/list/

Could you describe your management and leadership style? Mentorship is such an important theme in leadership – both mentoring and being mentored. Could you please tell us about your experiences about both? Do you still have mentors that you go to?

I made my management classes at the Executive School of the University of Saint Gallen.[8] But, I do not believe that this is so essential. Leadership has to do with personality, credibility, a certain wisdom. You cannot learn this at the university today, at least not with the system as it works today. To form a personality, your character, the first 15 years when you grow up in your family, your schooling with others, and the first five years of your professional career are most important. I think I learnt the most from my brothers and sisters, my mother and father, and from my first chefs, Daniel Wettstein and Albert Breu. Mentorship has become a program, but it is better and more sustainable when you can get the necessary resources as a natural part of your life.

Do you have any strategic plans for developing your Abbey for the next five to ten years?

Yes, we have strategic plans. On the one hand, our strategy is part of the management plan of the UNESCO world heritage site Abbey of Saint Gall, and, on the other hand, we are developing micro-strategies in fields such as cataloging, conservation or manuscript digitization.

Which part of your job as the director do you find most rewarding? What is the most frustrating?

As I said, my job is a real dream job. The only thing that sometimes frustrates me, are people that do not understand at all what my dream is about. But, they also motivate. I am a bit of a rebel. Opposition makes me grow.

Do you know if many young people who graduated with a degree in History, Latin, Religious Studies or Library Science are inspired to become a monastery librarian like you? If not, could you tell me why?

The number of students who know Latin and work on the Middle Ages is sinking. There are not so many positions like the director of the Abbey Library of Saint Gall, you cannot plan this. So, many people think this a not a very promising track for professional life. Moreover, the still active monasteries try to keep the

---

8 University of Saint Gall – Homepage. Available at: https://www.unisg.ch/en

task of the library within the personal of the convent, because it has a lot to do with the identity of a community. If we look at it this way, and given the fact, that there were over 30 applications for my positions, we can say, that it is certainly attractive, but the number of specialist who work consequently to get this job is, naturally, not so big.

What are the futures for the monastery libraries in Europe with long history and valuable collections like the St. Gall, Melk and the Admont Abbey Library?

These collections are treasures in their own right, basic for European thinking, spirituality and ethics, indispensable for the history of communities and the states. And, it is important that they stay in their places of origin, in their wonderful buildings, that belong to this kind of reading culture. These great monastic libraries will remain landmarks and touristic attractions. However, their future in the library context seems a bit open, since they are not so much part of the dynamics we see in the university libraries or the big public libraries. It is important that they get the resources to make their collections accessible to a new and younger public.

If a young person is aspiring to become a monastery librarian like you, what kind of processional advices in terms of career path would you give him/her?

Keep your scholarly skills alive and your mind independent, work hard, remain open for spirituality, love history, manuscripts, books and abbeys, and stay in touch with the monasteries and their libraries.

Further readings

Abbey Library of St. Gallen - Stiftsbibliothek St. Gallen. Available at: http://www.stibi.ch/en-us/info/exhibition.aspx

Abbey of St. Gall - UNESCO World Heritage Centre. Available at: http://whc.unesco.org/en/list/268

Convent of St Gall (UNESCO/NHK) [YouTube]. Available at: https://www.youtube.com/watch?v=bmnYMEB_XCM

28 Oliver Urquhart Irvine

The Librarian & Assistant Keeper, The Queen's Archives

Introduction

In 2013, a job advertisement was placed by the Royal Collection Department of the Royal Household of the Sovereign of the United Kingdom to recruit a Royal Librarian – to succeed the soon-to-be-retired Lady Jane Roberts, who was appointed to take up the same role in 2002.

Many would even say it is a "dream job" of any bookworms, as the Royal Librarian is responsible for the care and maintenance of an exceptionally large and valuable collection of books, manuscripts and other artifacts in the Royal Library, established in the 1830s at the instigation of William IV. The Royal Library encompasses a collection of immeasurable cultural, historical as well as artistic values that spread across all the palaces, both occupied and unoccupied, i.e., including the largest group of drawings by Leonardo da Vinci. Other collection highlights include personal and political documents relating to the monarchy from the reign of George III onwards, as well as small group of Sovereigns' manuscripts dating from the 16th and 17th centuries. Since the establishment of the Royal Archives at the Windsor Castle in 1911, the Royal Librarian has also been responsible for the day-to-day management of the Royal Archives answering to the Keeper of the Royal Archives. In addition to overseeing the daily operations of the Library and the Royal Archives, the Royal Librarian is also expected to be seasoned bibliophile, as well as an exceptional scholar who possesses in-depth knowledge of history (particularly British), bibliography, and academic research, etc.

Oliver Urquhart Irvine, formerly of the British Library, is the current Royal Librarian and Assistant Keeper of the Queen's Archives. An Art History major from the University of London and the University of Amsterdam, Irvine spent a number of years working for the auction house Christie's and other commercial booksellers before joining the British Library. In the following interview, Irvine discusses the diverse skill set, and academic knowledge that are required for enabling the Royal Library to continue to contribute to the world of scholarship and research in the 21st century.

Fig. 28.1 + 28.2: Queen Elizabeth II is shown items from the George III Collection by Royal Librarian Oliver Urquhart Irvine (Photo: Royal Collection Trust).

Fig. 28.3: Royal Library, Windsor Castle (Photo: Royal Collection Trust).

Is this your very first time to be invited to give an interview about your job as the Librarian and Assistant Keeper of The Queen's Archives?

Yes it is – the first time.

Did you need to obtain permission from Her Majesty The Queen before proceeding with this interview?

I briefed before proceeding with this interview.

Could we begin this interview by first introducing yourself, for example, your education background and professional training?

After leaving school, and knowing already that I wanted to work with books and manuscripts, I studied History of Art at the Courtauld Institute of Art[1], part of

---

[1] Courtauld Institute of Art – Homepage. Available at: http://courtauld.ac.uk/

the University of London. I then pursued a second degree at the University of Amsterdam[2] in Early Modern History of Art and Archaeology. This was eventually followed by studying law then completing two post-graduate diplomas in the field of Art and Law. I am fortunate enough to have seen aspects of the bibliographical world outside the usual route for a librarian, including two years as a specialist in books and manuscripts for an auction house, six years in the antiquarian book trade, and nine years at the British Library.[3]

Do you come from a family of librarians, art historians or history scholars?

No, there have been engineers, schoolteachers, doctors, nurses, though my grandmother was an historian by training and inclination.

Could you describe your current role and areas of responsibilities as the Royal Librarian, and Assistant Keeper of The Queen's Archives? In addition, what kind of professional knowledge, technical skills and personality traits that are necessary for serving as the Royal Librarian and Assistant Keeper of The Queen's Archives?

The Royal Library (United Kingdom) is the official Library of the Sovereigns of the United Kingdom, and the Royal Archives are the Private Archives of The Queen and the [British] Royal Family.[4] Together they form one of the greatest documentary repositories for the history of the Royal Family and of the monarchy in Britain, certainly for the last 300 years. They both have, in different ways, as their primary purpose to support the work of The Queen. The Royal Library and Royal Archives are about the provision, management, and permanent retention of information, and because they are also significant and historic collections they are also made available external for research and for public benefit. The collections are also used on State occasions, for example during State Visits from foreign powers, to illustrate the relationship between the UK and the Royal Family and the visiting country.

The role requires a knowledge of both the latest library and archival standards and practices and significant curatorial expertise, but above all it looks out to the world and the organization and people that it supports, whether the work of Her Majesty The Queen and the Royal Household, or researchers and the public, across the UK, the Commonwealth and the rest of the world.

---

2 University of Amsterdam – Homepage. Available at: http://www.uva.nl/en/home
3 The British Library – Homepage. Available at: http://www.bl.uk/
4 The Royal Family – Homepage. Available at: https://www.royal.uk/

Have you always worked in libraries? Could you tell us more about your path to becoming the Royal Librarian and Assistant Keeper of The Queen's Archives? Did you apply for the job via open recruitment? If so, at the job interview, who was on the recruitment selection panel?

I have not always worked in libraries, but I have always worked with books, manuscripts and archives. My first "cataloging" experience – merely a listing really – I undertook aged 14 in the library at school. I was fortunate enough to be educated at a school with two very good libraries and a bookshop, and as schoolboy I was interested in all three, but did not really become involved until a rugby accident aged 14 had me on crutches for nine months, and not knowing what to do with me the school asked the school librarian, Dom Anselm Cramer OSB, if I could be occupied. This was my first real experience of thinking about books as ideas, as objects, as things to be described and understood, as to the importance of provenance and use and re-use.

Throughout my time as an undergraduate in London, I worked my university vacations in the book department at the London head office of the auction house Christie's[5] and it is there that I learned how to catalog quickly, accurately, and effectively. After completing my post-graduate degree from the University of Amsterdam, Christie's invited me to become a specialist in the books and manuscripts department in London, and for two years I cataloged vast numbers of books, under the supervision of the now International Director of the Book Department, Meg Ford, in almost every European language and in Latin and Greek, and traveled around the country visiting, and cataloging and valuing private libraries. Looking back this was effectively my apprenticeship in learning about the book and the history of the book.

I left Christie's to work in the Early English Department as a bookseller for the Royal Warrant holders, Maggs Bros Ltd.[6], then in Berkeley Square, Mayfair London, and now in Bedford Square, near the British Museum.[7] If Christie's had been an apprenticeship in general cataloging in a really intensive way, then Maggs was the opportunity to deepen and refine an understanding of the history of the book, and learn from Robert Harding FSA how to catalog, and describe in depth not just the text but historic bindings, how to extract the true significance of provenance of any particular volume.

---

5 Christie's – Homepage. Available at: http://www.christies.com/
6 Maggs Bros Ltd. – Homepage. Available at: https://www.maggs.com/
7 The British Museum – Homepage. Available at: http://www.britishmuseum.org/

I became so interested in the question of ownership that while at Maggs Bros Ltd. I studied for a Graduate Diploma in Law in the evenings, and coincidentally just as I completed this the British Library advertised for the first ever full-time post in the UK devoted to the question of cultural property, then and now a developing area of law and collections management. This was a significant role, the remit being to manage and develop a strategy for all aspects of the British Library's immense collections where ownership was contested. Recent international conventions and new UK Law meant that this had become a substantial area of policy and research for all institutions, in particular for the British Library. This also gave me direct experience of contributing to UK Government consultations, of implementing standards of good practice, and of training all staff to whom it applied in the law as related to the management of special collections.

Material affected included that with gaps in provenance for the period 1933–1945, among which was the Beneventan Missal, the first item to be returned to its previous owner under the Holocaust (Return of Cultural Objects) Act 2009. No less significant than legally framed cases were those where restitution or repatriation was not necessarily sought but where competing interests had to be carefully managed, whether arising from religious significance or simply from the place of production. This role gave me a very broad insight into all the British Library's collections and collecting history of the nation in all its forms, in particular Britain's history in relation to Africa, South and South East Asia and the Far East. After a brief spell working for the British Library Board's secretariat as responsible for international matters with the inspirational Andy Stephens OBE, I became Head (Keeper) of the Asian and African Department and eventually secured, as Head of the British Library-Qatar Foundation Partnership[8], what was then the largest single collection-based collaboration for the British Library, worth £8.7M, to make available online bilingually in English and Arabic, 500,000 pages of archival material relating to the Gulf and 25,000 pages of the most significant medieval Arabic science held by the British Library.

It was while leading the partnership with the Qatar Foundation[9] that I received a call from Buckingham Palace[10] asking me if I would be interested in considering applying for the role of Royal Librarian. The post was advertised publicly and I duly applied, and after several interviews, including with The Queen's

---

8 British Library-Qatar Foundation Partnership – Homepage. Available at: http://www.bl.uk/qatar/
9 Qatar Foundation – Homepage. Available at: https://www.qf.org.qa/
10 Buckingham Palace – Homepage. Available at: https://www.royal.uk/royal-residences-buckingham-palace

Private Secretary, Sir Christopher Geidt, in which capacity he is also Keeper of The Queen's Archives, and another trustee of the Royal Collection Trust[11], Dame Rosalind Savill, I was appointed as the ninth Royal Librarian since its re-formation under William IV in the 1830s. My immediate predecessor had unusually not also been the Assistant Keeper of The Queen's Archives in addition to being appointed Royal Librarian I was also shortly afterwards appointed as Assistant Keeper.

The Royal Library was assembled in 1836. Could you tell me what classification scheme and subject headings have you and your predecessors been using for describing the Royal Library collections?

The current Royal Library was established by William IV (r. 183037) in a series of three rooms adapted from the State Apartments at Windsor Castle. The Royal Library is not the first official library of the monarchy. Earlier Royal Libraries were presented to the nation in 1757 by George II (the Old Royal Library), and in 1823 by George IV (the King's Library). Both collections now form a core part for the British Library. William IV did not establish the Royal Library from scratch. At his accession, he had access to the private libraries of George III, and of George IV at Carlton House. Both kings were avid book collectors and their libraries contained a wide array of materials. William IV brought these libraries together at Windsor and successive monarch have added to them substantially.

The classification history of the Royal Library is still largely a product of the mid-19th century and remains highly effective for the management of the collection. However, it is now also cataloged on an in-house electronic database, which has previously not followed any applicable external standard, and at no point in the past, with the exception of the incunabula in the Library, have any records been shared on union catalogs in either printed or electronic form. At the time of writing, the records relating to printed books in the Royal Library are being converted to being MARC-format compatible with a view to the data contained in the Royal Library being more widely available. The incunabula have recently been the subject of a re-cataloging project and are available on the Incunabula Short-Title Catalog. The staff of the Library are now working their way through the next tranches of the collection in broad chronological groups to complete date process of converting the records, and preparing them for being made publicly available beyond the scope of Royal Collection website.

---

[11] Royal Collection Trust – Homepage. Available at: https://www.royalcollection.org.uk/

What is the current size of the collections of the Royal Library and of The Queen's Archives? Could you also describe what you deem are the highlights these two collections? Or are there simply too many to be listed out one by one?

The Royal Library is responsible for approximately 205,000 books, manuscripts, coins, medals and insignia. The Library has expanded to include not only material collected by members of the Royal Family, but its collection also reflects the work of the Royal Household, Royal Collection Trust and the particular interest of successive Librarians. The individual highlights are very numerous and include the Sobieski Hours, made by the Master of the Bedford Hours, the Mainz Psalter, the first book to be printed in color, and the second to be printed with moveable type, unique examples of the printing of William Caxton, innumerable examples of the very finest manifestation of the book, whether the finest bindings, the most technologically accomplished production, or the most textually significant works. Among the treasures are diplomatic gifts from other nations including magnificent oriental and Islamic manuscripts, or presentation copies of landmark works, such as *Emma* by Jane Austen or *South* by Shackleton. However, perhaps more significant than all this are three interconnected, distinguishing features for the Library's collections – that they reflect the interests and activities and intellectual context for successive monarchs, that many of the books have some distinguishing feature arising from their provenance, for example annotations by royal owners, presentation inscriptions revealing the relationship between the monarchy, and the life and work of the peoples of Great Britain and the world, and thirdly that the books can be seen in the context of the correspondence held in the archives to which the book attests a particular relationship or event.

The Royal Archives was founded in 1914 and is a private archive, which offers public access to historical papers and academic study, while protecting the personal private papers of The Queen and members of the Royal Family. The archival collection reflects the changing world and the monarchy's relationship to it, and contains, among its significant collection, the papers of the last Stuarts in exile, George III, George IV, and those of late monarchs and members of the Royal Family, including the correspondence and journals of Queen Victoria.

The Archives is therefore quite different in character to the Library, but like all archives is above all significant for being a primary source for Britain's shared past with the rest of the world and for being the first-hand, direct, commentary of those involved at every level. The Royal Archives is not simply the papers of the sovereigns themselves, but of their officials, courtiers, advisors and employees, etc. It contains letters from correspondents around the world, many of whom are household names, and who had profound effect on the United Kingdom, and its relationship with the rest of the world. It is also a domestic archive of the organization of a series of households, covering everything from kitchen garden records, livestock books, education, travel, and so on. It is thus an archive of the great moments of the nation as well as one of social history, and as such is capable of supporting the widest definition of inter-disciplinary research and public engagement.

Does your Library work closely with other libraries across England? What about the rest of the world, including the Commonwealth? If so, could you tell us about such cross-national or global collaborative projects? What are some highlights?

Historically, the Royal Library has not worked closely with other libraries, however this is changing and the work to publish online material relating to the Hanoverian dynasty – the Georgian Papers[12] – from both the Library and Archives has been a significant opportunity to begin to work collaboratively with other libraries and special collections in the UK and overseas. This collaboration already extends to King's College London[13] in the UK, the College of William and Mary[14] in the US, also in the US the Omohundro Institute of Early American History & Culture[15], the Library of Congress[16], and Mount Vernon Library.[17] More locally, we have a series of regular staff meetings with the staff managing the internationally significant collection at Eton College[18] Library, and there are clear collection connections with the library and archives at Lambeth Palace[19], and of course with the British Library.

In the field of hand-bookbinding we have recently launched the first UK apprenticeship scheme for more than 40 years. The Royal Library is one of the few remaining libraries in the world with not just a conservation department but also a working bindery, not only repairing and preserving existing books, but also making new bindings, for example for State Gifts made for Her Majesty to present to visiting Heads of State. The scheme is supported by a number of charities and education bodies, and is a national response to a very significant skills shortage in this area.

---

[12] Georgian Papers Program – Homepage. Available at: https://www.royalcollection.org.uk/georgian-papers-programme#/
[13] King's College London – Homepage. Available at: http://www.kcl.ac.uk/
[14] College of William and Mary – Homepage. Available at: http://www.wm.edu/
[15] Omohundro Institute of Early American History & Culture – Homepage. Available at: https://oieahc.wm.edu/
[16] Library of Congress – Homepage. Available at: https://www.loc.gov/
[17] Mount Vernon Library – Homepage. Available at: http://www.mountvernonwa.gov/library
[18] Eton College – Homepage. Available at: http://www.etoncollege.com/CollegeLibrary.aspx
[19] Lambeth Palace – Homepage. Available at: www.org/pages/visit-lambeth-palace.html

A lesser-known tale about one of the most famous partnerships in crime fiction Sherlock Holmes and Dr John Watson was by Walker Books in collaboration with the Royal Collection Trust. Could you tell us more about your role in this unique project?

Among the more surprising and charming parts of the library is the contents of Queen Mary's Dolls' House[20] Library. Queen Mary commissioned the dolls' house after the First World War as a way of encouraging and promoting British craftsmanship and industry. Significantly, Queen Mary had more than 170 blank miniature volumes commissioned from the renowned London bookbinders Sangorski & Sutcliffe, and these were sent to leading authors of the day, including A.E. Housman, Thomas Hardy, and of course Conan Doyle, and were to be returned for inclusion in the dolls' house library. There they remain to this day. Conan Doyle wrote a new work for his miniature volume, the conceit of the story being that Watson had finally worked out how Sherlock Holmes made his clever deductions. When I started as Royal Librarian, colleagues in the Royal Library had already identified this as publishing opportunity and Royal Collection Trust publishing had found a printer capable of reproducing the work life-size. Shortly after, I started the miniature facsimile was published and my role was simply to promote its significance.

According to you, "Significantly, Queen Mary had more than 170 blank miniature volumes commissioned from the renowned London bookbinders Sangorski & Sutcliffe, and these were sent to leading authors of the day, including A.E. Housman, Thomas Hardy, and of course Conan Doyle, and were to be returned for inclusion in the dolls' house library." – since they were blank miniature volumes – why were they sent to A.E. Housman, Thomas Hardy, and Conan Doyle, and were later returned – what purpose would it serve?

The Dolls House was a project to encourage and celebrate British trade, craftsmanship and enterprise in all its forms in the decade following the First World War. The books in the Dolls House represent some of the finest miniature bindings of the period as well as containing number of new literary works, including for example Conan Doyle's *How Watson Learned the Trick*.

In 2012, the Archives successfully completed a project to scan Queen Victoria's journals, and made them available online as a special project for the Diamond Jubilee. Could you tell us more about this project? What kind of technology was used in the

---

[20] Queen Mary's Dolls' House – Homepage. Available at: http://46.236.36.161/queenmarysdollshouse/home.html

digitization process and made available online? What were the users' comments and responses?

This was a highly significant project for the Royal Archives led by my predecessor as Assistant Keeper, David Ryan LVO (and also Director of Records for the Royal Household), being the first time that material from the Royal Archives was digitized and made available online, the first collaborative project with commercial (ProQuest) and university partners (the Bodleian Library at Oxford University). The entire body of Queen Victoria's journals, a remarkable body of material covering the major part of the 19th-century and comprising some 50,000 pages, were fully transcribed and published in 2012 and made freely available in UK web domain, and for a modest subscription elsewhere. The material was all scanned at Windsor Castle using contractors and was launched to immediate success and received a number of awards.

Who are the majority users of Queen's Victoria's online journal? What were the users' comments and responses?

The Journals have very wide appeal and cover a very significant portion of the 19th-century. The online resource regular sees significant 'spikes' in the access numbers immediately following popular history or historical drama series, for example, and we know they are frequently consulted and enjoyed by general public and scholars alike.

Quite recently, a 200-year old book of poetry gifted to George III and letters from Rear Admiral Sir Samuel Hood written during the American War of Independence are among a treasure trove of documents released by the Royal Archives. The collection, which was amassed by George III and had been under lock and key was digitized and launched to much publicity. How does the Royal Collection Department decide which part of this collection to be digitized and be made available for online access?

Launched on 1 April 2015 by Her Majesty The Queen, the Georgian Papers Program is transforming access to papers in the Royal Archives and Royal Library covering the period 1714–1837. By 2020 free digital access will be available to all the material, both private and official, relating to Britain's Hanoverian monarchs. At the heart of the Program is a partnership between the Royal Archives and Royal Library with King's College London. King's both frames multidisciplinary academic interpretation of the material and brings to bear its own track record of leadership in the development of digital access. It also has relevant collections that will feature in the partnership. The Omohundro Institute of Early American History and Culture and the College of William & Mary are sharing in this work as primary Program partners for the USA.

Including the papers of George I, II, III, and IV and William IV, as well as other members of the Royal Family, politicians, courtiers and the Privy Purse, the Program promises to deepen our understanding and provide new insights into Britain's role in the world, its relationships with other European states, colonial America and the United States of America, as well as British politics, the Enlightenment, science, food, art collecting and patronage, life at court and the education of royal children. Careful checking has revealed that only 15% of the 350,000 pages have ever been published before. This will be augmented with a further 100,000 pages of manuscript material from the Royal Library.

Decisions about which parts of the archives to release online are made by the Librarian and Assistant Keeper with recommendation being made to the Keeper and to HM.

Please describe the staffing structure at the Royal Library and the Queen's Archives. Do you have staff working under you?

The team is based at Windsor Castle, though we have responsibility for all the Libraries in all the residences – material can be found in more than 260 rooms in nine of the occupied and unoccupied palaces. The team comprises a mix of qualified librarians and archivists, as well curatorial and project-based staff, bookbinders and conservators, equivalent in total to approximately 18 full-time equivalent employees, and in addition a number of volunteers and former members of staff continuing to assist on specific projects.

Could you describe your typical day at work? Is there ever a typical day at work?

No one day is alike and there is never a typical day at work. Every brings a mix of strategic professional library and archive matters – questions of access or collections management for example – as well as curatorial decisions such exhibitions or the preparation of displays, or research matters for the work of other departments of the Royal Household, or dealing with the work supporting external academic collaborations or visiting researchers or showing HM's guests around the Library. While the majority of time is spent at Windsor Castle, all the other libraries need visiting on a regular basis, and this would include traveling to the Isle of Wight, or Norfolk or Scotland, for example.

Who are the majority of users of the Queen's Archives? That is, who comes to see you about the Queen's Archives?

A significant user of the Archives is naturally the Royal Household, including of course colleagues in the Royal Collection researching the history and use of the fine and decorative art in the Royal Collection. The Archives has been open to external researchers for historical research and educational purposes for some time, but in July 2016 we opened the first dedicated research room, creating a twelve-fold increase in our capacity to support research, and at the same time we updated the access to policy to focus on the information sought, and whether we were the only holder of that information. We also developed with our academic partners a number of visiting fellowships and professorships open to anyone to apply for and managed by our external partners. In support of this increased access, the first exhibition focusing on the Royal Archives was held in 2015 and the first history of the collection was published that year, and the first guide to the collections for users of the Library and Archives was published in 2016.

Since you are the Royal Librarian, do you report directly to Her Majesty The Queen? If so, who is responsible for conducting your job performance appraisal at the end of the year?

As Royal Librarian my performance is appraised by the Surveyor of The Queen's Pictures.

For your work as the Assistant Keeper of The Queen's Archives, do you report directly to the Private Secretary to the Sovereign?

Yes, the Private Secretary is also the Keeper of The Queen's Archives, and his authority in that role is carried by me as Assistant Keeper. In that respect, my performance is appraised by the Private Secretary.

Lady Jane Roberts was your predecessor as the Royal Library (2002–2013). How were the job duties of the Royal Librarian handed down to you from Lady Jane Roberts in 2014?

There was no formal handover of responsibilities, but Lady Roberts and her predecessor Oliver Everett, the Royal Librarian Emeritus (and who was also Assistant Keeper) have both been generous with their time and in sharing their experiences.

Would you agree that organizing major exhibitions to be showcased during the official visit of a foreign head of state is the most major and taxing task on the Royal Librarian's job description?

This is certainly one of the most enjoyable and taxing of the regular tasks that fall to the Royal Librarian. The requirement to master regularly the shared history of Britain and a succession of foreign powers is a great intellectual challenge, and the chance to expose parts of the collections not normally seen, and perhaps not usually considered as candidates for public exhibitions focused on aesthetic subjects, is a real and rewarding task. Each display must reflect the diplomatic themes of the State Visit, reveal the complexity, and richness of Britain's shared history with the visiting country yet not be a history lesson. The display is also an opportunity to reflect upon the personal involvement of the Royal Family, sometimes over many centuries, and the interests of the visiting head of state, as well as to touch upon the major diplomatic and trade themes under consideration, and to show material in the Royal Collection and Royal Archives of particular personal interest to the visiting head of state.

During the state visits – everything is timed to the second, and everything has to be executed with utmost precision. As the Royal Librarian, do you have some kind of rundown that you need to work out with The Queen's Private Office well in advance – so that you could follow it like a checklist on the day of the state visit?

While the Librarian's Display for a State Visit is coordinated and lead by The Librarian, it is of course part of a much bigger and complicated program of organization. We work to a regular and well-defined set of tasks to produce the display, and this process is of course continuously improved. The real challenge and opportunity with each display is to mine the Royal Collection, Royal Library and Royal Archives for any given country, and to find material that speaks to the relationship between Her Majesty The Queen and Great Britain on the one hand, the visiting country on the other.

Which part(s) of your job as the Royal Library and the Assistant Keeper of The Queen's Archives do you find most rewarding? What is most frustrating? What are the major challenges that you and your colleagues are currently facing?

The sheer variety of the role is tremendously stimulating as is the huge scope chronologically, geographically, and subject wise of the collections. Perhaps most rewarding of all is making the Library and Archives really achieve its full potential in support of the work of the Crown and for the benefit of the nation, whether by working as the official library or private archive of The Queen, by publishing the historic collections online, by contributing to exhibitions, by supporting the work of the British diplomatic effort through the Librarian's displays for State Visits, or simply, by taking an item off the shelf and telling someone something new about it or a researcher enriching our own understanding of the collection.

Like any working and growing library and archives, the Royal Library and Royal Archives are no exception to the common challenges facing all those work with collections rich in information: issues of storage and preservation, stewardship (making discoverable), the opportunities and challenges of providing proper access and running an effective library and archive service, and of course collection and data security. All four of those over-arching challenges apply equally to the digital as to the paper collections.

Further readings

HRH The Prince of Wales and the Royal Librarian discuss Frogmore House interiors [YouTube]. Available at: https://www.youtube.com/watch?v=wtKl0TO78OY.
Royal Library and Royal Archives – Royal Collection Trust – Homepage. Available at: https://www.royalcollection.org.uk/about/working-for-us/our-roles/royal-library-and-royal-archives.
Take a tour of the Royal Library's Treasures and Curiosities [YouTube]. Available at: https://www.youtube.com/watch?v=I6CWwNaf6c4&t=1688s.
Walker, Tim. (2013). Wanted: Royal librarian to look after the Queen's 125,000 titles. *UK News*. Available at: http://www.telegraph.co.uk/news/uknews/theroyalfamily/10163060/Wanted-Royal-librarian-to-look-after-the-Queens-125000-titles.html.

Conclusion

Urban, cultural and public spaces provide interaction for citizens. The significance of creating and retaining cultural spaces are considered one of the most important strategies for establishing urban cultural landscapes. Cultural centers have influential roles to play in shaping the public culture via providing cultural, educational and recreational activities in both short-term and long-term periods for the citizens, as well as providing social services related to needs and welfare of the local communities as a whole (Izadi & Mohammadi, 2016).[1] The typologies of cultural spaces are social space, neighborhood space – human space; community space and existential space (recognized as lived space by Relph, 1976).[2]

According to Izadi & Mohammadi (2016), cultural and social spaces neighborhoods, as parts of thriving urban spaces, are considered as having the most potential in the development of citizenship culture due to enjoying potentials and capacities. As pointed out by several library directors appearing in this book, one of the most essential social values / functions of a public library is to develop citizenship culture for reducing various socio-cultural inequalities, as well as to contribute to the realization of sustainable development of urban culture and society as a whole. National and public libraries belong to the same category of cultural institutions, such as theatre halls, art galleries, opera houses, museums, etc. In this context, libraries as public social spaces continue to contribute to the overall development of quality interactions and communications amongst citizens, naturally having the potentials to enhance the sense of belonging to the space and identity, as well as supplying emotional needs of the community as a whole.

In that sense, a public library's role in supporting the development of cultural spaces and collective and urban entertainments is considered important in the process of cultural sustainable development of the city. In many countries, libraries, as cultural assets of the nations / neighborhoods, are sometimes, unfortunately, under-recognized. In order to improve the situation, libraries need to be incorporated into the existing cultural policy infrastructures of the whole nation or city. As indicated by several library directors appearing in this book, many cities have already institutionalized a role for their libraries in the cultural lives of the urban neighborhoods or even the whole nation.

Cultural spaces are considered as one set of the main instruments of cultural development in current societies and are burdened significant responsibility in developing human forces.

---

[1] Izadi, M. & Mohammadi, J. (2016). The roles of neighborhood cultural spaces in the development of citizenship culture. *Modern Applied Science*, 10(3): 89–94.
[2] Relph, E. (1976). *Place and Pacelessness*. London, U.K.: Pion.

> Cultural spaces, as one set of the main important institutions for cultural services, have important functions in increasing the literacy and culture level of societies. Then establishment of such spaces and the mode of their distribution in the neighborhoods are, directly or indirectly, effective on the degree of individuals' reference and use of these spaces. (Izadi & Mohammadi, 2016, p. 91).[3]

As mentioned previously, libraries (city libraries in particular) undoubtedly play a communal socialization role – that is a neighbor socio-cultural space that helps foster the development of citizenship, culture and recreation, etc. According to Choi & Dae Geun (2013), a cultural space is recognized as a space or facility that can directly produce and educate some cultural products in everyday life or where citizens can come and appreciate arts and culture. In fact, the library is not just simple physical social place, but a space in which the locality and cultural activities are organically connected for the production and enjoyment of both high and low culture. Therefore, the role of the library as a physical social space will inevitably and continue to change along with the change of times (Choi & Dae Geun, 2013).[4] In sum, the roles of libraries as cultural spaces symbolized a place characteristic where people perceived and use urban spaces. In addition to their functional values, the significance of libraries as public spaces, together with their sociocultural activities have established the place meaning, and a sense of belonging to users, as well as the communities they serve.

This book does not intend to be comprehensive in breath; nevertheless, it has covered a number of leading national and public libraries in many different countries, including: Argentina, Austria, Canada, Germany, Latvia, Montenegro, Qatar, Spain, Switzerland, the United Kingdom and the United States. The national and public libraries appearing in this book exhibit considerable diversity in their architectural design, physical size, collection, funding, structure, missions, clientele, as well as functions, etc. The varying sociocultural, political and economic landscapes these libraries are situated in, the diversity in the user populations, as well as their rapidly changing needs and expectations have also been discussed.

The ultimate goal of any library is to provide good services – that is, offering quality services to all categories and levels of users, regardless of their social status, economic income, education level, age, gender, nationality, ethnic origin, religious beliefs, etc. In this regard, fulfilling the reading, information, learning needs of their city's inhabitants, as well as satisfying the social and recreational

---

[3] Izadi, M. & Mohammadi, J. (2016). The roles of nehgiborhood cultural spaces in the development of citizenship culture. *Modern Applied Science*, 10(3): 89–94.

[4] Choi, J. R., & Dae Geun, L. (2013). Case study of cultural space to revitalize local community. *International Journal of History and Culture*, 1(1): 1–14.

needs of the local community at all levels has become the "gold standard" for libraries worldwide. Apparently, national and public libraries across the world are desperately reinventing themselves by increasingly becoming vibrant, engaging and attractive community hubs, focusing on the need to foster digital literacy – in order to measure to the ideal world of everyone being digital fluent. In that sense, a library is a critical institution for the kind of community people say they want to live in, a space where those people could – theoretically, anyway – learn and gather – with or without printed books.

In fact, there are already many innovations happening amongst libraries featured in this book; for example, space station-like library architecture, bookstore / Starbucks-like interior design, collaborative learning spaces (with movable furniture), maker labs, bookless spaces, free lunches for underprivileged children, use of book bikes to recruit new members, the intergenerational and cross-cultural interaction programs for seniors and new immigrants to connect with the community in a meaningful way, as well as numerous multi-purpose facilities, with all sorts of innovative offerings and services, etc.

National libraries versus public libraries

The public library is often regarded as the people's university. They are physical public spaces dedicated to serve as the local gateway to unlimited knowledge, and they are sometimes referred as "sanctuaries" of free learning for all people – providing endless opportunities for a wide range of intellectual and creative endeavor, as well as for other lifelong learning, recreational and social opportunities. Furthermore, when one considers that the most vulnerable and underserved city-dwellers are also those who generally do not have easy access to the Internet, the need for a free and publicly connected space like the public library becomes even clearer.

On the other hand, specifically established by the government of a county, a national library is designed to serve as the primary repository of information. The world's national libraries all share a common mission, that is, to collect, record, organize, store, preserve in perpetuity, and to provide access to their nation's documentary heritage. In other words, the most essential task of a national library is that they are responsible for acquiring, preserving and making accessible the publications (of all kinds) of the country. For this reason, publishers are required by law to provide a copy or copies of every book published to the national library. For the sake of serving as a repository for rare, valuable, and significant works, most of these national libraries do not circulate their collections. In short, national libraries are at best a contribution to civilization, representing a cultural history of a nation, or even just a vulnerable storage of valuable materials of national cultural heritage. In that sense, a good national library is often regarded as a legitimate source of national pride. However, national libraries have some particular challenges. As indicated by the interviewees who served as library directors of former Soviet satellite states, being government-funded and seen as representative of the whole country, many libraries in Eastern Europe during the Soviet era were seriously affected by the ideology of the Communist regimes, such as austerity, corruption, or political propaganda, etc.

Libraries in the post-Communist era

Many national and public libraries in Eastern Europe have had a rich heritage of collecting and preserving materials in the domains of national and foreign history, literature, art, and science, etc. Unfortunately, during the Communist regimes, libraries in general were expected to serve as propaganda tools for the former USSR government's Marxist ideology. In fact, the process of social reform, which started in the early 1990s, has targeted organizations in all fields such as schools, universities, hospitals, orphanages, documentation centers, and also libraries, etc. Having experienced one of the most repressive dictatorships, which ended by the popular revolt of 1989, has led to the abolition of censorship and of government-controlled media – eventually led to an unprecedented surge in book publishing both original works and translations, which originally served the propagandistic goals of the communist government.

Professional librarians previously working in former Soviet satellite states, their responsibilities were reduced to shelving books, assigning call numbers, and keeping a vigilant eye on the users in the reading room and blindly implement the decisions made by the communist party leadership at a national or local level. The decentralization of the entire Communist bureaucracy involves radical changes at the macro/societal level and at the micro/institutional level in all sectors of society: economic, technological, social, environmental, political, cultural, and educational, etc. Librarians from the former USSR have established increased contacts with Western librarians over the past few decades. They have already absorbed the current mania for automation in their libraries. Under the Soviet rule, national and public libraries in Eastern Europe were oppressed by censorship, but the services that were available were traditionally free. Now that the Communist ideological restrictions have been lifted, new ones take their place, such as challenges of preserving collections that have been neglected for decades. During the post-Communist era, there is a strong desire among the former Soviet libraries to promote change from a system of limited access to information to a more open system that focuses on quality library services, operations, and organization in many respects. In their efforts to overcome the Communist legacy to the LIS profession and practices, many libraries in the post-Communist era have been implementing a more Western (that is more democratic and participative) managerial styles and services.

Fostering an on-going culture of social engagement in the digital age

Despite the convenience brought by Internet connectivity, as well as the different online platforms and mobile social network applications currently available in the market, the values and social functions of the physical library can never be replaced. As mentioned previously, public libraries are still regarded as one of the most valued and trusted resources at the heart of communities, for the reason that they have the potentials to foster learning and social, cultural and economic wellbeing of the community as a whole. Meanwhile, libraries cannot stand still in a changing world and many are exploring different ways of working – re-imagining the range of functions and services they can fulfil. As highlighted by the interviewees appearing in this book, the library is often regarded as a social public space where the community could come together and "live life in public" – a precursor to people engaging in an on-going conversations about the future of their own community or city. Libraries are gradually evolving from a "warehouse-like" repository to a place (either physical or virtual) that emphasises on librarians as information providers – in other words, accomplishing another goal of the library, that is placing users rather than books as the center of the library (Chapman, 1993).[5] It is true that providing a shared, communal space can be a great and important offering for many neighborhoods. However, social engagement should never be a one-time process or event. In other words, libraries must find new ways to leverage public spaces, of all kinds, to draw people and ideas together – not just in one-off events, but more consistently as a part of the daily behaviour, decisions and choices that defines our city's culture.

Leadership qualities and library directors

"Leadership is often regarded as the single most critical factor in the success or failure of institutions" (Bass, 1990, p. 8).[6] Scholtes (1998), who suggests: "There is no formula for leadership. Leadership consists of more than the approaches, capabilities, and attributes talked about in books." To which he adds: "Leadership

---

[5] Chapman, R.F. (1993). Personnel development in U. S. libraries. *Biblioteca*, 4, pp. 60–62 (in Romanian).
[6] Bass, B.M. (1999). "Two decades of research and development in transformational leadership." *European Journal of Work and Organizational Psychology*, 8(1): 9–26.

is an art, an inner journal, a network of relationships, a mastery of methods, and much, much more" (Scholtes, 1998, p. 372).[7] Meanwhile, Michele Darling predicts the leader of the future will mentor, encourage, guide and support rather than "bark orders." Leaders will have to be able to "share vision, a sense of purpose and direction" (p. 477).[8]

Leadership plays an important role in the overall success, as well as the future survival of any organization – regardless of whether it is for profit or non-profit, a corporate or cultural / education organization, etc. It has been said that, "You cannot be a leader, and ask other people to follow you, unless you know how to follow, too." Erskine Bowles (American businessman and White House Chief of Staff), describes the role of leadership as a process for influencing a group of people to meet the organizational goals (Northouse 2007).[9] Meanwhile, Spitzberg (1986) observed that the meaning of leadership may depend on the kinds of institutions or services in which it is practiced.[10] According to Knott (1997), leadership is a process that is fundamental to the practice of librarianship.[11] There is no exception for Leadership in the LIS sector. In fact, leadership can be seen as a decisive factor in library development (Robbins & Coulter, 2012).[12]

Crismond and Leisner (1988) clarified that nobody qualified for that list merely because of excelling in just one aspect of leadership. They contended – from the initial random surveys and from subsequent telephone interviews with nine of those top ten leaders – that each leader "demonstrated a broad vision over time, combining commitment, determination, intelligence, and decision-making abilities to see that dreams come true" as well as courage and risk taking, openness to others, and political aptitude (Crismond and Leisner, 1988, p. 123).[13]

All the library leaders appearing in this book have demonstrated that having a broader organizational view, being able to see their responsibilities extended

---

[7] Scholtes, P.R. (1998). *The Leader's Handbook: A Guide to Inspiring your People and Managing the Daily Workflow*. New York, N.Y.: McGraw-Hill.
[8] Darling, Michele. (1995). A new vision of leadership." In J. Thomas Wren (Ed.). *Leader's Companion: Insights on Leadership Through the Ages* (pp. 472–48). New York, N.Y.: Free Press.
[9] Northouse, P.G. (2007). *Leadership: Theory and Practice*. 4th ed. Thousand Oaks, Calif.: Sage.
[10] Spitzberg, I.J. Jr (1986), "Questioning leadership", unpublished manuscript, quoted by Bass, B. (1990), Bass and Stogdill's Handbook of Leadership: A Survey of Theory and Research, Free Press, Riverside, NJ, pp. 11 and 1086.
[11] Knott, W. (1997), "Public library leadership: meetings and the mechanics of growth." *Colorado Libraries*, 23: pp. 30–32.
[12] Robbins, S.P. & Coulter, M. (2012). *Management*. 11th ed. Boston, Mass.: Prentice Hall.
[13] Crismond, L.F. & Leisner, A.B. (1988). "The top ten public library leaders: a survey." *Public Libraries*, 27: 122–4.

beyond the sheer finances into human resources, information technology, and the daily operations – are some of the most important traits and attributes that make a successful library director in the digital age. They must also be able to build strong teams in the face of drastic changes in user behaviour and expectations, keep up with the latest technologies, and finally, demonstrate strong business acumen of a corporate CEO. This is where successful leaders tap into their strong communication skills, clearly explaining to each employee his or her career path and role in the company's mission, then supporting employees as they build their leadership skills and prepare for greater responsibilities.

Evolution of leadership in librarianship

According to Lomer & Rogers (1983), officers from outside the library and staff within the library agreed that the leadership of the chief librarian was the most important factor in the way the library operated and was developed. In practical terms, the chief librarian is always the most important influence on the way the library is run and it is his professional approach, which has most effect on the service.[14]

This book features a series of interviews with library directors practicing in many different parts of the world, discussing in details the common attributes of successful and authentic transformative leadership and management styles. Even though the funding levels are decreasing for many libraries, the quality of library staff, their professionalism, their dedication and innovative programming have undoubtedly helped their libraries and their own profession achieve an even higher stature and recognition. More importantly, successful leadership attributes, such as vision, effective communication, creativity, integrity are absolutely essential, and will never become out-dated or go out of style.

Successful library leaders – common traits and attributes

Unarguably, strong leaders with vision and the ability to empower employees are needed to develop and lead future libraries. For this reason, leadership skills that incorporate both purpose and vision, as well as having the capacity to develop and implement strategies are absolutely indispensable to address various challenges in times of change and uncertainty. The library directors appearing in this book indicate that under the digital age, libraries have evolved into even more complex, multi-layered, multi-purpose and multi-functional community-centered spaces.

---

14 Lomer, M. and Rogers, S. (1983). *The Public Library and the Local Authority: Organization and Management*. Institute of Local Government Studies, Birmingham, U.K: University of Birmingham.

They are sometimes referred as vibrant "community hubs" or "heart of the city" that have the potentials to support the entire community in many respects, including newcomer services, educational programming, seniors services and employment support, and in particular the lifelong learning of individuals.

According to Adrienne LaFrance (Staff Writer, The Atlantic), many libraries already offer a lot of technological services – the size and importance of these areas may just continue to grow in the future:

> *Today's libraries are already community spaces with rooms full of books and machines – many libraries have printers, copiers, computers, and microfiche terminals. But if the trend in American libraries is toward relative booklessness, when – and how quickly – do print volumes become searchable or downloadable only online? Perhaps the library of the future will consist of five coffee-shop-sized locations spread across a town, instead of one larger, centralized building. These physical spaces would become the main draw of a library; the books people want to check out would all be available to download from anywhere with an Internet connection.*[15]

In the next ten years, the rapid development in communications technology would promise even more changes – such drastic changes that would undoubtedly challenge every notion of how a library is supposed to "function", "serve" or even how the physical library building, as well as its virtual counterpart should be designed. Great leaders of any organizations, including the director of a library are the ones who care about the people he/she works with, and most importantly, the communities they serve. An individual library director's competence, his/her contributions and commitments are unarguably central to the overall success of entire library organization. That is why it is most crucial for library leaders to stay on top of industry trends and remain open to new ideas, and more importantly adaptable to change and innovation – in other words, one must be able to take charge constructively by utilising various leading-edge technologies to achieve new kinds and levels of services – thereby creating new and creative ways to engage the community. Being willing to take risks and to try new ventures are equally central for leadership in the field of librarianship, if it needs to be successful.

Michele Darling predicts the leader of the future will mentor, encourage, guide and support rather than "bark orders." Leaders will have to be able to "share vision, a sense of purpose and direction" (Darling, 477). Darling stresses

---

15 Olmstead, Gracy. (2015). What should the 21st-century library look like? *The American Conservative*. Available at: http://www.theamericanconservative.com/olmstead/what-should-the-21st-century-library-look-like/

that "Power doesn't accrue to those who hoard it. Real power is obtained only by those who give it away" (Darling, 477).[16]

The organizational culture of any libraries should at all times be focused on service. For this reason, it is essential that the vision of the organization's leadership must be founded on the same set of principles or focus on service to the public. Furthermore, future planning for the library is about vision and aspiration. Having a vision and a commitment to librarianship ideals are the primary qualities needed by any library leaders. A vision would mean having a clear picture of the organizational future – that is, where the services and how the entire library organization should be going in the next five to ten years. He or she should have the ability to communicate that vision clearly to all levels of library staff, and more importantly having the commitment and drive to implement that vision, by translating it into everyday practicalities.

Peter Drucker (Austrian-born American management consultant, educator, and author) described it this way:

> *Leadership is about lifting a person's vision to higher sights, the raising of a person's performance to a higher standard, the building of a personality beyond its normal limitations.*

Strong leadership skills are developed through experience, and can allow individuals to impart knowledge and guidance to others with confidence via motivation. As highlighted by Admiral James B. Stockdale:

> *Leadership must be based on goodwill. Goodwill does not mean posturing and, least of all, pandering to the mob. It means obvious and wholehearted commitment to helping followers. What we need for leaders are men of the heart who are so helpful that they, in effect, do away with the need of their jobs. But leaders like that are never out of a job, never out of followers. Strange as it sounds, great leaders gain authority by giving it away.*

All such qualities are, in fact, parallel to the concept of "servant leadership", defined by Robert Greenleaf – that is, it "begins with the natural feeling that one wants to serve, to serve first. Then conscious choice brings one to aspire to lead. That person is sharply different from one who is leader first, perhaps because of the need to assuage an unusual power drive or to acquire material possessions" (Greenleaf, 918–23).

---

16 Darling, Michele. (1995). A new vision of leadership." In J. Thomas Wren (Ed.). *Leader's Companion: Insights on Leadership Through the Ages* (pp. 472–48). New York, N.Y.: Free Press.

Library directors as servant leaders

In the context of librarianship, being a servant leader would mean offering an "inclusive vision"; listening carefully to others; persuading through reason; setting, leading employees working at all levels of the organization, not just the senior management, will be making decisions that affect the library's missions and future. Servant leadership is also a way to encourage healthier organizations and to rid the people in them of energy-depleting dependency and self-interest. The leader acts so that all will benefit and serves well regardless of the rate of pay. Servant leadership will continue to be the driving force in a dynamic environment that is driven by constantly evolving societal expectations. Commitment to adding value to society, to the service of communities, including an emphasis on motivation and on positive personal values, such as integrity.

In other words, leadership by empowerment; the more open-door and participative style of management which foster communications between senior management and staff will continue to be the keystone of many library organizations. For this reason, fostering strong relationships with co-workers is most invaluable. As pointed out by Bennis (2003):

> *The speed with which change and innovation happen is forcing organizations to abandon their top-down processes, and the new information channels allow decisions to be taken nearer to the coalface and quicker (xiii).*[17]

Libraries as cultural centers are considered as the most important elements in developing the strategy of urban cultural planning in the process of cultural sustainable development of the city. Changes in reading culture, publishing industry, modes of learning, and scholarly communications have defined new roles for the libraries. Being able to lead people in the direction that the community wants, will also be some of the most desirable qualities in a library leader. Furthermore, library directors need to keep learning. Succession planning in libraries should be considered, and conducted so that the next generation of leaders can inherit, and develop the achievements of the previous library leadership. As a result, all library directors need to continue learning, and they need to pass on that learning to the next generation – so that we could develop the seasoned directors we need to move the LIS profession and their libraries into the next decade or century. Libraries need reasoned, outspoken, and well-articulated leaders, if it is to flourish in a digital future. To conclude this book, I would like

---

17 Bennis, Warren. (1999). *Managing People is like Herding Cats*. Provo UT: Publishers Press.

to quote a message from an online lecture given by Pam Sandlian Smith (Director at Anythink Libraries), which summarizes the values of libraries and librarianship in the 21st century:

> *Libraries are places that support creativity, community, innovation, and entrepreneurialism. We are the cornerstones of democracy. Everyone has a seat at the table, and we treat everyone with the same respect and dignity – whether you are a millionaire, or whether you are that boy who was homeless. So that next time somebody says to you, 'Why do we need a library?' I ask you to pause and reflect, and I hope you will think, 'Who else is gonna do this?'*

About the authors

Dr. Patrick Lo, Ed.D.
Patrick Lo is currently serving as Associate Professor at the Faculty of Library, Information & Media Science, the University of Tsukuba in Japan. He earned his Doctor of Education from the University of Bristol (U.K.), and has a Master of Arts in Design Management from the Hong Kong Polytechnic University, a Master of Library & Information Science from McGill University (Canada), and a Bachelor of Fine Arts from Mount Allison University (Canada).

He also took part in a one-year academic exchange at the University of Tübingen in Germany from 1990–91. He is efficient in Chinese (both Cantonese and Putonghua), English and German. Dr. Patrick Lo has presented about 100 research papers and project reports focusing on librarianship, humanities, and education at different local and international workgroup meetings, seminars, conferences, etc., including: Mainland China, Hong Kong, Austria, France, Germany, Italy, Japan, Korea, Turkey, United States, and Sweden, and at institutions including the Library of Congress (U.S.), Austrian National Library (Vienna), University of Vienna, National Library of France (Paris), National Institute of Informatics (Japan), Konrad-Zuse-Center for Information Technology (Berlin), etc. His research interests and areas of specialty include: comparative studies in library and information science (LIS); art and design librarianship and information literacy.

Allan Cho
Allan Cho is the Digital Humanities Librarian at UBC's Walter C. Koerner Library's Humanities and Social Sciences division.

His work supports the digital scholarship on the UBC campus. Allan has MLIS and M.Ed degrees from the University of British Columbia, and an MA in History from the UBC History department where his thesis, "The Hong Kong Wuxia movie: identity and politics, 1966–1976," focused on the rise of the Hong Kong swordplay films across the Chinese diaspora during turbulent period of the Cultural Revolution. He is also an instructor in the Department of Library & Information Technology at the University of Fraser Valley in British Columbia, Canada.

Dr. Dickson Chiu, Ph.D.
Dickson K.W. Chiu received the B.Sc. (Hons.) degree in Computer Studies from the University of Hong Kong in 1987. He received the M.Sc. (1994) and the Ph.D. (2000) degrees in Computer Science from the Hong Kong University of Science and Technology (HKUST). He started his own computer company while studying part-time. He is now teaching at the University of Hong Kong and has also taught at several universities in Hong Kong.

His research interest is in library and information management with a cross-disciplinary approach, involving workflows, software engineering, information technologies, management, security, and databases. The results have been widely published in over 200 papers in international journals and conference proceedings (most of them have been indexed by SCI, SCI-E, EI, and SSCI), including many practical master and undergraduate project results.

www.ingramcontent.com/pod-product-compliance
Lightning Source LLC
Chambersburg PA
CBHW021338300426
44114CB00012B/994